The Modern Snp

THE MODERN SNP

FROM PROTEST TO POWER

EDITED BY GERRY HASSAN

EDINBURGH UNIVERSITY PRESS

To Tom Nairn, Nigel Smith and Jean Urquhart –
for their inspiration, grace and principle

© in this edition Edinburgh University Press, 2009
© in the individual contributions is retained by the authors

Edinburgh University Press Ltd
22 George Square, Edinburgh
www.euppublishing.com

Typeset in Goudy by
Servis Filmsetting Ltd, Stockport, Cheshire, and
printed and bound in Great Britain by
Athenaeum Press Ltd, Gateshead

A CIP record for this book is available from the British Library

ISBN 978 0 7486 3990 8 (hardback)
ISBN 978 0 7486 3991 5 (paperback)

The right of the contributors to be identified as authors of this work has been
asserted in accordance with the Copyright, Designs and Patents Act 1988.

Contents

Notes on the Contributors   vii

1. The Making of the Modern SNP: From Protest to Power
   Gerry Hassan   1

2. The Early Years: From the Inter-War Period to the Mid-1960s
   Richard Finlay   19

3. From Breakthrough to Mainstream: The Politics of Potential
   and Blackmail
   James Mitchell   31

4. Women's Political Representation and the SNP: Gendered
   Paradoxes and Puzzles
   Fiona Mackay and Meryl Kenny   42

5. Devolution, the SNP and the Electorate
   John Curtice   55

6. Who are the SNP Members?
   James Mitchell, Robert Johns and Lynn Bennie   68

7. The SNP and the Scottish Parliament: The Start of a New Sang?
   Colin Mackay   79

8. The SNP and Westminster
   Isobel Lindsay   93

9. SNP Economic Strategy: Neo-Liberalism with a Heart
   Jim Cuthbert and Margaret Cuthbert   105

10. Social Justice and the SNP
    Stephen Maxwell   120

11. The SNP, Cultural Policy and the Idea of the 'Creative
    Economy'
    Philip Schlesinger   135

12. The Auld Enemies: Scottish Nationalism and Scottish Labour
    Gerry Hassan   147

13. The Journey from the 79 Group to the Modern SNP
    David Torrance   162

14. The SNP and UK Relations
    Alex Wright   177

15. Degrees of Independence: SNP Thinking in an International
    Context
    Eve Hepburn   190

16. Nationalist Movements in Comparative Perspective
    Michael Keating   204

Index   219

Notes on the Contributors

Lynn Bennie is Senior Lecturer in Politics in the Department of Politics and International Relations, School of Social Science, University of Aberdeen. Her research interests include elections and political parties, environmental politics and political participation. She is the co-author of *How Scotland Votes* (1997) and author of *Understanding Political Participation: Green Party Membership in Scotland* (2004).

John Curtice is Professor of Politics at Strathclyde University, Research Consultant with the Scottish Centre for Social Research, Deputy Director of the Centre for Research and Social Trends (CREST) and Director of the Social Statistic Laboratory. His publications include *Has Devolution Delivered?* (2006) and *Devolution – Scottish Answers to Scottish Questions* (2003), along with several studies of UK politics and voting, including *The Rise of New Labour* (2001), *Labour's Last Chance?* (1994) and *How Britain Votes* (1985).

Jim Cuthbert studied mathematics, economics and statistics at Glasgow University and then took a D.Phil. at Sussex University in probability theory. After lecturing in statistics at Glasgow University, he joined the United Kingdom civil service in 1974 and worked in statistics in the Scottish Office and the Treasury. He was latterly Scottish Office Chief Statistician. After leaving the civil service in 1997, he has pursued a number of interests, including research and consultancy. His research is particularly in the areas of Scotland's public finances and the Scottish economy, and in certain aspects of purchasing power parities. Much of this research has been produced in collaboration with his wife, Margaret Cuthbert. Copies of most of the papers they have co-authored since 1997 can be found on their website at www.cuthbert1.pwp.blueyonder. co.uk

Margaret Cuthbert is an independent researcher whose major area of research has been public expenditure in Scotland. She edited and contributed to *Public Expenditure in Scotland*, one of the few economics texts on Scotland written in the period after the first devolution referendum. With Jim Cuthbert she worked for a number of years on the philosophy underpinning the determination of government expenditure and revenues in Scotland (GERS), and on the improvement of the GERS data and analysis. Current work includes critiques of the private finance initiative, of devolved and reserved spending and their associated powers, and of free care for the elderly.

Richard Finlay is Professor of Scottish History and Head of Department at the University of Strathclyde. He is the author of *Independent and Free: Scottish Politics and the Origins of the SNP 1918–1945* (1994) and *Modern Scotland 1914–2000* (2004). He is currently working on Anglo-Scottish relations since the Union of 1707.

Gerry Hassan is a writer, broadcaster and commentator on Scottish and UK politics and the author and editor of numerous books and publications. His books include *The Scottish Labour Party: History, Institutions and Ideas* (2004) and *After Blair: British Politics after the New Labour Decade* (2007). He is a Senior Research Associate at Demos and was head of their Scotland 2020 and Glasgow 2020 programmes leading to the publications *Scotland 2020: Hopeful Stories for a Northern Nation* (2005) and *The Dreaming City: Glasgow 2020 and the Power of Mass Imagination* (2007). He is a Honorary Research Fellow at Glasgow Caledonian University, an associate editor with the ideas journal *Renewal* and a frequent contributor in the Scottish and UK media. Gerry can be contacted at www.gerryhassan.com

Eve Hepburn is a Leverhulme Fellow in Politics at the University of Edinburgh. She is Co-editor of *Regional and Federal Studies* and Academic Coordinator of the ECPR Standing Group on Federalism and Regionalism. Her research explores the dynamics of regional party systems, multi-level governance, and nationalist parties in Europe and Canada. She has authored *Using Europe: Territorial Strategies in a Multi-level System* (2010), edited *New Challenges for Stateless Nationalists and Regionalists* (special issue of *Regional and Federal Studies*, 2009) and published several articles in journals such as *West European Politics, Cambridge Journal of Regions, Economy and Society* and *German Politics*.

Robert Johns is Lecturer in Politics at the University of Strathclyde. His research is in the fields of political psychology and electoral behaviour, and he has recently worked on major survey studies of the Scottish electorate and Scottish National Party members.

Michael Keating is Professor of Politics at the European University Institute in Florence and at the University of Aberdeen. Between 1988 and 1999 he was Professor of Political Science at the University of Western Ontario and before that was Senior Lecturer at the University of Strathclyde. He has taught in England, France, the United States and Spain. Author of numerous books and articles on European politics, nationalism, regionalism and public policy, his most recent book is *The Independence of Scotland* (2009) and a second edition of his book *The Government of Scotland* will be published by Edinburgh University Press in 2010.

Meryl Kenny is an ESRC Postdoctoral Fellow in the Department of Politics and International Relations at the University of Edinburgh. Current research focuses on feminist and new institutional theory and gender and political recruitment in the United Kingdom. Her recent publications include articles in *Politics and Gender, Scottish Affairs* and *Politics*.

Isobel Lindsay was a national office-bearer of the SNP during the 1970s and 1980s. She was Convener of the Campaign for a Scottish Parliament and an executive member of the Scottish Constitutional Convention. Lecturer in Sociology at the University of Strathclyde until she retired, she is currently Vice-Chair of Scottish CND and Convener of Scotland's for Peace.

Colin Mackay has been Political Editor for seven of Scotland's biggest commercial radio stations since 1999. Previously he worked for the BBC producing *Good Morning Scotland* and *Good Morning Ulster*. After the first Scottish Parliament election Colin took up his current post covering Holyrood for Radio Clyde, Forth, Northsound, Tay, Westsound, Border, and Moray Firth Radio. He is also a regular political commentator on television. He was IRN reporter of the year in the 2007 and his election coverage has won two gold medals at the New York Radio Festival.

Fiona Mackay is Senior Lecturer in Politics at the University of Edinburgh. Current research focuses on gender and constitutional change in the UK. She co-authored *Women, Politics and Constitutional Change* (2007), authored *Love and Politics* (2001), and co-edited *The Changing Politics of Gender Equality in Britain* (2002) and *Women and Contemporary Scottish Politics* (2001).

Stephen Maxwell was the SNP's national press officer between 1973 and 1977, and subsequently a Lothian Regional Councillor and Party Vice Chairman for Policy and for Local Government. He holds degrees from Cambridge University and the London School of Economics and has been a researcher and lecturer at universities in England and Scotland. Until October 2009 he was Associate Director of the Scottish Council for Voluntary Organisations and has held many volunteer posts with Scottish voluntary organisations.

James Mitchell is Professor of Politics at Strathclyde University. His most recent book, *Devolution in the United Kingdom*, was published in 2009 and he is co-author with Rob Johns, David Denver and Charles Pattie of a study of the 2007 Scottish elections to be published in early 2010. He has written extensively on the SNP and is co-author with Rob Johns and Lynn Bennie a book on the SNP to be published in late 2010. Previous books include *Conservatives and the Union* (1990), *Strategies for Self-Government: The Campaigns for a Scottish Parliament* (1996) and *Governing Scotland: The Invention of Administrative Devolution* (2003).

Philip Schlesinger is Professor in Cultural Policy at the University of Glasgow, where he directs the Centre for Cultural Policy Research. He is currently working on creative economy policies and cultural practices. An editor of *Media, Culture and Society* journal, he is author of *Media, State and Nation* (Sage 1991) and co-author of *Open Scotland?* (2001). He is a Fellow of the Royal Society of Edinburgh and an Academician of the Academy of Social Sciences and currently Chairman of the Ofcom Advisory Committee for Scotland.

David Torrance is a freelance writer, broadcaster and journalist. He is the author of three books on Scottish political history including '*We in Scotland*': *Thatcherism in a Cold Climate* (2009). He reports on the Scottish Parliament for STV, and contributes political commentary to a wide range of publications including *The Scotsman*, *The Herald* and *The Times*.

Alex Wright is a lecturer in politics at the University of Dundee. His published works include an edited volume, *Scotland: The Challenge of Devolution* (2000), *Who Governs Scotland?* (2005) and a co-authored book with David Gowland and Arthur Turner, *Britain and European Integration since 1945: On the Sidelines* (2009). He was a member of the Scottish Consumer Council (1998–2002) and an Assessor for the Commissioner of Public Appointments in Scotland (2002–7).

CHAPTER I

The Making of the Modern SNP:
From Protest to Power

Gerry Hassan

The Scottish National Party celebrates its 75th anniversary this year in good heart and shape. Established in 1934 as the amalgamation of two parties – the National Party of Scotland and the Scottish Party – it now finds itself in the unprecedented position of being Scotland's government after winning the 2007 Scottish Parliament elections, the first set of national elections the party has won in its history.

The SNP has, in the last 40 years, moved from being a marginal force often ridiculed, patronised and caricatured by opponents to a force which is both respected and feared, and which has defined and reshaped Scottish politics, brought the Scottish dimension centre stage and forced other political parties to respond on their terms.

It is now the accepted wisdom to state that 'modern Scottish politics' began with Winnie Ewing's victory in the Hamilton by-election in 1967. If this is true then modern politics can be defined in at least three distinct phases: firstly, 1967–79, taking us from Hamilton through the devolution decade; secondly, 1979–97, the Thatcher/Major years; and finally the election of New Labour in 1997 leading to the establishment of the Scottish Parliament in 1999 and the election of a SNP minority administration in 2007.

From this argument of Scottish politics post-Hamilton the modern SNP as we know it has been a long time coming with several milestones along the way. There was the party's reaction and then slow clawback from the shock of 1979, the re-emergence of the Scottish question in 1987 and the arrival of the Blair government committed to legislating for a Scottish Parliament. The contemporary SNP is a very different party from the one which sensationally broke through in the 1960s and was such an important force in the 1970s.

The journey of Scottish politics since the mid-1960s operates at a much deeper level as well. It was no accident that the SNP along with

1

Plaid Cymru erupted onto the Scottish and Welsh political scene in the months of 1966–7, for it occurred at the time of the high tide and then disillusion with the Wilson government after its 1966 election, an era of 'comatose constitutional orthodoxy' and 'bland electoral complacency' in the Scottish and Welsh Labour establishments (Marquand 2008: 222). This period of, first, Plaid Cymru winning Carmarthen and, then, the SNP winning Hamilton coincided with a fundamental crisis of British social democracy, from which it has never recovered. The road from Wilson's humiliation with the November 1967 devaluation, two weeks after Winnie Ewing's victory, takes us directly to the 1976 IMF crisis, the final burial of Croslandite social democracy, the ascendancy of Thatcherism and the creation of Blair's New Labour (Hassan 2007). The emergence of Scottish and Welsh nationalism were a product of the crisis of the British state and economy and the UK's place in the global economy (Nairn 2003).

Remembering the SNP:
Histories, Cultures and Peoples

Despite the widespread influence of the SNP in Scottish and UK politics the contemporary SNP has been significantly under-researched in Scotland, as have all the mainstream political parties. The most influential and prominent research into the SNP has studied Scottish nationalism and the party as a sub-set of this: seen in the work of Hanham (1969), Brand (1978) and Mitchell (1996). These works have covered a range of areas including the dynamics between Scottish nationalism culturally and politically, the influence of literary nationalism in the inter-war years, the emergence and establishment of the SNP and examination of where it drew support, the party's role in the campaign for self-government, and the relationship between minority (Scottish) and majority (British) nationalism in the UK.

There has been only one history of the entire period of the party's existence, namely Lynch (2002), while Finlay's (1994) research concentrated on the early years of the party. A number of senior SNP politicians have produced autobiographies from the early to middle period: figures such as John MacCormick (1955), Wendy Wood (1970), and William Wolfe (1973), and MPs such as Winnie Ewing (2004), Donald Stewart (1994) and Jim Sillars (1996). With the exception of Dick Douglas's autobiography of Robert McIntyre (1996), there is a complete lack of serious biographies about any SNP figures, including Alex Salmond. This reflects a wider Scottish pattern whereby the only senior Scottish political figures that earn the right of autobiographies are those who have established themselves as 'British figures' such as Gordon Brown, Robin Cook and Menzies Campbell.

Therefore, the exclusive focus of the published work on the party has been a historical angle with a conspicuous absence of analysing and understanding the contemporary SNP that this book hopes in part to remedy.

POWER AND PLACE MAKING AND THE SNP

The SNP's evolution from being the small party it was pre-1967 took it through many changes – explored by Richard Finlay and James Mitchell in their respective chapters. The party in the 1940s and 1950s, post-John MacCormick's departure to set up the Scottish Convention, was one of 'true believers' with an oligarchial leadership and centralisation of power (Brand 1978: 278). This slowly changed as the party grew and won increasing support and began to develop a more informal and collegiate style.

The modern SNP that arrived on the political scene in the 1960s was one of a party in flux: with a new, mass membership, a more consensual form of leadership and a form of campaigning and energy which changed the nature of the by-election in Scotland in a manner the Liberals did in England. The party's breakthrough since 1967 onward gave it a new sense of purpose, which particularly in the 1974–9 parliament gave it enormous attention, but also scrutiny and pressure. The party did not escape from this experience unscathed and this is explored by a number of contributors to this volume. Power in the party in the 1960s and 1970s was held diffusely with two alternating power centres in the party: the Westminster leadership and the party National Executive Committee. At points in the 1974–9 parliament these two groups were in conflict and loggerheads, as seen for example with the crucial endgame of the Callaghan government.

In the late 1980s and early 1990s the party became more professional. This was accentuated by the leadership of Alex Salmond from 1990 to 2000 and by the Salmond–Mike Russell preparations for the first Scottish Parliament elections in 1999. The party in a number of respects seemed to be aspiring to copy the New Labour organisational model of politics in those first elections, but it took the interregnum of John Swinney's leadership to put effective structures in place which modernised the party. This unleashed ferrous resistance in some sections of the party with a leadership challenge in 2003 from Bill Wilson, and one SNP member saying after the contest about Swinney's changes: 'He is going down the road of Labour and the Tories. It is a sign of weak leadership and it will destroy the soul of the party' (*The Times*, 23 November 2003). The preparations for the 2007 Scottish Parliament elections with Alex Salmond in charge saw the final comprehensive transformation and modernisation of the SNP as a campaigning, electoral and communication force with an impressive IT and voter ID strategy which, for the first time, saw the SNP able to out-professionalise Labour (Guthrie 2003).

This overhauling of the SNP in terms of internal power and capacity relates to the place of the party in the political system. In the 1970s the SNP had self-proclaimed centre-left policies: its February 1974 manifesto called itself a 'programme of social democracy', while the October 1974 manifesto was subtitled 'A Programme for Social Democracy'. However, there was still a degree of ambiguity at the heart of the party with some politicians calling the party 'centre-left', others 'centrist' and the Party Election Broadcast in the October 1974 election stating, 'I've voted once for Both Sides Now, For Right and Left, and yet somehow, It's their illusions I recall' (Bayne 1991: 55). The party were nervous of explicitly embracing a social democratic philosophy.

After the 1987 election the party began to become more comfortable asserting a social democratic outlook. The party's identity became genuinely anchored on the centre-left, reflecting wider changes in Scotland and the fusing of the national dimension and centre-left politics. However, there are a number of problems with taking this account at face value. Before going further it would be useful to offer some definition of social democracy which can still be understood by the left's traditional values of 'liberty, equality, fraternity'. Social democracy is centred on government intervention and regulation, to make society fairer and less unequal, and on an ideal of freedom which embraces economic and social rights. Tony Blair, Gordon Brown and Gerhard Schröder have been associated with the forces of 'new social democracy' which once promised so much and which can be measured by their own mantra to 'not retreat before the tide of neo-liberalism: acquisitive individualism is a brutal and crippled view of humanity' (Cornford and Hewitt 1994: 251); by these words it can only be seen as a humiliating failure.

First, the party leadership at key points in this transformation, post-1987 and the 1999 elections being the best examples, decided to articulate what seemed like an unproblematic version of social democracy. This was driven in both cases by a positioning strategy and place-making sense in the Scottish political environment, attempting to outflank Labour on the left. Therefore the party was, in its attempts to challenge New Labour in the run-in to the 1999 elections, uncritically supportive of a whole host of producer interests, higher public spending across a range of areas, and against modernisation of public services. One of the central problems at this time was that the party had decided to unconditionally become social democratic when this tradition was now in widespread crisis across the globe and in retreat across most of Western Europe in the face of the neo-liberal onslaught inspired by Margaret Thatcher and Ronald Reagan.

Second, this led the party's social democratic embrace to become mediated and qualified by neo-liberalism and the economic and social orthodoxies of the age. Neo-liberalism can be understood as the worldwide crusade for a narrow notion of 'freedom' which has in the last 30 years centred on marketisation, inequality and a model of corporate governance which rewards business elites (Doogan 2009).

The Nationalist leadership became advocates of what Jim and Margaret Cuthbert call in their chapter 'neo-liberalism with a heart', which in many respects is not that different from Blair/Brown New Labour. It is true that even when the party were uncritically embracing social democratic policies in 1999, there were still elements of neo-liberalism, as in the advocacy of the Laffer Curve, one of the key staples of Reaganomics, by Jim Mather. Yet by 2007 this influence had gone much further with the party embracing a 'Scotland plc' agenda of independence based significantly on the financial sector, light-touch regulation and not challenging vested interests – all of which has been thrown in the air by the global economic crises of 2008–9.

A different interpretation of the above events and the SNP's transformation can be found utilising Henry Drucker's idea of 'doctrine and ethos' which he used in his path-breaking analysis of British Labour (Drucker 1979). The SNP's 'doctrine' is formally social democratic, mixed with an accommodation with neo-liberalism, while its 'ethos', the party's sense of itself, is Scottish nationalist. This has at times articulated an 'I believe in Scotland' outlook which has perceived those who are not SNP sympathisers as being in some sense 'anti-Scottish'. This has over the years infuriated unionist parties who have seen this as the Nationalists claiming they have exclusive ownership of 'Scotland'; such an outlook can be seen in the SNP slogan in the 1960s, 'Put Scotland First', which, in the words of the party, 'no other party can use because the National Party is the only Scottish political party' (Hanham 1969: 205).

This takes us to the notion of what is the 'party soul', in the sense of Eric Shaw's words 'what endows a party with its sense of being or . . . its utopia'. This utopia 'may never be fully attainable but the striving towards it gives meaning to its sacrifices' (Shaw 2007: 40).

This 'utopia' in the Scottish National Party is the idea of Scottish statehood and independence which carries more weight than any sense of left or right. This is not in any sense to diminish the extent to which SNP members and activists see themselves and their party as firmly and without qualification on the centre-left, and particularly versus the failures of the New Labour 'near-left' experience, but merely to address the issue of what motivates and informs the party's soul.

Where did Scottish Nationalist voters come from, and how did the party change through the years since its first breakthrough? Post-1967 the party was associated with winning support in 'new towns' such as Cumbernauld, Glenrothes and East Kilbride, the 'new working class' as seen in Hamilton and West Lothian, and younger voters. According to a 1968 *Scotsman* survey, SNP support was more representative of the population socio-economically than the two main parties, although weaker in managerial and professional groups (Hanham 1969: 188–9).

Similar surveys in 1974 showed that while Labour and the Conservatives were still 'class parties', the SNP was not. The party won support from those with weak religious and class identities, and was not strong amongst Catholics and those aged over 45. It gained the votes of young voters, the self-employed, workers in small establishments and people with experience of unemployment, either personally or in their own family (Miller 1981: 144, 147).

By 1992 SNP support began more closely to resemble Labour's than at any previous election, winning more support in the West of Scotland, among working-class voters and in the Catholic community than previously, while still in each being significantly behind Labour (Mitchell 1996: 291). In the first Scottish Parliament elections SNP support increasingly became representative of Scotland as a whole, but the party still found it difficult to win constituency seats, particularly in the West of Scotland. This underlined that the main obstacle to Nationalist advance was the attachment of a sufficiently large part of Scotland, albeit declining, to Scottish Labour.

In the 2007 elections the SNP won its first ever national elections, narrowly both in votes and seats: 32.9% of constituency votes to 32.1% for Labour, winning 47 seats to Labour's 46 (see Table 1.1). The SNP gained more votes from men than women, proving unable to close the historic 'gender gap' in support for the Nationalists (as Fiona Mackay and Meryl Kenny explore in their contribution), amongst younger voters (and 18–24-year-olds in particular) and amongst skilled manual workers, although the party's support remained much more broad based in 'class' terms than Labour. The social base of SNP support in 2007, as explored by John Curtice in his chapter, varies relatively little across Scotland – from owner occupiers to council tenants, Catholics to Protestants – with only one group voting by a majority SNP (private rented tenants). There was still evidence of a reluctance in Labour's heartlands to vote SNP with

Table 1.1 Scottish Parliament Election results (% of votes)

	Constituency			Regional		
	1999	2003	2007	1999	2003	2007
Labour	38.8	34.6	32.1	33.6	29.3	29.2
SNP	28.7	23.8	32.9	27.3	20.9	31.0
Conservative	15.6	16.6	16.6	15.4	15.5	13.9
Lib Dem	14.2	15.4	16.2	12.4	11.8	11.3
Greens	0.0	0.0	0.1	3.6	6.9	4.0
Others	2.7	9.6	2.1	7.7	15.6	10.6

Source: Herbert et al. (2007), SPICe Briefing

Table 1.2 Westminster election results in Scotland, 1997–2005

	1997	2001	2005
Labour	45.6	43.2	39.5
SNP	22.1	20.1	17.7
Conservative	17.5	15.6	15.8
Lib Dem	13.0	16.4	22.6
Others	1.9	4.7	5.1

Source: Rallings and Thrasher (2006)

Table 1.3 European Parliament election results, 1979–2009

	1979	1984	1989	1994	1999	2004	2009
Labour	33.0	40.7	41.9	42.5	28.7	26.4	20.8
SNP	19.4	17.8	25.6	32.6	27.2	19.7	29.1
Conservative	33.7	25.7	20.9	14.5	19.8	17.8	16.8
Lib Dem	14.0	15.6	4.3	7.2	9.8	13.1	11.5
Green	–	0.2	7.2	1.6	5.8	6.8	7.3
Others	–	–	–	2.5	8.9	16.3	14.5

Source: Hassan and Fraser (2004); UK Office of the European Parliament (2009)

Table 1.4 Local government election results, 1995–2007

	1995	1999	2003	2007
Labour	43.8	36.6	32.9	28.1
SNP	26.2	28.9	24.3	27.9
Conservative	11.3	13.7	15.2	15.6
Lib Dem	9.7	12.7	14.6	12.7
Ind	7.6	6.5	9.5	10.9
Others	1.5	1.7	3.6	4.9

Source: Denver and Bochel (1995; 2007)

the party's only gains in West and Central Scotland: Glasgow Govan, Kilmarnock and Cunninghame North from Labour and Falkirk West from Independent. Labour won 28 of the 33 constituency seats in Glasgow and West/Central Scotland to the SNP's 4 and Conservative 1; the rest of the country returned 9 Labour, 17 SNP, 11 Lib Dems and 3 Conservative out of 40 constituencies.[1] While the SNP have still to make advances in large parts of the West of Scotland, huge progress has been made, and the strength of voters' attachment to Scottish Labour does now appear to be critically weakening.

The pattern of SNP support at Westminster, European and local government elections (Tables 1.2 to 2.4) presents a complex picture. At Westminster elections the Nationalists secured second place in votes in 1997 for the first time since October 1974. They held onto second place in 2001 despite losing votes, but in 2005 slipped into third place behind the Lib Dems. The pattern at European and local government elections is a more positive one. The 2009 Euro elections saw the Nationalists finish ahead of Labour for the first time, while in the 2007 council elections the party finished just behind Labour in votes, but ahead in council seats, aided by the introduction of the Single Transferable Vote (STV).

One conclusion emerging from the different elections is that where the Nationalists have pulled ahead or are level pegging with Labour, this is as much to do with Labour weakness as SNP popularity. The SNP's Scottish Parliament constituency vote in 2007 (32.9%) is only a little above the party's Westminster peak of October 1974 (30.4%) – the difference being the decline in Labour's vote. The party's current European and local government shares of the vote have previously been bested by the party in the 1994 and 1999 elections respectively. Just as one of the major contributory factors of Labour dominance in the 1980s was Conservative decline and weakness, now one of the major factors in SNP strength is Labour decline and weakness in an increasingly multi-party political environment.

Understanding the SNP: Scottish Nationalism and Nationalism

There has historically been a lack of intellectual activity and thinking within the SNP; although this is a truism that can be levelled at all Scotland's main political parties, remembering Wendy Alexander's argument that 'one of the last times the Labour movement in Scotland made a real intellectual contribution to the UK Labour Party was around . . . 1906' (*Daily Telegraph*, 30 September 2002). This was a bit harsh, as the party had a particularly fertile period in the 1920s, but broadly correct. The SNP combines this with little substantial work or intellectual curiosity in the area of policy.

The 1970s was an exception to this, witnessing a period of great activity and creativity on the part of Scottish Nationalists with the publication of *The Radical Approach* (Kennedy 1976) and *Power and Manoeuvrability* (Carty and McCall Smith 1978); and the journals *Scottish International Review* and *Question* explored progressive issues about Scotland's politics, culture and place in the world. The late 1990s and early 21st century will be seen in hindsight as another positive period for the SNP, but of a very different kind, seeing no comparable publications from the Nationalist canon setting the agenda. Pre-2007, there was the well-intentioned work of Kenny MacAskill (2004) alongside Mike Russell's advocacy of a host of predictable right-wing and neo-liberal platitudes (MacLeod and Russell 2006).

The late 1980s and early 1990s saw the Scottish Centre for Economic and Social Research publish an ambitious series of independent papers by thinkers such as Christopher Harvie and James Mitchell, but this was undertaken on a shoestring and proved to be unsustainable. This difficulty can be seen today in the lack of institutional support for the party whether it is in civil society, newspapers and media, business or think tanks. Labour has historically had a rich array of support across Scottish civil society which has given it a major advantage versus its competitors. This has sustained its role as the leading party of the nation, blurred boundaries between state and non-state and allowed a party which at its core was not that strong and without a mass membership to achieve hegemony (Hassan 2004).

This leads to the question of who owns 'Scottish nationalism', with the SNP on occasion seeing Scottish Nationalism and nationalism as synonymous. The journey from Gordon Brown's *Red Paper on Scotland* (1975) – a set of essays (including one by Vince Cable) which began as a critique of Ted Heath's Conservative government in Scotland, and which became through delay and dithering a collection which addressed the rise of the SNP in the two 1974 elections – to *A Claim of Right for Scotland* (Dudley Edwards 1989) collection, saw a significant part of the Scottish political community re-appraise and articulate a generous, inclusive version of Scottish nationalism. Interestingly, and not by accident, both volumes were all male in composition, the Brown collection containing 29 male contributors, illustrating the gender-insensitive nature of a section of Scotland which proclaimed its progressive credentials. However, to many in the SNP these were not Nationalist perspectives, but documents which invoked a quasi-nationalist language but were really influenced by unionist thinking. Chris McLean gave voice to this in his response to *A*

Claim of Right, seeing that for all its radical rhetoric it supported the UK constitution and British sovereignty (McLean 1989).

The SNP has consistently had problems with intellectuals and thinkers, but this is not unusual in party politics. Tom Nairn and Neal Ascherson are two examples of nationalist thinkers who have had problems with Scottish Nationalism. Neil MacCormick is the exception to the rule and that rare example of someone who combined an intellectual life with elected office. His writing influenced the SNP's recent thinking about independence and the Scottish government's 'National Conversation' (MacCormick 1999). Nairn for many years had a difficult relationship with the party, his writings on nationalism being revered across the globe but uncelebrated at home and unacknowledged by the Nationalists. This has shifted in recent years with Alex Salmond as First Minister inviting Nairn to give a prestigious Lothian Lecture and embracing him as one of the leading Scottish Nationalist thinkers (Nairn 2008).

The Devolution Years and the Coming to Power of the SNP

Pre-devolution, the history of the SNP was that of occasional by-election victories,[2] followed by hype, the party getting carried away with its own rhetoric, and then disappointment. This was the pattern of 1979 and 1992. Post-devolution, the reality of the SNP and Scottish politics has utterly changed. The SNP are a permanent fixture on the landscape. Not only has George Robertson's prediction that 'devolution will kill Scottish Nationalism stone dead' been proven wrong, it has given it a platform, a plausible strategy and the trappings, prestige and resources of office.

The appeal of the Nationalists slowly changed over the course of devolution, sometimes imperceptibly, sometimes dramatically. Initially, the party did not seem to know what it wanted to do with its new resources: was it there to make a success of devolution on the road to independence, or show its failures? Slowly the answer came in two forms: firstly, the sheer unattractiveness of much of Labour rule of Scotland; and secondly, under Alex Salmond's leadership from 2004, the transformation of the SNP's message on Scotland. Previously the party had often stressed what was wrong in Scotland, an essentially negative message suited to the long years of Thatcherism, but borne of an oppositionalist mindset. Salmond recognised that the party needed to tell a more positive story, of the potential of Scotland as a self-governing nation. Faced with a mostly uninspiring Labour campaign in 2007, the SNP's uplifting account struck a very different tone.

Many different forces, influences and individuals came together and pushed for a different approach in the long run-up to 2007. There was the work done by the Really Effective Development Company, a business development company. There were activities drawing upon American 'positive psychologist' Martin Seligman and in particular his book, *Learned Optimism* (Seligman 1990).[3] There was also the move of people to the SNP, shocked with the style and substance of the Labour–Lib Dem coalition. This coalesced into the desire for a different kind of party, a different kind of campaigning and message, and for a different kind of Alex Salmond, all of which he and the party leadership embraced. Allied to this was a hunger to win and a belief that the 2007 elections offered a huge opportunity to an SNP which was serious, professional and focused. This Nationalist transformation completely surprised and wrong-footed Labour.

The nature of the Scottish Nationalists in office has seen several commentators such as Iain Macwhirter proclaim that the party 'seems to have done more to further social democratic values in ten months than Labour managed in ten years' (Macwhirter 2008). This has become less marked over time, with the SNP appearing as the same uneasy compromise between centre-left values and that of neo-liberalism as Labour – as witnessed in the party's unsavoury promotion of American multi-millionaire Donald Trump, its funding from Brian Souter and its proposals for privatising forestry. Yet, there was also something very different and more progressive about the SNP from the outset in office which has remained: the tone, style and content of Alex Salmond's minority administration was one of 'Scotland's Government' as it proclaimed, aspiring to be the national voice of Scotland, in contrast to the timid Labour–Lib Dem Executive which preceded it.

From the outset the new administration was, in Chris Harvie's words, 'eager to please strategic lobbies' such as COSLA, while 'familiar begging bowls were briskly filled' (Harvie 2008: 39–40). In many respects in detail and policy the SNP administration has had a patchy record. As a minority administration the party has had to be deft and pragmatic in the Scottish Parliament, and in 2007–8 only seven Scottish bills were passed, compared with ten Sewel motions which give Westminster permission to legislate for Scotland (*The Times*, 12 May 2009).

In particular there was the absence, pre-crash, of any plausible explanation of political economy, beyond the inanities of the 'knowledge economy' with its talk of 'smarter Scotland' and 'competitive advantage' (Salmond 2008a); but in that, as many things, the Nationalists mirrored mainstream conventional politics. Across economic, social and cultural policy, as Jim and Margaret Cuthbert, Stephen Maxwell and Philip

Schlesinger make clear in their contributions, there has been a sense of the SNP going along with existing ideas and conventional wisdom, rather than being innovative. Such challenges are always difficult in a small policy-making community, whether devolved or independent.

AFTER BRITAIN?

There is the issue of how the SNP wish to be judged in office and what would success look like on its terms. Does the party have a 'national project' in terms of the kind of Scottish society it would like to see? What ambitions does it have for and beyond the idea of independence?

The issue of independence – so long and indeed still mocked by unionist politicians as 'eccentric' and not 'mainstream' – and the debate between it and the Union is one of the main fault-lines of Scottish politics. Indeed, after the demise of socialism it could be argued it is the central one. Surprisingly, apart from some SNP thinking in the 1970s there has been scant detailed thinking by the party or others about independence with (apart from Neil MacCormick) the primary exception in recent years being the London-based Constitution Unit, which produced an important study that focused more on legal and process issues and ignored politics (Murkens et al. 2002).

The contemporary case for independence put by the SNP until recently gave a central place to Scotland's financial institutions and the success of the small independent nations surrounding Scotland. This all changed with the global crises of 2008–9 and the banking meltdown which saw massive UK government intervention and nationalisation of the banks. Alex Salmond had previously invoked 'an arc of prosperity' including Iceland and Ireland (Salmond 2008b), which was now called by his opponents 'an arc of insolvency', given the perilous state of both economies. It was clear that the argument for independence would have to be substantially rethought.

The meaning of Scottish autonomy, statehood and sovereignty is central to independence and is explored by Alex Wright in his contribution examining the SNP's understanding of 'Britain'. We now live in an age defined by the fluidity and movement of power and authority – the mantra of the globalisers – alongside an ever-increasing concentration of power in political, business and media elites. These contradictory movements are of relevance to the Scottish experience, the future of the UK and how the dynamics of the European dimension evolve.

The old absolutist claims of statehood and sovereignty articulated by Tory Eurosceptics and Labour 'little Englanders' are increasingly irrelevant to the world described above. Some Scottish Nationalists hold out similar simplistic viewpoints, but despite Labour and Tory rhetoric against the Nationalists, claiming that the cause of independence runs counter to the age of globalisation, the main body politic of the SNP has adapted much more convincingly to the times than have the two main UK parties.

The nature of the British state and its ancient obsessions with sovereignty have shown that, even after more than a decade of Labour government supposedly committed to reform and a 'new politics', it has proven incapable of radically reforming and democratising itself. The crises of the British parliamentary democracy and state which engulfed politics in May 2009 showed a deep crisis of politics and the political classes, while at the same time, a post-British set of identities and politics has slowly been evolving (Gardiner 2004).

The European dimension has proven increasingly problematic to the British state since the entry of the UK to then EEC in 1973. The election of a David Cameron Conservative government in the future would see the return of an explicitly Eurosceptic agenda, hostile to further European integration and in favour of repatriating powers to Westminster. Such a course would have huge consequences in Scotland with Scottish political, business and civic institutions openly aligning themselves with Europe rather than the UK. This would be an accentuation of the shift evident in the latter days of the Thatcher era, but much more pronounced, and one which would strengthen the case for independence.

Europe matters enormously to the SNP and the argument for independence. It takes independence out from being an insular argument and sets it in a wider, modern context, something explored by Eve Hepburn and Michael Keating in their chapters. Europe underlines the problematic nature of the British state and its inability to share sovereignty and embrace European integration.

There is now a growing literature across the world about the role of small nations and devolved nations, regions and territories in an age of interdependence and shared sovereignty (Keating 2001). This addresses the limits of sovereignty and the prospects and limitations of 'post-sovereignty'. Such debates show the need to rethink and reimagine the case for independence, along with the argument for the UK as well. Independence has become a more fluid concept, about sharing and pooling sovereignty in new alliances and networks, from Europe to elsewhere. The nature of the UK state similarly has to face these challenges and respond in ways which, for all the rhetoric from UK governments, Labour and Tory, it has not done convincingly.

This is now a debate about change and reform rather than the status quo, witnessed in the workings of the Calman Commission and Scottish government's 'National Conversation'. These initiatives are being driven by wider social forces illustrating that the UK is on the move to a destination as yet unknown which is not under the control of the British government. The direction is undoubtedly in favour of a looser set of arrangements, which will involve decentralism, fragmentation and multiple levels of authority that could entail Scottish independence or new forms of autonomy. What is clear is that some accounts of this get carried away in a post-modern sense of change and fluidity that fails to acknowledge the unreformed nature of the British state, which will act as a major brake on any future change, unless overcome.

While domestic policy will prove the most important, there is also the arena of defence and foreign policy, seen in such concerns as British nuclear weapons being sited on the Clyde, the Euro-sceptic, pro-Atlanticist role of the British state which led us into the quagmires of Iraq and Afghanistan, and the wider militarisation of Scotland. SNP policy provides a direct threat to powerful geo-political interests in the UK government, those of US and NATO, who would pose major obstacles to Scotland negotiating a different path to where it currently is.

Some commentators claim that the SNP's cause of independence does not really matter and that it is either a small parochial issue or an ultimately bourgeois concern. The sociologist Michael Mann gives voice to this when he dismisses a range of 'stateless nations' with the question, 'Does it finally matter whether Quebec remains part of Canada, or Scotland part of the United Kingdom, or Catalonia part of Spain?', and then goes on:

> If Quebec, Scotland or Catalonia separate from their imperial ruler, people will not die or be driven from their homes. Rather they will worry about the consequences for investment and employment, what languages they will learn, or whether a tiny country would ever qualify for the World Cup finals . . . For the past decade the Québécois, Scots and Catalans have been dithering at election time, unable to decide whether they really do want independence. It doesn't matter much, one way or the other, either for them or for their supposed exploiters. (Mann 2005: 525)

Mann surely protesteth too much. Scotland has had a relatively privileged experience in the modern capitalist age in comparison to lots of examples: the ethnic cleansing of Bosnia-Herzegovina, genocide in Darfur or the suffering of the Palestinians at the hands of one of the world's most powerful military machines, the Israelis.

What cannot be ignored is the nature of the British state and the role Britain continues to play across the world while it still professes to be 'the Mother of Parliaments'. The British state is not the benign entity Fabian socialists used to think it was, but an 'Empire State' (Barnett 1997). This state places itself in the nexus of a geo-political alliance which aids those with power and wealth in the world, while happily embracing its subordinate role in the American military project, colluding in torture in 'the war on terror' and two unwinnable wars. Britain's nuclear weapons would become a controversial subject in any independence discussions (Chalmers and Walker 2001); they are both 'a political hornet's nest' and offer 'real bargaining power for Scotland' (Murkens et al. 2002: 89, 90). There are potential similarities with this and the end of the Soviet Union which witnessed discussions between the Russians and Ukrainians over nuclear weapons and the Soviet Black Sea Fleet. All this shows that Scottish independence matters at Scottish, UK and international levels.

The SNP's contribution to these processes will be vitally important at a Scottish and UK level. However, the Nationalists will need to recognise that this debate is not just about writing and imagining 'a new Scottish constitution' in Tom Nairn terms, but filling out and articulating a 'national project' about the kind of Scotland and society people want to live in, and how government and institutions align themselves with those values.

This book is published at a crucial time for Scottish politics, but also for the UK and wider global economy. A UK general election is on the cards which could see the return of the Conservatives which will throw up all sorts of questions: about the devolution settlement and nature of power in the UK, particularly in light of the economic crash in the UK, about future public spending constraints, and about the systematic crisis of the British political system, which amounts to a far-reaching crisis of the British state. The SNP has contributed hugely to the vitality and energy of Scotland and Scottish political life in recent years and under devolution. This book hopes to offer insights into and analysis of that journey and the possibilities ahead.

NOTES

1. The Glasgow, West of Scotland and Central Scotland regional constituencies, along with the four seats of Ayrshire and South Lanarkshire, make up the 33 seats.
2. The SNP's reputation in winning parliamentary by-elections is based on the seismic and totemic nature of a few victories. From Motherwell in 1945 to Glenrothes in 2008, the SNP has fought 74 Westminster and Scottish Parliament by-elections and won 6: Motherwell, Hamilton, Glasgow Govan (twice), Perth & Kinross and Glasgow East.
3. Details of the Really Effective Development Company can be found at www.redco. uk. Martin Seligman's work in 'positive psychology' has been hugely influential the world over, but this has not prevented him being implicated in the role American

psychologists have played in 'the war on terror'. See: http://www.americantorture.com/labels/DDD.htm

REFERENCES

Barnett, A. (1997), *This Time: Our Constitutional Revolution*, London, Vintage.

Bayne, I. O. (1991), 'The Impact of 1979 on the SNP', in Gallacher, T. (ed.), *Nationalism in the Nineties*, Edinburgh, Polygon, pp. 46–65.

Brand, J. (1978), *The Nationalist Movement in Scotland*, London, Routledge and Kegan Paul.

Brown, G. (ed.) (1975), *The Red Paper on Scotland*, Edinburgh, Edinburgh Student Publications Board.

Carty, T. and McCall Smith, A. (eds) (1978), *Power and Manoeuvrability: The International Implications of an Independent Scotland*, Edinburgh, Q Press.

Chalmers, M. and Walker, W. (2001), *The UK, Nuclear Weapons and the Scottish Question*, East Linton, Tuckwell Press.

Cornford, J. and Hewitt, P. (1994), 'Dos and Don'ts for Social Democrats', in Miliband, D. (ed.), *Reinventing the Left*, Cambridge, Polity Press, pp. 251–4.

Denver, D. and Bochel, H. (1995), 'Catastrophe for the Conservatives: The Council Elections of 1995', *Scottish Affairs*, No. 13, pp. 15–26.

Denver, D. and Bochel, H. (2007), 'A Quiet Revolution: STV and the Scottish Council Elections of 2007', *Scottish Affairs*, No. 61, pp. 1–18.

Doogan, K. (2009), *New Capitalism? The Transformation of Work*, Cambridge, Polity Press.

Douglas, D. (1996), *At the Helm: The Life and Times of Dr. Robert McIntyre*, Portessie, NPFI Publications.

Drucker, H. M. (1979), *Doctrine and Ethos in the Labour Party*, London, George Allen and Unwin.

Dudley Edwards, O. (1989) (ed.), *A Claim of Right for Scotland*, Edinburgh, Polygon.

Ewing, W. (2004), *Stop the World: The Autobiography of Winnie Ewing*, Edinburgh, Birlinn.

Finlay, R. J. (1994), *Independent and Free: Scottish Politics and the Origins of the Scottish National Party 1918–1945*, Edinburgh, John Donald.

Gardiner, M. (2004), *The Cultural Roots of British Devolution*, Edinburgh, Edinburgh University Press.

Guthrie, G. (2003), *The SNP Electoral Systems Review*, unpublished paper.

Hanham, H. J. (1969), *Scottish Nationalism*, London, Faber and Faber.

Harvie, C. (2008), 'A Year with Salmond', *Scottish Affairs*, No. 65, pp. 38–46.

Hassan, G. (ed.) (2004), *The Scottish Labour Party: History, Institutions and Ideas*, Edinburgh, Edinburgh University Press.

Hassan, G. (2007), 'Labour, Concepts of Britishness, "Nation" and "State"', in Hassan, G. (ed.), *After Blair: Politics after the New Labour Decade*, London, Lawrence and Wishart, pp. 75–93.

Hassan, G. and Fraser, D. (2004), *The Political Guide to Modern Scotland*, London, Politico's Publishing.

Herbert, S., Burnside, R., Earle, M., Edwards, T., Foley, T. and McIver, I. (2007), *Election 2007*, SPICe Briefing, Edinburgh, Scottish Parliament, Research Paper 07/21.

Keating, M. (2001), *Plurinational Democracy: Stateless Nations in a Post-Sovereignty Era*, Oxford, Oxford University Press.

Kennedy, G. (ed.) (1976), *The Radical Approach: Papers on an Independent Scotland*, Edinburgh, Palingenesis Press.

Lynch, P. (2002), *SNP: The History of the Scottish National Party*, Cardiff, Welsh Academic Press.

MacAskill, K. (2004), *Building A Nation: Post-Devolution Nationalism*, Edinburgh, Luath Press.

MacCormick, J. (1955), *The Flag in the Wind: The Story of the National Movement*, London, Victor Gollancz.

MacCormick, N. (1999), *Questioning Sovereignty: Law, State, and Nation in the European Commonwealth*, Oxford, Oxford University Press.

MacLeod, D. and Russell, M. (2006), *Grasping the Thistle: How Scotland Must React to the Three Key Challenges of the Twenty First Century*, Glendaruel, Argyll Publishing.

Macwhirter, I. (2008), 'Brown's blue rinse obscures Labour's true colours', *Sunday Herald*, 6 April.

McLean, C. (1989), 'Claim of Right or Cap in Hand?', in Dudley Edwards, O. (ed.), *A Claim of Right for Scotland*, Edinburgh, Polygon, pp. 110–18.

Mann, M. (2005), *The Dark Side of Democracy: Explaining Ethnic Cleansing*, Cambridge, Cambridge University Press.

Marquand, D. (2008), *Britain since 1918: The Strange Career of British Democracy*, London, Weidenfeld and Nicolson.

Miller, W. L. (1981), *The End of British Politics? Scots and English Political Behaviour in the Seventies*, Oxford, Clarendon Press.

Mitchell, J. (1996), *Strategies for Self-Government: The Campaigns for a Scottish Parliament*, Edinburgh, Polygon.

Murkens, J. E. with Jones, P. and Keating, M. (2002), *Scottish Independence: A Practical Guide*, Edinburgh, Edinburgh University Press.

Nairn, T. (2003), *The Break-Up of Britain: Crisis and Neo-nationalism*, 3rd edn, Glasgow/Melbourne, Big Thinking/Common Ground.

Nairn, T. (2008), 'Globalisation and Nationalism: The New Deal', Lothian Lecture, Edinburgh, http://www.opendemocracy.net/article/globalisation/institutions_government/nationalism_the_new_deal

Rallings, C. and Thrasher, M. (2006), *British Electoral Facts 1832–2006*, Aldershot, Ashgate.

Salmond, A. (2008a), 'Speech to National Economic Forum', 6 February, http://www.scotland.gov.uk/News/This-Week/Speeches/First-Minister/nat-econ-forum

Salmond, A. (2008b), 'Scotland Can Be One of World's Wealthiest Countries', SNP, 6 February, http://www.snp.org/node/7499

Seligman, M. E. P. (1990), *Learned Optimism: How to Change Your Mind and Your Life*, New York, Pocket Books.

Shaw, E. (2007), *Losing Labour's Soul: New Labour and the Blair Government 1997–2007*, London, Routledge.

Sillars, J. (1986), *Scotland: The Case for Optimism*, Edinburgh, Polygon.

Stewart, D. (1994), *A Scot at Westminster*, Sydney, Nova Scotia, Catalone Press.

UK Office of the European Parliament (2009), *Results of 2009 European Elections in the UK*, http://www.europarl.org.uk/section/european-elections/results-2009-european-elections-uk#scotland

Wolfe, W. (1973), *Scotland Lives: The Quest for Independence*, Edinburgh, Reprographia.

Wood, W. (1970), *Yours Sincerely for Scotland*, London, Arthur Barker.

CHAPTER 2

The Early Years: From the Inter-War Period to the Mid-1960s

Richard Finlay

In examining the development of the SNP from its inception to its electoral breakthrough in the mid-1960s, two themes soon become apparent. The first is that throughout this time the notion of Scottish self-government often was interpreted as political devolution in which a Scottish parliament would legislate on domestic matters while working within the framework of the British state, but others took it to mean political independence in which there would exist a separate Scottish nation state. Furthermore, the term could also encompass anything in between.

For much of this period in the party's history, the issue was confused and pragmatists could live with either definition in the belief that it would be a step further towards their goal. More often than not it was separatists who believed that devolution could act as a stepping stone towards independence. This issue of pragmatism or principle has cast a long shadow over the SNP and is important in explaining the party's standoffishness with the Scottish Constitutional Convention in the 1990s and the decision to endorse the Yes, Yes vote in the referendum in 1997.

The second theme that emerges is the question of political identity and how a single-issue movement should engage with the political process in which parties arm themselves with a wide range of socio-economic policies and target their message at particular sectional or class interests. The extent to which the SNP should act as an independent political party that engaged with the entirety of the normal political party process, or operate as a pressure group to influence the existing political parties who could be made to accommodate Scottish self-government as part of their policies, was one that weighed heavily on Nationalist activists.

By definition, a single-issue party is at a disadvantage when it comes to winning electoral support in that its particular issue must be of such significance that the voter would prioritise it above all others. Yet, without demonstrating that an issue has popular support, normal political parties will ignore it. At the heart of this dilemma is the simple proposition that a single-issue political party would find it difficult to mobilise popular support compared to a pressure group that would leave conventional politicking to the established parties. That said, the issue would then be at the mercy of political parties to implement the policy because in the British political process the electoral mandate lies with political parties.

The early history of the SNP was dominated by these competing strategies of either seeking a cast-iron electoral mandate by means of a dedicated political party, which was slow and protracted, or the pressure group method which was quicker and less costly, but also less secure. The early history of the SNP is further complicated by the fact that these two themes tended to intertwine and overlap among different party members.

In the Beginning

The origins of the Scottish National Party can be traced back to the altered political circumstances of the period following the end of the First World War (Finlay 1994). Home rule had been an article of faith among the leftist radical tradition that encompassed both the Labour and Liberal parties and although Henry Cowan's bill had reached the statute book before the war, the Speaker's Conference on devolution in 1919 let it drop. Although Scottish home rule commanded a wide range of support, much of it was nominal and for those keen protagonists of the policy, the key issue was how to translate this into political action. For some in the Labour and Liberal parties, the issue was one that was best served by the existing political parties who would promote it as part of their wider political agenda. For a significant minority, however, the issue was one that they believed could cross the party political divide and should be exempt from the normal cut and thrust of party political divisions.

Harking back to the pressure group strategies which had been a marked feature of pre-war Liberal political culture, the Scottish Home Rule Association took the decision to canvass prospective candidates at elections and by-elections and, according to who they thought was most committed to the cause, would endorse that candidate irrespective of party. By and the large the Scottish Home Rule Association was reasonably content with this system as most contests involved either a Labour or Liberal candidate who paid lip service to the idea of creating a Scottish parliament.

The advent of a minority Labour government, however, changed things. The competition between the priorities of a Labour government and the issue of home rule was revealed starkly when a bill was talked out and the government did little to revive it. The Labour government's failure to push the issue led to an ideological split within the devolutionist camp, between those who believed that home rule could be attained by working with and within the conventional political parties, and those who believed that some form of direct action was necessary to demonstrate that the issue commanded so much support among the electorate that failure to take the issue could have electoral consequences. The failure of a private member's bill in 1927 effectively killed off any faith among activists in the Association that reliance on the Labour Party was likely to succeed in the near future.

The pre-war notion that Scottish self-government would be contained within an overall British government and that a Scottish parliament would only be responsible for domestic issues also came under fire from a vocal minority. The experience of Ireland worked on the proto-nationalist movement in two ways. First, it widened the parameters of what self-government should mean and for some this meant pushing for complete independence, as was the case with Irish republicanism, or almost complete independence, as was the case with the white dominion colonies of the British Empire.

Second, it dented faith in the ability or willingness of conventional British political parties to take the issue seriously. In the melting-pot of Scottish nationalism after the First World War, those who were unconvinced in the suitability of devolution and those who believed that British political parties were unable or unwilling to bring about constitutional change found agreement in the need to set up a new political party, even though there were manifest ideological incompatibilities about how far self-government should go. Frustration with the existing political status quo in Scotland provided a temporary bond. The National Party of Scotland was created from four organisations: the Scots National League, the Scottish National Movement, the Glasgow University Student Nationalist Association and activists in the Scottish Home Rule Association.

The Scots National League was modelled to a large extent on Irish republicanism in that it believed that the Scottish relationship with the British state was colonial and that it should seek a mandate for independence from the Scottish electorate. The Scottish National Movement was a one-man band led by Lewis Spence, who can best be described as a nationalist maverick whose Anglophobia was an embarrassment to mainstream nationalists. The Glasgow University Scottish Nationalist Association was led by the charismatic John MacCormick, who had pulled off the publicity stunt of nearly electing the novelist Compton MacKenzie as Rector of Glasgow University in a contest with Prime Minister Stanley Baldwin in 1928.

On the whole, the Association was fairly devolutionist and not particularly fixed in terms of ideology or strategy. The Scottish Home Rule

Association was led by veteran socialist Roland Muirhead, who was largely devolutionist but passionate on the idea that the Scots should determine their own political future. Muirhead's frustration with the Labour Party's dominance within the Home Rule Association was the trigger to explore the creation of a separate party. By using trade union affiliation, the Scottish Trade Union Congress was able to block any move towards a more radical strategy that would put it at odds with the Labour Party, to the immense displeasure of Muirhead and the leading activists.

PARTY MOVES

The National Party of Scotland (NPS) was born out of this unlikely mixture in April 1928. When the party failed to deliver the electoral dividend that its members hoped, its ideological divisions began to open. In essence, the division can be characterised as being between moderates who pushed a devolutionist strategy and fundamentalists who pushed for outright independence. Overlapping and crossing this division there were differences in terms of party strategy, with those who advocated a pressure group approach and those who believed that the party had to win an electoral mandate by contesting elections. Muirhead, for example, thought that the NPS would only have to inflict sufficient electoral damage on the Labour Party in the short term in order to bring about a change of heart.

This policy came to nought and if anything it hardened Labour attitudes against home rule, especially as the NPS intervened in a number of key by-elections following the 1931 general election in which Labour was wiped out in Scotland. In 1932, an intervention in the Dunbartonshire by-election kept Thomas Johnston out of parliament, which many Labour activists who were favourable to home rule thought was unforgivable and a spectacular own goal.

In any case, Labour had shifted its position on home rule. The policy was largely an inherited article of faith in the radical tradition, but by the late 1920s it was clear that the extent of Scottish socio-economic problems were such that it required the greater resources of the British state to bring about an effective remedy. A Scottish parliament it was believed, would have insufficient access to economic power to achieve the restructuring that was needed. A Scottish parliament would reside over a Scotland devastated by poverty and unemployment but would not have access to the levers of power to do anything about it. The future, John Wheatley argued, lay in greater centralised state planning at a British level.

Initially, the division between fundamentalists and moderates absorbed most energy as each side blamed the other for the party's poor electoral performance with claims that extremism was frightening the electorate away and counterclaims that the message of nationalism was not being pushed hard enough. The 'colourful' aspect of nationalism was the one that attracted most media attention and projections as to what a future Scotland would be like under the fundamentalists provided political satirists with a field day. Visions of kilted sailors in a Scottish navy and tartan-clad goose-steppers did little to help the party's credibility. As a result of growing discontent at the party's electoral performance, a series of purges removed the fundamentalist wing and consolidated the moderates in a position of leadership.

The belief that moderatism was necessary had also been spurred on by the emergence of a right-leaning group in 1932 – the Scottish Party – which could boast a more establishment-minded leadership. The Scottish Party revolved around a group of disgruntled Tories in Cathcart, the editor of the *Daily Record*, R. D. Anderson, the former Lord Provost of Inverness, Sir Alexander MacEwen and the maverick peer, the Duke of Montrose. Connected to this group and operating in the background was Andrew Dewar Gibb, a former Conservative candidate and professor of law at Glasgow University, and the journalist George Malcolm Thomson. It was these two who provided the moderate body of nationalism with its intellectual backbone. The Scottish Party was devolutionist and claimed that a critical factor in bringing the party into existence was to counter the separatism and republicanism which was perceived to come from the National Party of Scotland.

For moderates in the NPS, the emergence of the Scottish Party was seen as an opportunity to broaden the appeal of the nationalist movement and reach out to the mainstream of Scottish society. As the full impact of the Great Depression took its course and its effects on the Scottish economy became more pronounced, increasingly mainstream voices were heard as to what was perceived to be unfair treatment of Scotland. Fears were raised as to the future of Scotland's identity and that the nation was in terminal decline. The growing sense of unease was one that moderates felt could be harnessed to electoral purposes and even figures within the Scottish authorities believed that nationalism had the potential to become a serious political force. Although lacking an active membership, the Scottish Party did well in the merger of the two organisations and secured many of the leadership positions. For moderates in the NPS, such as John MacCormick and Neil Gunn, the Scottish Party would be able to give a veneer of respectability to the nationalist movement and capitalise on what appeared to be sympathetic elements within the Scottish establishment.

THE SNP ARRIVES

The two parties united in 1934 to become the Scottish National Party in 1934. The electoral contest which aided the prospect of a new party had occurred the previous year in 1933 in a by-election in Kilmarnock, when the NPS supported the Scottish Party candidate, Alexander MacEwen. With his polling 17% of the vote, this seemed to show some promise. This initial optimism, however, was misplaced as the divisions over objectives and strategy which had plagued the National Party assumed the same prominence within the new organisations, especially when the party showed its poor electoral performance (Finlay 1994; Mitchell 1996).

In the 1935 general election the party contested seven seats and in each of the ones in which a previous nationalist had fought, the performance was worse. The best performances were in the Western Isles and Inverness by John MacCormick and Alexander MacEwen and this gave a boost to those who argued that radicalism and separatism were still a problem for the party. The extent to which self-government should be pushed was constantly watered down to accommodate those who believed that devolution ought to be the primary goal of the party and those who believed that anything more radical would frighten away potential support.

By the mid-1930s, the ideological bickering, poor electoral performance and a dwindling membership meant that the party was barely capable of functioning as a credible political organisation. The inability to find the funds to contest elections prompted a re-emergence of the question of tactics and strategy as to whether it might be better to act as an umbrella organisation and pressure group for the cause of home rule. The party had already conceded that members could belong to other political parties and that contesting elections was beyond the means of the organisation.

The fact that the party was no longer deemed a threat by Labour led to a softening of attitudes to home rule, although this was in fact motivated more by the way in which the working class had been systematically frozen out of the political decision-making process in Scotland with the advent of greater administrative devolution. The growing power of central government was a concern for Labour activists who were alarmed at the proliferation of corporatism in Scottish society, which had an anti-Labour and trade union bias. Some form of democratic accountability, it was believed, would check these trends and bring Labour in from the political cold. It is important to emphasise this was a political development that was merely a pragmatic response by the Labour Party to changes in government administration in Scotland – not the result either of a deep-seated commitment to the principal of devolution, or of pressure from the nationalist movement.

Indeed, it is more the case that it was Nationalist impotence that encouraged Labour's flirtation with home rule safe in the knowledge that any policy change or reversal would have limited electoral consequences.

By the eve of the Second World War, the SNP was in a fairly hopeless position. Just before war was declared, the energetic and able John MacCormick began to push the idea of a Scottish Convention that would act as a cross-party organisation that would mould a consensus on the issue of self-government. The Liberal Party was fairly enthusiastic, and some Labour home rulers expressed an interest, but the advent of war put the project on hold. Meanwhile, MacCormick and the leadership had taken their eye off the ball with regard to party sentiment and the rank and file had pushed for more strenuous measures, including an anti-conscription policy to be maintained until the British government agreed to implement home rule. Lax discipline also meant that many fundamentalists were able to drift back to the party and were able to coalesce around this issue.

The war also revived the opportunities for electoral politics. The wartime truce between the established parties, in which they agreed not to contest by-elections against one another, did not apply to the SNP and it was believed that this could be used strategically to put pressure on the government and highlight the cause. In 1940, such an opportunity presented itself in Argyll where the SNP launched a campaign against the sitting Tory Party and were able to do well because of government unpopularity. It seemed as if the electoral strategy was up and running again, but in 1942 in a by-election in Cathcart it ran into the sands with a dismal performance.

At the same time, Douglas Young went on trial for refusing to be conscripted and he acted as a rallying point for activists keen to pursue a more vigorous policy. The appointment of Thomas Johnston as the wartime Secretary of State also helped to take the wind out of the Nationalist sails. Johnston was able to use his position to air Scottish grievances and was not averse from banging the Nationalist drum in order to put pressure on cabinet colleagues. His creation of the Scottish Grand Committee and its sitting in Edinburgh together with the Committee of the Ex-Secretaries of State seemed to fly the Nationalist flag.

In 1942, frustration with the political impasse spilled over at the annual conference when the moderate leadership was ousted by the fundamentalists who demanded a more vigorous policy. This led to secession by MacCormick and his followers, who went off to form the Scottish National Convention. The Nationalist camp was effectively divided into two camps: one that advocated a cross-party approach that would use pressure group tactics; and one that returned to the founding ideals of the

National Party of Scotland, seeking an electoral mandate as an independent political party. The rump of the SNP scored a number of points for the remainder of the war by coming close in the Kirkcaldy by-election in 1944 and by winning the 1945 Motherwell by-election, in which Robert McIntyre was returned as the first ever SNP Member of Parliament.

In the immediate post-war era, the National Convention scored the big success with the signing of the National Covenant, which claimed to have attracted two million supporters. In part, this can be explained by the fact that Johnston's banging of the Nationalist drum during the war, and the fact that the Labour Party was still nominally committed to home rule, did create a positive expectation among the population for greater devolution. At this juncture it seemed as if the cross-party, pressure group approach was more successful in that it could mobilise support more quickly than the conventional independent party approach. The problem for the Convention was how to translate this popular support into political action.

While the idea of Scottish home rule could always find a large number willing to support it, the problem was to determine where this came in the list of political priorities. For the Labour Party, home rule could not be easily accommodated with a greater role for British state intervention and planning in social and economic planning. Nationalisation and the Welfare State had been designed as a universal British policy to create a better and fairer British society and Scottish home rule was not relevant to this process.

While this was increasingly apparent to Labour politicians, it was not necessarily apparent to the population at large, but if people were forced to choose between them, there was no doubt which would take precedent. The was understood by Hector McNeil, the Scottish Secretary of State, who simply challenged MacCormick on the basis that if home rule was so popular people could vote for it by returning MPs and demonstrating that the Convention had a democratically elected mandate. This tactic effectively burst the Convention bubble, although the issue would rumble on and MacCormick would further lower his stock with the Labour Party and government by contesting the Paisley by-election as an independent nationalist candidate with Liberal support. He lost.

AFTER THE CONVENTION:
THE RETURN OF THE PARTY

The failure of the Convention left the SNP as the sole flag bearers of political nationalism in Scotland (Finlay 1997). The fragility of the cross-party pressure group approach had been tested and found wanting. It was a vindication of the original policy that the only way Scottish self-government could be attained was by a dedicated political party for that purpose which would seek an electoral mandate. While the Convention approach had the apparent advantage of circumventing the problems associated with establishing a separate political party, at the end of the day it would always lack political credibility.

In the short term, however, this did not help the SNP, as the collapse of the Convention was a body blow to the Nationalist movement and many members of the SNP had actively participated in the Convention. Having won the intellectual argument, the SNP found itself in a most inhospitable climate in post-war Scotland. The advent of consensus politics and the role of government intervention in key areas of economic and social policy had the effect of marginalising the Nationalist case. This was especially true after 1951 when a Tory government ended rationing and began to loosen the reins of austerity which had been imposed from the war.

In so far as 'nationalist' issues such as the use of the numeral in Queen Elizabeth's coronation in 1953 made the political agenda, it was not so significant that it could be used to make capital for the SNP's cause. In any case, the Conservatives made most of the running in raising the Nationalist agenda by denouncing nationalisation and excessive central government control in Scotland. In Edinburgh in 1948, Winston Churchill came close to advocating Scottish Nationalism as a response to state socialism and nationalisation. SNP electoral performance was fairly dismal throughout the 1950s and early 1960s and the party contested few seats and regarded a saved deposit as a good result.

The 1950s and early 1960s, however, was a period when the Party could build up a clear identity, formulate a coherent electoral strategy and begin the time-consuming process of constructing an effective organisation. Most of the leaders at this time, such as Robert McIntyre, Arthur Donaldson, James Halliday and Tom Gibson, had witnessed the party's tendency to internecine warfare in the past and were determined to avoid it in the future. Discipline was enforced and the party was quick to dump extremists and those who promoted violent means.

Although the party conference of 1948 had stipulated the goal of the SNP was to attain political independence from the United Kingdom, it is clear at the time of the National Convention that not all members agreed with this. Many chose to belong to both the SNP and the National Convention.

The withering of the Convention put this to bed as the party made independence its key objective and enforced this throughout the membership. It also began to formulate clearer policies that would demonstrate the socio-economic impact of independence on Scottish society. The party also sought to give its socio-economic policies a distinctive flavour to mark them out as different from the Conservatives and Labour. A broadly social democratic ethos was created which sought to locate the SNP in the political centre and the party sought to position itself as suspicious of both big government and big business.

To a large extent, the party sought out the consensus in Scottish politics in order to cast its electoral net as widely as possible. Much of this was simply determined by the fact that unpopular policies, or policies that did not attract widespread support, would damage the appeal of independence. Yet, one difficulty was that by appealing to the middle ground, it had little to offer that was distinctive. In international politics, it advocated neutrality along Swedish and Irish lines. This explains why the party has had historic difficulties over NATO and the European Union. It also drew parallels with the economic performance of the smaller western European nations and sought to emulate their success. It also acted as a champion of the Scottish national interest and much criticism was levelled against any perceived bias against Scotland.

Much of the SNP's critique at this time involved drawing attention to Scotland's comparative economic performance relative to the rest of the United Kingdom and it was in this arena that the party had most success. Although the party sought to present itself as one that offered positive solutions to Scottish problems, it was easier to make more political impact by highlighting Scottish grievances. At the time, it was difficult for the SNP to carve out any policies that could compete against the Labour or Conservative parties, both of which used British state intervention in economic and social policy to good effect. As the electoral agenda was largely dominated by jobs, housing and wages, the British parties made most of the running. The SNP, however, did begin to build up its party apparatus and organisation. Regular conferences and a core of activist members were able to form a nucleus around which the party could later expand in the 1960s.

PREPARING FOR THE BREAKTHROUGH

By the mid-1960s, the external environment was beginning to change in favour of the SNP. Increasing government intervention was unable to mask the relative poor performance of the Scottish economy and its failure to keep pace with the rest of the United Kingdom. Crucially, wages and standards of living were still lagging behind and far from ameliorating this social economic discontent; increased government intervention simply raised expectations and led to greater demands on Scottish politicians to deliver more. It was against this background of greater expectation that the

Labour Party was able to notch up an impressive performance in Scotland in the general elections of 1964 and 1966, especially with the ambitious five-year plan for Scotland. In spite of planning, the economic climate did not improve as the government ran into balance-of-payment problems which culminated with devaluation in 1967 (Finlay 2004: Hutchinson 2001).

Other external factors worked to the advantage of the SNP. Both the Conservative and Labour parties in Scotland had paid insufficient attention to their organisation and tended to rely heavily on their British counterparts for leadership and direction. Membership declined and the selection of candidates for elections tended to confirm the hackneyed stereotypes of both parties. The Tory Party became more gentrified, while Labour was dominated by former trade union activists and local councillors. The creation of new towns and the relocation of population through overspill broke down traditional territorial political loyalties, especially for the Labour Party. The decline of heavy industries, and their association with political loyalties revolving around either trade union affiliation with Labour or skilled working-class Toryism, undermined the extent to which political loyalties could be taken for granted. Light manufacturing, sales and services and other new types of employment were not imbued with traditional political loyalties. Paradoxically, it was in the new urban settlements, among the new types of employment created by British state intervention, that the SNP found its most fertile ground.

The '60s counter-culture had a limited impact in Scotland but, for a new generation of political activists, the staid Conservative and Labour parties did not offer much in the way of dynamism. Labour's collaboration with the decision to site nuclear weapons in Scotland left anti-nuclear activists the choice of either the SNP or the Liberal Party. The SNP recruited a new generation of activists who were more in tune with aspects of the counter-culture and nationalism was given intellectual respectability with leftist notions of anti-colonialism.

The idea that the Scots were subject to a form of English imperialism was given some degree of currency by the experience of the Highland Clearances and parallels that could be drawn with Ireland. It was during this time that the SNP was able to reinvent itself and move towards a dynamic younger image that contrasted favourably with the Labour Party. The party's logo of a combination of the St Andrew's cross and the thistle was adopted and the SNP also paid more attention to local issues. Furthermore, at a time in the mid-1960s when the membership of the SNP was growing, that of the Labour and Conservative parties had stagnated. This was particularly the case with the Labour Party, where a handful of members were left to run large constituencies.

SNP activism, enthusiasm and dynamism helped the party to grow successful local branches that began to make an impact in the immediate locality. Labour and Tory complacency failed to take seriously the Nationalism inroads that were being made in local government and by-elections before the Hamilton by-election in 1967. At the general election of 1966, the SNP contested 23 seats and, although it only polled 5% of the vote (totalling 128,474 votes), the fact that the party was in a position to organise and fund such an extensive campaign should have sent alarm bells ringing in the Scottish political establishment. In the following year at the Pollok by-election the party notched up 28% of the poll and lost the seat for Labour to let the Conservatives win; and in the local elections in May the SNP received an impressive 60,000 votes in Glasgow, though the first-past-the-post system meant they won no seats. Across Scotland they polled over 144,000 votes, or nearly 16% of the vote. So when the SNP went on to overturn a Labour majority in Hamilton in November, there had been signs that the party had been building up support and that Labour complacency was misguided.

Although support for the SNP would oscillate erratically for the next thirty years and the party would face trying times, the twin issues – of sticking with independence as the prime political objective and attaining this through a popular electoral mandate by contesting elections as an independent political party – if occasionally wobbled, never wavered. The success of the late 1960s and early 1970s were crucial in putting to bed the divisions that had plagued the party in its formative years.

REFERENCES

Finlay, R. J. (1994), *Independent and Free: Scottish Politics and the Origins of the Scottish National Party, 1918–1945*, Edinburgh, John Donald.

Finlay, R. J. (1997), *A Partnership for Good? Scottish Politics and the Union Since 1880*, Edinburgh, John Donald.

Finlay, R. J. (2004), *Modern Scotland, 1914–2000*, London, Profile.

Hutchison, I. G. C. (2001), *Scottish Politics in the Twentieth Century*, Basingstoke, Palgrave Macmillan.

Mitchell, J. (1996), *Strategies for Self-Government: The Campaigns for a Scottish Parliament*, Edinburgh, Polygon.

CHAPTER 3

From Breakthrough to Mainstream: The Politics of Potential and Blackmail

James Mitchell

INTRODUCTION

The Scottish National Party had struggled to become part of the mainstream of Scottish politics for most of its existence. The Hamilton by-election in 1967 was an important milestone in the party's development. But, contrary to the hopes of SNP members, it did not bring the party into the mainstream. It would remain outside the political mainstream until the establishment of the Scottish Parliament. The SNP may have become a parliamentary party but it retained the characteristics of an extra-parliamentary party. This presented more challenges than opportunities. It may have been a familiar part of Scottish politics by the time devolution was established, but it had had a precarious existence.

HAMILTON AND THE BEGINNING OF MODERN SCOTTISH POLITICS

The election of Winnie Ewing as Hamilton's MP marked the beginning of a new era in Scottish politics. On the political fringes from its inception 40 years before, the SNP had finally broken through. Robert McIntyre, Ewing's great hero, had briefly held Motherwell at the end of the Second World War but this result was widely seen as aberrant. Hamilton, on the other hand, was a harbinger of change and would mark the start of continuous SNP presence in the Commons.

Not for the last time, the SNP's interpretation of the result left no room for managing expectations. The party went into the 1970 general election with unrealistic expectations, only to be disappointed with what was a reasonable result. Even more significant than Hamilton's impact on the SNP was its impact on the wider world of politics. Westminster and Whitehall exhibited signs of panic and no event in 20th-century Scottish politics provoked more awareness of the Scottish dimension than this by-election. As one Treasury official remarked to colleagues within weeks of Hamilton, 'The election of Mrs Ewing has galvanised the Scottish MPs into asking a flood of questions on this topic' (TNA T328/227). Scotland moved closer to the centre of politics and, though it would recede in importance over the years, it would rarely return to the backwaters of the pre-Hamilton era.

Modern Scottish politics was born. The party system underwent dramatic change. The decline of class and partisan alignment facilitated the rise of the SNP. The old two-party system that had dominated post-war politics gave way to a party system in which Labour was dominant, due partly to the electoral system, and the Conservatives, Liberals and SNP each vied to be Labour's main challenger. Over the next 40 years, the SNP struggled to achieve this status though at times it came close to doing so.

Class would no longer be quite the dominant cleavage in Scottish politics. Scotland's constitutional status would become more important, at times cutting across and at other times reinforcing the class cleavage. But most important of all, parties needed to be seen to act in Scotland's interests in this era as never before. Scotland's interests may have been nebulous and the battle to define Scottish interests was as important as acting in these interests, but any party that failed to engage in this battle, preferring to present themselves as exclusively acting in the interests of either the UK as a whole or some sectional interest, would suffer electorally. In time, Scottish interests became almost synonymous with supporting a Scottish parliament; but that was still well in the future when Ewing won Hamilton.

ENTERING THE MAINSTREAM

The remarkable ease with which Holyrood has insinuated itself into the life of Scottish politics is in marked contrast to the SNP's rise to prominence. Sartori (1976) referred to two sources of relevance for a party: governing potential and blackmail potential. The SNP had no governing potential pre-devolution, though there were times when it thought it might secure sufficient support for a mandate for independence. But with the brief exception of a period in the mid–late 1970s, this was fanciful. Its blackmail potential as a parliamentary party was rarely significant, though the potential existed during the late 1970s when the Labour government lost its overall Commons majority. Its real blackmail potential pre-devolution was the electoral threat it posed to other parties. Winnie Ewing has frequently recounted Michael Foot's comment to her that it was not the eleven SNP MPs who were elected in October 1974 who worried him but the many Labour seats in which the SNP occupied second place.

The blackmail potential of taking votes from other parties was evident within a year of Hamilton. Ted Heath's 'Declaration of Perth' set out the Tories' plan for devolution. It was over-hyped and created expectations that the Tories had no intention of realising. A year later, Harold Wilson announced the establishment of the Royal Commission on the Constitution under Lord Crowther's chairmanship. Crowther was unsympathetic but on his death he was replaced by Lord Kilbrandon, a far more sympathetic Scottish judge. Established to 'spend years taking minutes', the Commission on the Constitution reported just as the SNP was on the rise again and helped thrust the constitution to the fore of Scottish politics to the SNP's advantage, but devolution would prove divisive and difficult for the SNP.

Until devolution, the SNP was the outsider, at times uncertain whether it even wanted to be part of the inside track or, at least, which inside track it aspired to be on. The SNP's blackmail potential was related almost exclusively to its capacity to win votes from other parties. Its main opponents saw the SNP as an upstart usurper, attempting to break into the settled politics of post-war Scotland. They were determined to present it as the outsider and they were aided in this by a strand of thinking within the SNP that preferred an oppositional approach to politics. In the 1970s, its MPs were keen to present themselves as a Scottish government-in-waiting while some members of the SNP executive had a different view. In the 1980s, the SNP's blackmail potential was negligible. A Conservative government with healthy majorities made concessions unlikely.

As Scotland's constitutional status rose to prominence, the SNP became relevant again. When John Major's government lost its effective overall majority, however, the SNP had boxed itself into a corner by opposing deals with Conservatives and its one effort to win a minor concession in the Maastricht legislation proved deeply divisive internally.

The problem the party confronted was that without a Scottish parliament it could only be oppositional. There were few electoral incentives in being responsible so long as it remained a minority in Westminster. Nonetheless, the electoral threat resulted in gains. As a senior Treasury official remarked in a private note in summer 1974, the idea of a Scottish Development Agency was 'intended to contain the pressure for benefits to Scotland "associated with" North Sea oil without, as we sincerely hope, an undue proportion of resources and environmental development in Scotland' (Mitchell 2009: 29). But it would be difficult to take credit for measures that others introduced.

Voluntary versus Professional Organisation

The party was ill prepared for the dramatic change in its fortunes signalled by Hamilton. It remained a voluntary organisation. It had no 'leader' but a chairman hemmed in constitutionally and ideologically by a party that was suspicious of leadership. Billy Wolfe, who chaired the SNP from 1969 to 1979, was overshadowed by Margo MacDonald, his deputy, and Donald Stewart, leader of the SNP parliamentary party, preferred Westminster and the Western Isles over mainland Scotland. There was no lack of charisma, enthusiasm or ideas, but an absence of discipline and means to channel the party's abundant energy in a clear direction.

The party had become a parliamentary party and future success depended on it adding to its number of MPs, but it refused to acknowledge the implications. The consequence was a series of rows between its MPs and the national executive, contradictory messages and an absence of strategy. Membership fluctuated wildly and SNP headquarters never had any idea how many members the party had. Figures would be issued but these were guesstimates multiplied by a large number.

The lack of professional staff and full-time politicians meant the party relied heavily on volunteers and a myriad of national office bearers, often elected for reasons other than competence in the matter for which they were elected. This did not make for a streamlined structure and a number of individuals over the years were put under pressure from employers to limit their public involvement. The commitment of activists whose careers suffered is often overlooked, but it played a very significant part in the development of the party.

Electoral Developments

The 1970 general election saw Labour regain Hamilton but the SNP took the Western Isles, the final result announced in that year's general election. Even though the SNP vote had risen, failure to win a seat would have been a serious setback for the party. Commentators saw the SNP as a flash party, the temporary beneficiary of protest voting rather than a sign of realignment in the electorate (McLean 1970). But, as time would tell, realignment was in process. The SNP managed to maintain a reasonable level of support in local elections and by-elections during the 1970–4 parliament, culminating in victory in Glasgow Govan in November 1973. Once more, the victor was a young, charismatic woman succeeding in what had been a safe Labour seat. Margo MacDonald would become the public face of the SNP despite holding the seat for less than four months and holding only the post of senior vice-chairman.

Complaints would be made by the SNP's opponents that it was a media confection. The SNP attracted more media attention than its electoral support warranted but no more than its ability to generate news. It was colourful, enlivened the political scene and was often in step with a mood for change. It led changes in political campaigning with car cavalcades, almost continuous campaigning and celebrity endorsements. Its opponents saw this as 'razzmatazz': flashy, ebullient double-talk designed to deceive.

Coincidences and luck – good and bad – affected the SNP's development as much as strategy. North Sea oil's part in the rise of the SNP continues to divide opinion but some evidence is irrefutable. The SNP's rise started before oil was discovered. Oil may have had an impact on the elections in 1974, but was subsequently of less value, and yet oil-fuelled Nationalism became one of the myths of modern Scottish politics. More relevant in the two elections in 1974 was the return of devolution to the agenda, aided by the report of the Royal Commission.

The backdrop of a severe economic crisis and an election in February preceded by a three-day week confounded the interpretation that the SNP was the beneficiary of some post-materialist politics (Inglehart 1977) emerging to replace the materialism of class politics. James Kellas had described the SNP at the 1970 election as 'something of a "Social-Democratic" party, rather more collectivist than the Liberals, yet apparently opposed to centralisation and bureaucracy' (Kellas 1971: 457) and the February and October 1974 manifestos both openly proclaimed the party's social democratic credentials. Scottish Nationalism was distinctly materialist, with its emphasis on 'Scotland's Oil'. Its arrival on the scene was less a sign of a new post-materialist politics than the marriage of old class politics with the previously submerged national question.

The party itself was divided on how it had achieved its breakthrough. Some elements within the SNP mistakenly assumed that because it had won more seats from the Conservatives than Labour in 1974 this meant that it had won more Conservative votes. Margo MacDonald, responsible for strategy, struggled to convince many key figures that the party had garnered together an anti-Tory coalition in these constituencies. The Conservative vote had held up reasonably well, making it relatively easy for these seats to be won back – leaving the SNP with only two, formerly Labour, seats in 1979. That year marked the nadir in SNP fortunes, though its vote would fall further at the next election, and cast a long shadow over the party. It was not only a poor result but the end of the dream for many Nationalists. There had been no by-elections in Scotland until the last year of the 1974–9 parliament. Three in succession in 1978 signalled the demise of the SNP. Labour held each seat and even Margo MacDonald, standing in Hamilton, could not stall the drift back to Labour. By-elections, so important to the party in its development, would have a damaging impact on morale as the devolution referendum and general election approached.

The party had decided at its 1976 Motherwell conference, with over 2,000 members in attendance, to back devolution. A resolution was proposed that reaffirmed SNP support for independence but included the phrase, 'though prepared to accept an assembly with limited powers as a possible stepping stone'. An amendment seeking to remove this phrase was defeated by 594 to 425 votes. Despite much indiscipline on a range of matters, the party succeeded in aligning itself behind devolution. It would prove a fateful alignment. The SNP would be associated with Labour's policy and suffer three years later.

By 1983, SNP support dipped again and the party appeared to be returning to its pre-Hamilton status. Commentators assumed that only the personal votes for Gordon Wilson and Donald Stewart allowed it to retain its toehold in parliament. At the next election in 1987, the party took three steps forward and two back. Labour regained the Western Isles when Stewart retired and Wilson was defeated in Dundee, but the party picked up three seats in areas of earlier success: Banff & Buchan, Moray and Angus. But this time, the party understood well that these seats had been won by building an anti-Tory majority. There would be less ambiguity, less room for its opponents to define the SNP's politics than in the 1970s. The party became more self-consciously left wing.

Within a year, a by-election in Glasgow Govan offered the SNP an opportunity. The seat had changed considerably, including its boundaries, from the scene of Margo MacDonald's victory but there was symbolic value in contesting Govan for the SNP. Jim Sillars, MacDonald's husband, stood for the SNP and took the seat with a 33% swing. This was Sillars's second by-election victory. In March 1970, he easily held the South Ayrshire seat for Labour, contributing to knocking the wind out of the SNP's sails in the run-up to that year's general election. Eighteen years on, Sillars was in the SNP and creating more problems for the Labour Party than he had for the SNP in his previous incarnation. The context was all important. The Conservatives had been in power under Margaret Thatcher since 1979, fatally ignoring the Scottish dimension in the belief that devolution had gone forever.

Scottish politics became polarised in the late 1980s. The Scottish dimension had become almost synonymous with support for a parliament and a progressive, left-of-centre agenda. The SNP contributed to this development. Class and national identity aligned in potent ways as never before. But while the SNP could usually be relied on to create interest in by-elections, it still struggled to advance at general elections. In 1992, it was not only the SNP but also Labour and the Liberal Democrats who suffered from over-hype and unrealistic expectations.

There was no Tory wipe-out as many had predicted and the SNP saw its parliamentary representation remain at the same level as 1987, though its share of the vote increased by 50%. The Tory wipe-out came five years later and the SNP doubled its number of seats to six and with only a marginal increase in share of the vote. For the SNP, 6 seats out of 72 was slow progress in 30 years since becoming a parliamentary party, but the stage was now set for a new phase in Scottish politics with the election of the first Scottish Parliament in 1999. Two disadvantages suffered by the SNP in Westminster general elections would be removed. Westminster elections were UK-wide and fought using the first-past-the-post electoral system. Third parties were squeezed under simple plurality and the SNP was a third party contesting only about one-eighth of Westminster's seats. Media interest in Scotland was sporadic in UK elections. That and the electoral system changed with devolution. The SNP moved from being a bit player to becoming a contender over night.

Catch-all or Left of Centre?

The SNP continually wrestled with what kind of party it was, throughout its Westminster years. For some, being the 'national' party of Scotland meant being a catch-all party that should be ideologically 'lite' and appeal across the classes and sectional interests within the nation. Having elected representatives meant that the party would need to take positions on policies, but the catch-all element believed that these should be determined on the basis of whether policies were in Scotland's national interest. Others believed that the 'national interest' required elaboration and involved taking a clear ideological position. The party never fully resolved this tension. This was especially evident in the 1974–9 parliament. A coincidence of electoral and economic turbulence marked the parliament. The Labour government soon lost its overall majority and the SNP's parliamentary novices found themselves at the centre of attention more often than would otherwise have been the case. It was the party's first big test and it flunked it.

Partly because of the failure to appreciate the nature of its support and in pursuit of a catch-all strategy, the party in parliament went out of its way to appear equidistant between Labour and the Conservatives. By failing to define itself, it left others to define it instead. It was thus 'tartan Tory' in Labour heartlands and 'tartan Socialists' in Tory heartlands. This was less of a problem so long as voters thought in terms of Scottish interests, on which others struggled to compete with the SNP, but when the focus shifted to traditional left-right politics it was in trouble. Old left–right politics became important during 1974–9. As the Labour government set out to nationalise aircraft construction and shipbuilding and impose cuts in public services, SNP MPs could not fail to attract attention in the tight parliamentary arithmetic of minority government. Producing tables of parliamentary votes showing that SNP MPs had voted fairly evenly for and against the Labour government only underlined the lack of ideological ballast.

After 1979, the party returned to its early 1970s position. Gordon Wilson described the party's ideology as 'moderate left of centre' and in time this won support across the party. This was lost in internal debates, especially with 79 Group members' counter-productive efforts to portray the leadership as right wing but over time the party altered its image without having to alter its policies. It had always been on the left but it was to become self-consciously left wing by the mid–late 1980s. At times this appeared more tactical than deep-rooted, reflecting contemporarily the rhythms of politics. The SNP sought to outflank Labour on the left as the latter moved to the right in the early 1990s. The poll tax cemented this re-positioning and provided closure on the old 'tartan Tory' jibe. By 1997, the SNP had succeeded in defining itself on the left – but just at the point when the centre of political gravity was moving to the right.

The Shadow of 1979

The double whammy of the referendum defeat and election losses in 1979 had a devastating effect on the SNP. The party looked inward in search of scapegoats and answers. It found many of the former but none of the latter. The two most vociferous of many responses emerged over the months leading up to the party's annual conference in the autumn: fundamentalist opposition to dealings in assemblies, and the 79 Group. The SNP strategy that had been agreed in 1976 in Motherwell was in tatters. There was not going to be a Scottish assembly so long as Margaret Thatcher was in power. Those who had warned that devolution was a cul de sac were vindicated. Billy Wolfe announced his intention to stand down but Margo MacDonald decided to contest the deputy post.

It was no surprise that hardliners swept the floor in internal contests at the party's annual conference in 1979. Four senior members came forward initially to stand for the party chairmanship but this was whittled down to two, Gordon Wilson and Stephen Maxwell. Wilson had been active in the party since his student days, was behind its successful campaigns in 1974 and had retained his Dundee East seat at Westminster. Maxwell had been a regional councillor, had worked for the party and was a founder member of the 79 Group. More importantly, he was associated with devolution, having directed the SNP's 'Yes' campaign in the 1979 referendum. The result was a foregone conclusion. Wilson won by 530 votes to 117. MacDonald lost to Douglas Henderson, defeated MP for East Aberdeenshire, by 450 to 169. The party resolved that it would 'not engage in any more dealings in assemblies, devolution, or meaningful talks'. This would prove the most significant reaction to the 1979 result.

The other response was the 79 Group. The group's name was more appropriate than its members appreciated. It was reactive and internally focused. Its self-conscious radicalism brought to mind Bernard Crick's comment on 'student politics' (Crick 1982: 134) and, indeed, its membership drew overwhelmingly amongst students. However, it included a number of prominent members. It was a small but lively band of members who decided that the SNP needed a sharper left-wing image, a view shared by many in the party. Its main achievements were generating excitement amongst young members, who might otherwise have drifted away, and considerable media interest in the party at a time when the SNP was in the electoral doldrums. It would have earned a footnote in the history of modern Scottish politics but for the fact that it included Alex Salmond as a member. As with most of its senior members, Salmond's main aim was to alter the public's image of the party.

In the fevered atmosphere of SNP politics after 1979, the 79 Group and fundamentalism were twin responses and each would lose significance as the 1979 defeats receded from view. The 1983 election was a wake-up call for the party and a process of healing began. Fundamentalist Nationalism proved far more resilient and a challenge to the leadership. In fits and starts, the party moved out of the shadow of 1979. Its opponents preferred the inward-looking, fundamentalist SNP, as this posed less of an electoral threat. Gordon Wilson started the process of healing and this was carried through to conclusion by Alex Salmond. In August 1997, the party overwhelmingly backed support for devolution in the forthcoming referendum.

The SNP and Westminster after Devolution

A decision was taken that all SNP MPs would contest elections to the Scottish Parliament and for two years its MPs were also MSPs. This meant that the party had a core of experienced parliamentarians in the new

Scottish Parliament but it also meant that it could not devote the same attention to Westminster affairs as in the past. As the 2001 UK general election approached, the SNP found itself in an awkward position as far as Westminster was concerned. It was about to lose all its MPs and a completely new inexperienced set of candidates would be standing in their place. Added to this, its opponents argued that as the Scottish Parliament had been established, there was no need to vote for the SNP. The party was losing its relevance. It had gained governing potential in Holyrood but continued to have none at Westminster and its blackmail potential was deemed less relevant. Becoming a major party in the Scottish Parliament looked set to come at a cost at Westminster.

Alex Salmond's decision to stand down as leader in 2000 led to a decision to stand down from the Scottish Parliament and continue as an MP. The stated reason was to allow John Swinney, his successor, freedom to get on with the job of leading the party. It also meant that the Nationalists would still have a well-known figure standing in the Westminster elections and leading the Westminster group.

Salmond had long shown an interest in foreign affairs and cut out a role for himself at Westminster in this area. He was the first SNP politician to gain a formidable reputation in a field other than Scottish or constitutional politics. The SNP lost one of its seats in 2001 and saw its vote fall back on its 1997 performance. By 2005, its new MPs had begun to establish themselves but the party saw its vote fall back further. Though it gained one MP when Dundee East was won back after its loss eighteen years before, the SNP vote fell to the level it was at in 1979. The party had fallen behind the Liberal Democrats and was no longer Scotland's second party in votes or seats.

Suggestions were made in some quarters in the SNP that it should acknowledge that Holyrood was its primary focus and agree an electoral pact with the Greens. This plan never materialised. The party struggled to find a new relevance at Westminster. That slowly emerged as the party focused on retained matters, notably including foreign affairs but also highlighting some of Westminster's more unseemly sides as Angus McNeil, MP for the Western Isles, raised questions concerning cash for peerages. On his election as First Minster, Alex Salmond was replaced by Angus Robertson as group leader at Westminster. The SNP had once more managed to get through a difficult period as a Westminster party.

CONCLUSION

It would be three decades after Hamilton that Winnie Ewing, the Parliament's oldest member, opened the Scottish Parliament. Progress to that end had been neither certain nor linear. On entering the Commons, Ewing pressed Harold Wilson's Labour government to establish an inquiry into devolution while arguing for independence. The tension evident at the establishment of the SNP between those who favoured nothing less than independence and those who supported a stepping-stone approach did not trouble Ewing and the key figures in the SNP in the early years. Simply getting the issue onto the parliamentary agenda was sufficient evidence of progress. But when devolution moved onto the legislative agenda of the Westminster government it caused the SNP difficulties. The party included many members who feared that devolution would deflect support away from independence. The most striking feature of the SNP during the 30 years after the Hamilton by-election was that it succeeded in maintaining a parliamentary presence at all. It never fully made the transition from being an extra-parliamentary party. It was oppositional by necessity and relied heavily on voluntary efforts of its members, especially as compared with other parties.

This turbulent period in its history saw high hopes dashed and plenty of disillusionment and internal dissent, but idealism, not always supported by expectations of success, kept the party alive. In retrospect, the SNP's main achievement during these 30 years was its blackmail potential. In that respect, it operated more like a pressure group than a conventional political party seeking the offices of state. But its success as blackmailer meant that it gained governing potential after 1997.

References

Crick, B. (1982), *In Defence of Politics*, 2nd edn, London, Pelican.

Inglehart, R. (1977), *The Silent Revolution*, Princeton, Princeton University Press.

Kellas, J. G. (1971), 'Scottish Nationalism', in Butler, D. and Pinto-Duschinsky, M., *The British General Election of 1970*, London, Macmillan, pp. 446–62.

McLean, I. (1970), 'The Rise and Fall of the Scottish National Party', *Political Studies*, Vol. 18, pp. 367–72.

Mitchell, J. (2009), *Devolution in the United Kingdom*, Manchester, Manchester University Press.

Sartori, G. (1976), *Parties and Party Systems: A Framework for Analysis*, Cambridge, Cambridge University Press.

CHAPTER 4

Women's Political Representation and the SNP: Gendered Paradoxes and Puzzles

Fiona Mackay and Meryl Kenny

INTRODUCTION

The results of the 2007 Scottish Parliament elections were historic, with the SNP ending over 50 years of Labour dominance of Scottish politics. Yet, while the 2007 elections were remarkable, they also resulted in the first drop in the number of female MSPs since the creation of the parliament in 1999. In terms of the victorious SNP, the performance on women's representation was comparatively poor: a little over a quarter of SNP elected members were female (down from a high of 42.9% in 1999), compared with Labour's 50%. The SNP presents a number of gendered paradoxes. As a party, its public face has always included high profile – some would say iconic – women but internally, its party membership is male dominated. Unlike its competitor, Scottish Labour, and its comparator, Plaid Cymru, the SNP's internal debates about the under-representation of women as party office holders and electoral candidates appear to have been muted and party action limited. In terms of electoral politics, traditionally women have been less likely to vote for SNP than men. However – apart from a brief flirtation with a heather-hued image in the run-up to the 2003 elections – there has been little systematic effort at targeting women voters or linking the gender gap with issues of women's political under-representation. This chapter provides a pre-liminary account of women in the SNP – an under-researched group in an under-researched party. The primary focus is to report on candidate trends and electoral trends post-1999 as a foundation for future research.

According to Burness (1995; and forthcoming) women have long played a prominent role in the party (and its forerunner, the National Party of Scotland) with a long history as speakers, organisers and can-didates. In 1970 the SNP put up more women candidates than all its competitors combined and in 1974 it fielded the highest number of female candidates, although the overall numbers were small (10/19 and 8/21 respectively). The spectacular by-election successes of Winnie Ewing in 1967 and Margo MacDonald in 1973 did much in the public mind to associate the SNP at Westminster with young, dynamic women. Indeed, around a quarter of SNP MPs have been women although since 2005 there have been no women in the SNP Westminster parliamentary group (see Table 4.1). The first elections to the Scottish Parliament reaped a bumper crop of female parliamentarians: with 42.9% women MSPs, the SNP was second only to Labour. Women continued to play high-profile roles in the party in opposition: as shadow spokespersons, committee chairs and, from 2004, as leader of the parliamentary group. In power, two of the five Cabinet Secretaries appointed in 2007 were female, continuing the party's tradition of promoting young and talented women.

In contrast to this impressive public-facing track record, women comprise under a third of SNP party members, compared with many political parties where a roughly equal number of women and men hold party cards. The grassroots membership of the SNP is predominantly middle-aged or elderly men (see Mitchell et al. in this volume and Brand et al. 1994). We do not have the data to assess the trends in party office holding, an area where work clearly needs to be undertaken. Many of the high-profile elected women have held multiple offices at branch, constituency and national level. Winnie Ewing, for example, served both as party vice-president (1979–87) and president (1987–2005). However, anecdotal evidence suggests that, overall, the pattern is one of traditionally gendered lines.

The following section provides an overview of the Scottish Parliament elections 1999–2007, focusing particularly on trends of candidate selection and recruitment in the SNP over time. It suggests that the elections of 1999 and 2003 may come to be seen as the 'high tide' of women's representation in post-devolution Scotland, highlighting underlying gendered patterns of political recruitment that point in the direction of further decline (Mackay and Kenny, 2007). Why focus on the Scottish Parliament? Because devolution signalled the party's transition from a minor party to one of the two main parties in a multi-party system. Comparative experience suggests that women can often play a prominent role in small, movement-based parties, where the chances of electoral success are slim. However, women can be muscled aside and squeezed out when a party makes the transition into an electorally viable organisation with the potential to hold office and wield power (Randall 1987). The post-devolution performance of the SNP provides a good test for what happens to the issue of women's representation in changing political circumstances.

ELECTORAL RESULTS AND CANDIDATE TRENDS OVER TIME

In the third Scottish parliament elections, women took 43 out of 129 seats in Holyrood (33.3%),[1] compared with 39.5% in the 2003 elections and 37.2% in 1999. As Table 4.1 shows, 43 women and 86 men make up the 2007 Scottish Parliament. Women comprise 12 of 47 SNP MSPs (25.5%), 23 of 46 Labour MSPs (50%), 5 out of 17 Conservatives (29.4%), and 2 out of 16 Liberal Democrats (12.5%). The two Green MSPs elected are both male and the one Independent returned is a woman. For the first time, a minority ethnic MSP was elected, a male.[2]

To put each respective party's performance on women's representation in context, the percentage of Labour and SNP women MSPs both fell in 2007 (by 6% and 7.8% respectively), while the percentage of Conservative and Liberal Democrat women MSPs rose (by 7.2% and 0.7% respectively). Figure 4.1 charts the performance of the four main political parties on women's representation over time. The decline in SNP women MSPs over time is particularly dramatic and establishes the SNP as the only major Scottish political party to experience an overall decrease in the percentage of women MSPs over two subsequent elections, dropping from 42.9% women MSPs in 1999 to 33.3% in 2003, and finally to 25.5% in 2007. When compared to its primary rival, Scottish Labour, the SNP's party performance on women's representation closely matched Labour's in 1999 (42.9% to 50%), but, since then, the SNP has been at least 20 points behind its main competitor.

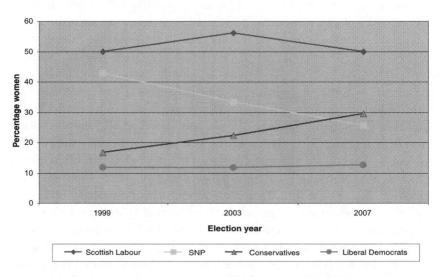

Figure 4.1 Proportion of women among MSPs, by party, 1999–2007

Table 4.1 SNP female MPs, 1967–2007

Name	Constituency	Dates as MP
Winnie Ewing	Hamilton, Lanarkshire	1967*–1970
	Moray & Nairn	1974–1979
Margo MacDonald	Govan	1973*– 74
Margaret Bain	East Dunbartonshire	Oct 1974–1979
(*later Margaret Ewing*)	Moray	1987–2001
Roseanna Cunningham	Perth & Kinross	1995*–2001
	(*Perth 1997–2001*)	
Annabelle Ewing	Perth	2001–2005

* *indicates by-election*
Source: Adapted from *Women in the House of Commons*. House of Commons
Information Office Factsheet M4, Appendix B (undated)

CANDIDATE SELECTION IN THE SNP: 1999–2007

Turning to candidate selection, in the run-up to the 2007 elections, women made up 36.1% of candidates overall (including SNP, Labour, Conservatives, Liberal Democrats, Greens and SSP/Solidarity). This translated into 33.3% of seats, meaning that women candidates were slightly less likely to be elected than their male counterparts. The percentage of women candidates in 2007 represents a slight increase from previous elections, but has translated into fewer seats for women overall. In 1999, women were 30.1% of candidates overall, which translated into 37.2% of seats. And in 2003, women were 31.7% of candidates, which translated into 39.5% of seats. Figure 4.2 disaggregates these figures by party, charting the performance of the four main Scottish political parties on numbers of women candidates over time.

Figure 4.2 highlights a wide range of performance amongst the different parties in the period 1999–2007. Scottish Labour has repeatedly selected a large proportion of female candidates, and at least 40% of its candidate places in both constituency seats and on the regional list have been consistently filled by women. In contrast, the SNP is the only party to see a major decrease in the number of women candidates in an election cycle, dropping from 21 women constituency candidates in 1999 to 16 in 2003 (from 28.8% to 21.9%) and dropping from 33 women list candidates to 19 women in 2003 (from 34.4% to 24.7%). In 2007, the SNP saw a substantial increase in the number of its women candidates overall – from 23.3% women candidates overall in 2003 to 31.5% women candidates in 2007 – which marks a return to its 1999 levels of women candidates.

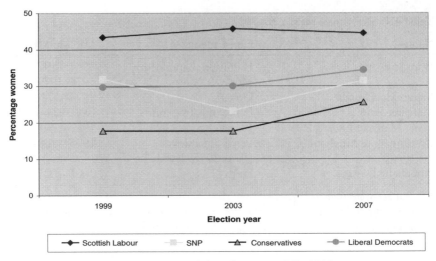

Figure 4.2 Proportion of women candidates by party, 1999–2007

However, this has not translated into an increased number of seats for women candidates.

Therefore, while women were perhaps slightly less successful as candidates overall in the 2007 elections, the evidence, once this is disaggregated by party, suggests that it has less to do with women as candidates and more to do with the seats or positions on the list in which women candidates are placed. Studies of women candidates in the United Kingdom repeatedly demonstrate that women do not receive an electoral penalty when running for office and that the selection process for parliamentary candidates is still the major factor explaining why so few women prospective candidates are elected (e.g. Norris et al. 1992; Rasmussen 1983; Studlar and Welch 1993; Welch and Studlar 1996). The success of prospective women candidates, then, depends not just on being selected, but on being selected for 'winnable' seats – in the Scottish case, winnable positions either in constituencies or on the regional list. We return to the issue of winnability in the following section.

PARTY MEASURES TO IMPROVE WOMEN'S REPRESENTATION

Research evidence in Scotland and elsewhere highlights the structural barriers that constrain prospective women candidates (e.g. Brown 2001a; 2001b; Chapman 1993; Shepherd-Robinson and Lovenduski 2002). Political parties can use a range of measures to counter these barriers.

These include reform to selection procedures to make them fairer and more transparent and to ensure that equal opportunities are taken into consideration; positive action measures such as balanced shortlists; and 'equality guarantees' – quota-type mechanisms such as 'all-women short-lists', 'twinning' constituency seats or applying gender templates such as 'zipping' to party lists (see for example Brown 2001c; Childs et al. 2005; Lovenduski 2005; Mackay 2004). Evidence suggests that strong equality guarantee measures are the most likely to result in substantial improvements in women's representation (see for example Caul 1999; 2001; Dahlerup 2006; Russell 2000) and also that the adoption of quota-type measures by one political party may lead to a 'contagion' effect in which other political parties respond by actively promoting women as well, either through formal or informal measures (Matland and Studlar 1996).

In the run-up to devolution in 1999, the issues of women's representation was high on the political agenda because of the 50/50 campaign run by women's organisations like Engender and the STUC Women's Committee, the lobbying efforts of women activists within political parties, and wider debates about the need for more inclusive and modern political institutions in the Scottish Constitutional Convention and beyond. SNP women were part of these discussions, although activists were reluctant to associate themselves too closely or publicly with the 50/50 campaign, given the SNP's formal non-involvement in the Convention. Responding to these pressures, the SNP debated using strong equality measures in the 1999 elections. A statement of principle supporting gender balance was approved by Party Conference in 1995, and the party leadership had publicly pledged to deliver gender balance at a 50/50 campaign rally in 1996 (McDonald et al. 2001). The gender balance mechanism of 'zipping' – whereby women and men are alternated on party lists – was brought before a Special Conference in 1998, but was defeated, by a narrow margin of 257 votes for and 282 against (Russell et al. 2002: 62).

This defeat reflects the long-standing opposition of the party grassroots to support quota-type mechanisms in either internal party contests or in candidate selection (Russell et al. 2002: 59), although the party has long been willing to support 'soft' positive action such as special training and informal encouragement. Yet, despite its decision not to use any strong equality measures, the SNP did implement proactive unofficial measures encouraging women to stand for election – for example, holding a women's training day for prospective parliamentary candidates and encouraging women to put themselves forward as candidates – and it also placed women at the upper end of their regional party lists (Brown 2001c). In addition, like their main rival, Labour, the SNP used an approved panel of candidates and employed equal opportunities procedures (Bradbury et al. 2000; Russell et al. 2002).

Since the first election, however, the SNP has done little or nothing to promote gender equality in candidate selection in terms of 'strong' measures that guarantee equality of outcomes. This is despite the introduction of permissive legislation by the UK government in 2001. In addition, there appears to have been little informal targeting and promotion within the party since 1999 (Mackay 2003; Mackay and Kenny 2007). In part, this can be understood as complacency engendered by the comparatively high levels achieved and the belief that discriminatory attitudes are a 'thing of the past'. The issue of women's representation has not retained high salience for any of the Scottish political parties, nor has it remained a matter on which parties competed.

By 2003, there were already signs that gains made – system wide – were fragile and liable to reversal. The number of women MSPs overall was predicted to fall in the second election, largely as a result of the significant reduction in the number of women selected as candidates by the SNP (Mackay 2003). However, against expectations, there was a small increase from 37.2% to 39.5%. This was largely as a result of the prominence of women candidates within the small parties such as the Scottish Socialist Party, and the subsequent success of those parties in the election. The strong performance of Labour women as incumbents also played a role in shoring up numbers. Therefore, rather than reflecting a systematic or system-wide improvement, gains were the result of accident rather than design, and progress remained fragile and contingent (Mackay 2003). With the collapse of the small party vote in 2007 – and the further downward slide in the number and positioning of the SNP's female candidates – it can be argued that an overall reduction in the number of women MSPs was inevitable.

In the run-up to the 2007 Scottish Parliament elections, the SNP did not use any equality guarantee measures – such as all-women shortlists or twinning – in the selection of candidates to contest constituency seats. Nor did it use any 'softer measures', such as gender-balanced shortlist policies used by both Scottish Labour and the Liberal Democrats in constituency selections. Overall, female SNP candidates were less likely to be selected to fight safe or winnable constituency seats (Mackay and Kenny 2007). For example, of the party's top five most winnable ('target') seats – all very marginal seats which had been held by a vote percentage majority of less than 5% – only one was contested by a woman.

In terms of the selection of candidates to be placed on the regional lists, the SNP operated an informal rule of thumb that the lists should be more

Table 4.2 Scottish Parliament, 2007 by party and type of seat

Party	Total seats constituency	Total seats list	Total MSPs
Labour	37	9	46
SNP	21	26	47
Cons	4	13	17
Lib Dems	11	5	16
Greens	0	2	2
Independent	0	1	1
Totals	**73**	**56**	**129**

or less gender balanced. In 2007, around a third of all places on the SNP regional lists went to women. However, these women were again generally placed in poor positions. In terms of election scenarios, it is the first and second place on each list that is most vital – and most likely to be won. In the case of the SNP – which generally wins more seats through the lists than through constituency seats – six of the eight regional lists were topped by men and seven of the eight regional lists also had men in second place. Only three of the top sixteen (first and second) slots were allotted to women (18.7%). Analysis of the regional lists also reveals underlying patterns of gendered turnover. In the 2007 elections, only two of the fifteen SNP list MSPs elected for the first time to the Scottish Parliament were women (13.33%). In the previous elections in 2003, all five of the SNP list MSPs elected for the first time to the Scottish Parliament were men.

The SNP and the Gender Voting Gap

Moving onto electoral trends (see Table 4.3), the gender gap in support for the SNP has been well documented, with fewer women than men casting their vote for the SNP since at least the 1970s (Paterson 2006). Women have also been consistently less supportive of independence than men, although overall trends fluctuate over time (Brown et al. 1998, Bromley et al. 2005). The trend post-devolution is less clear: as Paterson notes, in 1999, the level of support among male voters was about one half greater than amongst women. However, the 2003 elections saw a reversal of the gender gap, when female voters were slightly more likely than their male counterparts to support the SNP (18% compared with 15%). Lindsay Paterson (2006) suggests that the 2003 election results provide evidence of the party managing to reposition itself with female voters under the leadership of John Swinney. In September 2002 the SNP attempted to rebrand itself as a softer, more women-friendly party by unveiling a new heather-coloured party logo to supplement its trademark black-and-yellow brand insignia. The move was parodied in the media, with for example *Scotland on Sunday* observing:

> In the beginning was the SNP leader's ties, then there was his shirt, and now the entire party's colour scheme has followed suit. John Swinney has reinvented his part colours based on his own lilac-hued wardrobe and the hillsides of his Perthshire constituency. Party chiefs have decided that the SNP needs a softer, less macho scheme to attract women voters, who have traditionally been dubious about voting for the Nationalists. (cited in Dodds and Seawright 2004)

However, the 'make-over' was part of a serious attempt to tackle the electoral gender gap, based upon insights gained from internal polling and focus groups with female voters. For a short period (2000–3) there were efforts to mainstream gender into party policy, re-prioritise classic women's issues such as equal pay, and work on the party's macho image. Internal party debate on women's under-representation, which had been led by influential women in the run-up to devolution, continued in this period through the vehicle of a rejuvenated Women's Forum. However, these discussions and activities had no discernible effect upon the selection processes in the run-up to the 2003 elections (see previous section), nor did activists succeed in getting a mechanism (such as candidate gender quotas) progressed. In other words, activists seemed less successful than their counterparts in Scottish Labour, Labour UK or Plaid Cymru (McAllister 2001, Chaney et al. 2007) in linking party reforms with the issue of women's political under-representation, or using gender voting gaps as leverage to secure internal or external mechanisms to promote equality. Furthermore, the apparent success with women voters was overshadowed by internal convulsions and leadership challenges and wider perceptions that strategy and campaigning had been flawed.

There is no research to date on internal debates and strategy to tackle the gender gap in the post-Swinney period. However, figures from the 2007 Scottish elections show both a substantial increase in female support for the party and a widening of the gender gap as the increase in men's votes outstripped the increase in women's support. As Table 4.3 shows, 32% of the female electorate voted for the SNP in the constituency contests compared to 41% of the male electorate; 27% of women voters supported the SNP in the list contests compared with 35% of men voters. This translates into a nine-point gap in the constituency contests and an eight-point gap in the list contests. As such, this suggests a reassertion of previous patterns, albeit at much higher overall levels of support.

Table 4.3 SNP support by sex, 1979–2007

		Percentage supporting party				
	1979	1992 %	1997 %	**1999%**	2003%	**2007%**
Male	29	22	17	23	15	(constit) 41 (list) 35
Female	20	18	13	17	18	(constit) 32 (list) 27

Parliament election years in bold
Source: adapted from Table 4.5, Dodds and Seawright (2004); Table 4.1,
Paterson (2006); 2007 results taken from www.scottishelectionstudy.org.uk

CONCLUSIONS

These trends are worthy of further analysis; however, they do suggest that the SNP as a party continues to pose a number of gender paradoxes. Women have been present and prominent in the party since its inception. It has a long and impressive track record of recruiting and promoting women, including Nordic-levels of female MSPs in the first Scottish Parliament, and women have held high-profile leadership positions in both opposition and government. However, the transition to a major party has, after the first elections, been accompanied by an overall decline in women's representation. Furthermore, the party at grassroots level is disproportionately male. Finally, although electoral trends are uncertain post-1999, there is evidence that female voters still regard the SNP as a macho party.

This presents the party with several issues: first, the problem of how to attract women voters and party members; second, how to project a 'women-friendly' image; and third, how to tackle the decline in women's political representation. This prompts the question as to why there appears to have been so little attempt to date to 'couple' the issue of women's equal representation with processes of party modernisation and a more 'women-friendly' electoral strategy. Whilst there is some evidence of periodic changes to style and image and the occasional headlining of classic 'women's issues' in election campaigns, there has been no thoroughgoing effort to tackle the ongoing issues of women's political under-representation and women voters' perceptions of party machismo, despite the apparent electoral incentive. In the absence of systematic research on women and the SNP, we do not have the data to answer such questions. There are a number of possible explanations. The first is that of complacency: the idea that there is not a problem, given the long-standing presence of high-profile women in the party's political elite and the party's espoused support for equal opportunities. The second explanation relates to both capacity and agency and suggests there may be institutional and ideological barriers that discourage the mobilisation of party women around gender identities and gender-equity claims. Comparative evidence suggests that party women – particularly feminists – are critical actors in reform processes. Such actors are crucial in making the links and coupling processes of 'feminisation' to wider party processes of modernisation and reform. It is particularly puzzling that the party's projection of a modern, inclusive and tolerant nationalism has not provided – to date – the conditions for the growth of a feminist-accented nationalism, in contrast with comparator parties such as Plaid Cymru and Parti Québécois. It is clear that comparative research on the relationship between feminism and nationalist parties in Scotland, Wales, Quebec and other similar nations and regions would reap rich insight.

NOTES

1. The number of female MSPs has subsequently increased to 45 out of 129 MSPs (34.8%). Shirley-Anne Somerville (SNP) became regional member for the Lothians on 31 August 2007 following the resignation of Stefan Tymkewycz. Meanwhile, Anne McLaughlin (SNP) became regional member for Glasgow on 9 February 2009, replacing Bashir Ahmad. All figures in this chapter are based on initial election results.
2. Bashir Ahmad MSP (SNP) died in February 2009.

REFERENCES

Bradbury, J., Denver, D., Mitchell, J. and Bennie, L. (2000), 'Devolution and Party Change: Candidate Selection for the 1999 Scottish Parliament and Welsh Assembly Elections', *Journal of Legislative Studies*, 6 (3), pp. 51–72.

Brand, J., Mitchell, J. and Surridge, P. (1994), 'Social Constituency and Scottish Nationalism', *Political Studies*, 42 (4), pp. 616–29.

Bromley, C., Curtice, J. and Given, L (2005), *Public Attitudes to Devolution: The First Four Years*, http://www.natcen.ac.uk./natcen/pages/publications/P7457PDF.pdf

Brown, A. (2001a), 'Women and Politics in Scotland', in Breitenbach, E. and Mackay, F. (eds), *Women and Contemporary Scottish Politics: An Anthology*, Edinburgh, Polygon, pp. 197–212. (Originally published in *Parliamentary Affairs*, 49 (1), 1996.)

Brown, A. (2001b), 'Deepening Democracy: Women and the Scottish Parliament', in Breitenbach, E. and Mackay, F. (eds), *Women and Contemporary Scottish Politics: An Anthology*, Edinburgh, Polygon, pp. 213–29. (Originally published in *Regional and Federal Studies*, 8 (1), 1998.)

Brown, A. (2001c), 'Taking their Place in the New House: Women and the Scottish Parliament', in Breitenbach, E. and Mackay, F. (eds), *Women and Contemporary Scottish Politics: An Anthology*, Edinburgh, Polygon, pp. 241–7. (Originally published in *Scottish Affairs*, No. 28, summer.)

Brown, A., McCrone, D. and Paterson, L. (1998), *Politics and Society in Scotland*, Basingstoke, Macmillan.

Burness, C. (1995), 'Drunk Women don't look at Thistles: Women and the SNP 1934–94', *Scotlands*, 1 (2), pp. 131–54.

Burness, C. (forthcoming), 'Count up to Twenty-one: Scottish Women in Formal Politics, 1918–1990', in Thane, P. and Breitenbach, E. (eds), *Women and Citizenship in Britain and Ireland in the Twentieth Century: What Difference did the Vote Make?*, London, Continuum.

Caul, M. (1999), 'Women's Representation in Parliament: The Role of Political Parties', *Party Politics*, 5 (1), pp. 79–98.

Caul, M. (2001), 'Political Parties and the Adoption of Candidate Quotas: A Cross-National Analysis', *Journal of Politics*, 63 (4), pp. 1214–29.

Chaney, P., Mackay, F. and McAllister, L. (2007), *Women, Politics and Constitutional Change: The First Years of the National Assembly for Wales*, Cardiff, University of Wales Press.

Chapman, J. (1993), *Politics, Feminism, and the Reformation of Gender*, London, Routledge.

Childs, S., Lovenduski, J. and Campbell, R. (2005), *Women at the Top 2005: Changing Numbers, Changing Politics?*, London, Hansard Society.

Dahlerup, D. (2006), *Women, Quotas and Politics*, London, Routledge.

Dodds, A. and Seawright, M. (2004), 'The Politics of Identity: Scottish Nationalism', in O'Neill, M. (ed.), *Devolution and British Politics*, Harlow, Pearson Education, pp. 90–112.

House of Commons Information Office (undated), *Women in the House of Commons*, Factsheet M4.

Lovenduski, J. (2005), *Feminizing Politics*, Cambridge, Polity Press.

Mackay, F. (2003), 'Women and the 2003 Elections: Keeping up the Momentum', *Scottish Affairs*, No. 44, pp. 74–90.

Mackay, F. (2004), 'Gender and Political Representation in the UK: The State of the "Discipline"', *The British Journal of Politics and International Relations*, 6 (1), pp. 9–120.

Mackay, F. and Kenny, M. (2007), 'Women's Representation in the 2007 Scottish Parliament: Temporary Setback or Return to the Norm?', *Scottish Affairs*, No. 60, pp. 25–38.

Matland, R. E. and Studlar, D. (1996), 'The Contagion of Women Candidates in Single Member District and Proportional Representation Electoral Systems: Canada and Norway, *Journal of Politics*, 58 (3), pp. 707–33.

McAllister, L. (2001), *Plaid Cymru: The Emergence of a Political Party*, Bridgend, Seren.

McDonald, R., Alexander, M. and Sutherland, L. (2001), 'Networking for

Equality and a Scottish Parliament: The Women's Co-ordination Group and Organisational Alliances', in Breitenbach, E. and Mackay, F. (eds), *Women and Contemporary Scottish Politics*, Edinburgh, Polygon, pp. 231–40.

Norris, P., Vallance, E. and Lovenduski, J. (1992), 'Do Candidates Make a Difference? Gender, Race, Ideology and Incumbency', *Parliamentary Affairs*, 45, pp. 496–517.

Paterson, L. (2006), 'Sources of Support for the SNP', in Bromley, C., Curtice, J., McCrone, D. and Park, A. (eds), *Has Devolution Delivered?*, Edinburgh, Edinburgh University Press, pp. 46–68.

Randall, V. (1987), *Women and Politics: An International Perspective*, 2nd edn, Basingstoke, Macmillan.

Rasmussen, J. (1983), 'The Electoral Costs of Being a Woman at the 1979 British General Election', *Comparative Politics*, 15, pp. 462–75.

Russell, M. (2000), *Women's Representation in Elected Office: What can be Done within the Law?*, London, Constitution Unit.

Russell, M., Mackay, F. and McAllister, L. (2002), 'Women's Representation in the Scottish Parliament and National Assembly for Wales: Party Dynamics for Achieving Critical Mass', *Journal of Legislative Studies*, 8 (2), pp. 49–76.

Shepherd-Robinson, L. and Lovenduski, J. (2002), *Women and Candidate Selection in British Political Parties*, London, Fawcett.

Studlar, D. T. and Welch, S. (1993), 'A Giant Step for Womankind? Women Candidates and the 1992 General Election', in Denver, D., Norris, P., Broughton, D. and Rallings, C. (eds), *British Parties and Elections Yearbook 1993*, London, Harvester Wheatsheaf, pp. 216–28.

Welch, S. and Studlar, D. T. (1996), 'The Opportunity Structure for Women's Candidacies and Electability in Britain and the United States', *Political Research Quarterly*, 49, pp. 861–74.

CHAPTER 5

Devolution, the SNP and the Electorate

John Curtice

'Devolution,' famously quipped the former Labour Shadow Secretary of State for Scotland, George Robertson, 'will kill Nationalism stone dead.' Yet eight years after the founding of the Scottish Parliament in 1999, the SNP leader, Alex Salmond, was installed as Scotland's First Minister and a nationalist administration was formed for the first time. This chapter attempts to explain how in practice devolution threw an electoral lifeline to the SNP that eventually enabled it to come to power.

THE GEOGRAPHY OF SNP SUPPORT

The SNP first emerged as a substantial nationwide force following its initial breakthrough in the 1967 Hamilton by-election. Thereafter it began to stand in more or less every single Scottish constituency in UK general elections, whereas previously it had often fought little more than a handful. Moreover, as Table 5.1 shows, in so doing the party proved itself capable of commanding substantial shares of the popular vote. In October 1974, in particular, it won over 30%, thereby displacing the Conservatives from second place. Indeed, it was this electoral success that persuaded the then Labour Prime Minister, Harold Wilson, that his government needed to introduce some form of devolution in Scotland as a means of countering the nationalist threat, although in the event his efforts foundered after the 1979 referendum. Although the Nationalists never subsequently proved capable of emulating their October 1974 performance, they still proved capable of winning around a fifth of the vote.

However, the SNP consistently secured little reward in terms of seats relative to the votes it obtained. Even when running second in votes in October 1974 the party won only 11 of the 71 Scottish seats then in existence, or just 15% of the total. The Conservatives still managed to win 16 seats in that election, despite winning fewer votes than the SNP. Between

Table 5.1 UK election results in Scotland, 1970–2005

	% vote				
	Cons	Labour	Liberal/ Lib Dem	SNP	Other
1970	38.0	44.5	5.5	11.4	0.6
1974 (Feb)	32.9	36.6	7.9	21.9	0.6
1974 (Oct)	24.7	36.3	8.3	30.4	0.3
1979	31.4	41.5	9.0	17.3	0.8
1983	28.4	35.1	24.5	11.8	0.3
1987	24.0	42.4	19.2	14.0	0.3
1992	25.6	39.0	13.1	21.5	0.8
1997	17.5	45.6	13.0	22.1	1.9
2001	15.6	43.3	16.3	20.1	4.7
2005	15.8	38.9	22.6	17.7	5.1

Source: Rallings and Thrasher (2006)

1979 and 1992 the Nationalists only ever won two or three seats. That tally finally rose in 1997, though still only to six, even though the party once again secured more votes than the Conservatives. Meanwhile, this time the Liberal Democrats managed to win four more seats than the SNP despite coming fourth in votes.

The explanation for the difficulty the SNP had in translating votes into seats is simple. The party's vote was too evenly spread across Scotland. An indication of the degree to which this has persistently been the case is indicated in Table 5.2, which shows for each of the four main parties on each of three occasions a commonly used measure of variation, the standard deviation. The higher this figure the more a party's vote varied from one constituency to another. Evidently, while Labour's vote has always varied a great deal, and the degree of variation in the Conservative and Liberal Democrat vote has changed over time, the SNP vote has always been evenly spread. Moreover this quality was still a feature of its support at the time of the last Scottish Parliament election.

Unless a party is leading the pack in votes, having a geographically evenly spread vote is always a disadvantage if the first-past-the-post system is in place (Gudgin and Taylor 1979). Even if it is running second overall, a party with such a vote is likely to find itself second more or less everywhere and first almost nowhere. And if it is running third the seats it wins are likely to be sparse indeed, as testified by the experience of the Liberal Party and its successor parties for much of the post-war period. Meanwhile in contrast to the even spread of the SNP vote, support for

Table 5.2 Variation in party support in Scotland, 1974–2007

	Standard deviation of constituency support		
	Oct 1974	1997	2007
Conservative	11.2	8.3	9.3
Labour	15.1	17.3	13.8
Liberal/Lib Dem	9.2*	12.7	13.2
SNP	9.4	9.2	8.9

* Based only on the 68 constituencies fought by the Liberal Democrats at that election.
Source: author's calculations

Scotland's leading party has a strikingly uneven vote that means that typically the party either comes first in a constituency or else a long way behind. Relatively few votes are wasted coming a good second.

So prior to the advent of devolution, the scales were heavily tilted against the SNP in elections to the House of Commons. Even if the party secured a substantial share of the vote, the geographically even spread of its support meant that it struggled to secure significant representation at Westminster. This even spread was in fact a reflection of the fact that its level of support was more or less the same amongst voters in different demographic groups.[1] This is illustrated in Table 5.3, which shows the level of SNP voting amongst different groups at the time of the 1997 UK general election, as well as on the occasion of the 2007 Scottish Parliament election (for a fuller account of the history of the social basis of SNP support see Paterson 2006).

There are a few differences in Table 5.3 worth noting. In 1997 the SNP drew rather less support amongst women than it did amongst men. The ratio of men to women varies little between one part of Scotland and another, however, so this difference did not give rise to any geographical variation in SNP support. The party was somewhat less successful at securing support amongst Catholics, but by 1997 this pattern had become less striking than it had been previously (Seawright and Curtice, 1995).[2] The Nationalists also tended to do less well amongst graduates and older people, but otherwise there was no consistent link between either age or education and SNP support.

Above all, however, SNP support varied relatively little between those in different social classes or between owner-occupiers, on the one hand, and those in social housing on the other – and these are groups whose incidence does vary substantially across Scotland. In contrast, in 1997 Labour

Table 5.3 SNP Vote by demographic characteristics, 1997–2007

		1997 %	2007 %
Gender	Male	21	36
	Female	17	32
Age group	18–34	19	38
	35–59	22	36
	60 +	13	29
Social class	Employers and managers	16	32
	Intermediate	20	30
	Small employers/self-employed	17	32
	Lower supervisory/technical	21	29
	Semi-routine and routine	22	38
Highest	Degree	12	27
educational	Professional	18	40
qualification	Highers	16	32
	Standard grade	21	37
	None	23	34
Housing tenure	Owner occupier	17	32
	Social housing	25	36
	Private rental	10	53
Religion	Protestant	20	29
	Catholic	10	24
	None	23	40

Social class is based on respondent's occupation. In 1997, it is based on the Heath-Goldthorpe class schema (Erikson and Goldthorpe 1992; Goldthorpe and Heath 1992); in 2007 it is based on the National Statistics Social Economic Classification (NS-SEC) (Rose and Pevalin 2003). The two schemas are similar to each other.
2007 data are for those voters who said that the SNP was their first choice party in that year's Scottish parliament election.
Sources: Scottish Election Study 1997; Scottish Social Attitudes Survey 2007

won the support of just 33% of employers and managers, but no less than 65% of those in routine and semi-routine occupations. Equally, Labour support varied between 46% amongst owner occupiers and 64% amongst those in social housing. The equivalent differences in SNP support as shown in Table 5.3 are clearly mild in comparison.

THE SCOTTISH PARLIAMENT ELECTORAL SYSTEM

So, prior to devolution the SNP struggled to secure representation because, so long at least as it did not come first in votes, the single-member plurality voting system discriminated against its socially and

Table 5.4 Scottish Parliament election results in votes and seats, 1999–2007

	% Constituency vote (no. of seats)					
	1999		2003		2007	
SNP	28.7	(7)	23.8	(9)	32.9	(21)
Labour	38.8	(53)	34.6	(46)	32.2	(37)
Conservatives	15.6	(0)	16.6	(3)	16.6	(4)
Liberal Democrats	14.2	(12)	15.4	(13)	16.2	(11)
Greens	–	–	0.1	(0)	0.1	(0)
Scottish Socialists	1.0	(0)	6.2	(0)	0.0	(0)
Others	1.7	(1)	3.5	(2)	2.0	(0)
	% Regional list vote (no. of seats)					
	1999		2003		2007	
SNP	27.3	(28)	20.9	(18)	31.0	(26)
Labour	33.6	(3)	29.3	(4)	29.2	(9)
Conservatives	15.4	(18)	15.5	(15)	13.9	(13)
Liberal Democrats	12.4	(5)	11.8	(4)	11.3	(5)
Greens	3.6	(1)	6.9	(7)	4.0	(2)
Scottish Socialists	2.0	(1)	6.7	(6)	0.6	(0)
Others	5.7	(0)	8.9	(2)	10.0	(1)

Note: Greens did not fight any constituencies in 1999 or 2003.
Sources: Hassan and Fraser (2004); Electoral Commission (2007)

thus geographically evenly spread vote. However, devolution not only saw the advent of a new parliament but also a new electoral system. Following protracted negotiations in the early 1990s between Labour and the Liberal Democrats within the forum of the Scottish Constitutional Convention, the two parties agreed upon a system whereby the 72 existing first-past-the-post constituencies (with Orkney and Shetland divided into two separate constituencies) would be supplemented by 56 party list seats, allocated within each of eight regions such that the overall distribution of seats in each region, both constituency and list, would reflect as closely as possible the division of the vote between the parties. This Additional Member System helped meet the Liberal Democrats' long-standing preference for a more proportional electoral system, while giving Labour some reassurance that, should the SNP ever make a breakthrough and come first in votes, they could still fail to secure an overall majority in seats (Curtice 2006a).

As Table 5.4 shows, the introduction of the new electoral system is one key reason why the advent of devolution has provided an electoral lifeline to the SNP. As is apparent from the second column in Table 5.3 (above), since 1997 the party's vote has continued to be evenly spread across different demographic groups and thus (as shown in the final column of Table 5.2, above) evenly spread geographically too. Consequently, it has continued to find it difficult to win individual constituency seats. The party has been heavily dependent on the allocation of the additional, 'top-up' regional list seats. In the first term of the Scottish Parliament, for example, such seats accounted for no less than 28 of the 35 SNP representatives in the chamber. And in allocating the party so many seats, the list element of the new system enabled the party to become a substantial parliamentary force for the first time in its history.

The new system was also crucial to the party's ability to secure power in 2007. As can be seen from the last column in Table 5.4, even though the Labour party slipped narrowly behind the SNP in its share of the overall vote cast for individual constituency MSPs, it still won an overall majority – 37 out of 73 – of the constituency seats, while the SNP only secured 21 (albeit quite easily a record number). Although the system lacked sufficient list seats to correct the resulting disproportionality fully, in the event it had just enough to ensure that the SNP emerged with one more seat than Labour.[3] Labour's Scotland Act had provided the means for the SNP to gain power.

WINNING HOLYROOD VOTES

But the mechanics of the new electoral system are, of course, not a sufficient explanation of why the SNP has prospered under devolution. For one feature of Table 5.4 as compared with Table 5.1 is the fact the SNP's share of the vote has typically been higher in Scottish Parliament elections than it has been in contemporaneous Westminster contests. Thus, for example, in the first Scottish Parliament election in 1999 the party won 29% of the constituency vote, seven points above its score in the UK general election held two years previously. Similarly, in 2003 its share of the constituency vote was nearly four points higher than its vote in the preceding UK election, while in 2007 it was no less than fifteen points higher. Evidently the SNP find Scottish Parliament elections a relatively favourable environment in which to garner votes.

One possible explanation could be that, so far, Scottish Parliament elections have always occurred during the mid-term of a Westminster Parliament. Perhaps, therefore, such elections have been regarded by the electorate as occasions when they can send a protest note to London about the performance of the incumbent UK Labour government by voting for the SNP. However, although such behaviour is not entirely absent from

Table 5.5 Actual and hypothetical votes for Holyrood and Westminster, 1999–2007

	Difference in % vote	
	Constituency vote – hypothetical Westminster vote	Hypothetical constituency vote – Westminster vote
1999	+7	–
2001	–	+10
2003	+5	–
2005	–	+3
2007	+10	–

Source: Scottish Social Attitudes surveys

Scottish Parliament elections (Curtice 2006b; Curtice 2009; Curtice et al. 2009), in practice it is not a sufficient explanation for the SNP's relative success in Scottish Parliament elections.

Rather, irrespective of the current state of the Westminster electoral cycle, voters are more willing to vote for the SNP in elections to the Scottish Parliament than they are in elections to the UK House of Commons. This pattern was first identified in the earliest opinion polls, conducted in 1998, to ascertain voting intentions for both the Scottish Parliament and for a UK general election (see www.alba.org.uk) and it has been apparent in every survey conducted since.

It is illustrated further in Table 5.5. First of all this table shows, for each Scottish Parliament election, the difference between the proportion who say that they voted for the SNP in their local constituency contest and the proportion who say that they would have voted for the Nationalists if a Westminster election had been held that day. On each occasion it is apparent that considerably more people voted for the SNP in the Scottish contest than would have done in a UK general election. Second, this table also displays for the last two UK general elections the difference between the proportion who reported having voted for the SNP on that occasion and the proportion stating that they would have voted for the SNP on the constituency ballot if a Scottish Parliament election were being held instead. Here we can see that the proportion saying they would have voted for the SNP in a Holyrood contest is markedly above the proportion who actually did so in the general election in question.

So it seems that if we are to understand why the SNP has prospered to the extent that it has done in Scottish Parliament elections, we have to explain why voters find the party a more attractive option in such contests than they do in elections to the House of Commons. Table 5.6 gives us an initial clue as to why that might be the case. It shows what voters said was

Table 5.6 What matters to voters in different elections, 1999–2007

% say voted mostly on basis of what going on in	1999	2001	2003	2005	2007
Scotland	52	34	54	32	56
Britain as a whole	34	44	27	43	29

Source: Scottish Social Attitudes

uppermost in their minds when deciding how to vote, first, at each Scottish Parliament election and, second, at the last two UK general elections. In the two UK general elections rather more people said they voted mostly on the basis of what was going on in Britain as a whole than said they were looking primarily at developments in Scotland in particular. When Scottish Parliament elections were being contested, however, voters were apparently far more likely to be concerned with what was going on in Scotland.

Evidently, then, some voters regard UK general elections and Scottish Parliament elections differently. In a Westminster ballot they are concerned to identify who they think can provide good government for the whole of the UK, whereas in a Holyrood contest they ask themselves who seems to be best able to improve the condition of Scotland. And it should come as little surprise that the SNP are more likely to be regarded as able to provide good government for Scotland than they are for the UK as a whole.

The distinctively 'Scottish' tone to Scottish Parliament elections, and the way in which that tone profits the SNP, can, however, be demonstrated in a more striking matter. We have already seen from Table 5.3 (above) that the differences in the level of SNP support between different demographic groups were much the same in the Scottish Parliament election of 2007 as they had been in the Westminster contest of 1997. However, the same is not true if we chart the pattern of support for the SNP amongst those with different national identities.

This is demonstrated in Table 5.7. Respondents to the Scottish Social Attitudes surveys, from which these data are taken, were asked to state which of five possible combinations of being British and being Scottish best described themselves. This method of identifying national identity, known as the Moreno question (Moreno 1988), enables people both explicitly to state that they hold one of the two identities but not the other, or to acknowledge that they have some kind of dual identity. In the table we show, for each Scottish Parliament election and the last two UK general elections, what proportion of those in each category of response to the Moreno question said they had voted for the SNP.

Table 5.7 National Identity and Support for SNP, 1999–2007

National identity	% voted SNP				
	1999	2001	2003	2005	2007
Scottish not British	43	24	40	25	58
More Scottish than British	27	16	27	19	42
Equally Scottish and British	18	8	6	9	15
More British than Scottish	6	9	2	4	11
British not Scottish	6	3	1	2	7

Source: Scottish Social Attitudes

The variation from election to election in the level of support for the SNP is clearly greater in some categories than in others. At one end of the spectrum, amongst those who feel exclusively British, few have voted for the SNP in any kind of election. In contrast, at the other end, amongst those who only feel Scottish, support for the SNP has consistently been considerably higher in Scottish Parliament elections than in it has been in UK general elections. Equally, support for the SNP has also tended to be higher in Scottish Parliament elections, albeit less dramatically so, amongst those who feel 'more Scottish than British', whereas this has not been consistently true of those who regard themselves as 'more British than Scottish'.

So it seems that in Scottish Parliament elections the SNP are better able to acquire the support in particular of those with a strong sense of Scottish identity and weak sense, if any at all, of British identity. True, even on those occasions feeling Scottish is far from synonymous with voting for the SNP (Rosie and Bond 2003). However, it would seem that when faced with a purely Scottish election for a political institution that may be thought to symbolise Scotland's distinctive sense of nationhood, some voters with a strong sense of Scottish identity are more inclined to acknowledge or express that identity by voting for the SNP. As a result the SNP finds it easier to prosper in Scottish Parliament elections.

This phenomenon is, in fact, not unique to Scotland. Jeffery and Hough (2003) have shown that nationalist parties consistently tend to do better in sub-state elections where a distinctive sense of national identity exists. The architects of devolution might, perhaps, have been less confident in predicting that devolution would lead to the demise of Scottish Nationalism if they had been aware of experience in similar circumstances elsewhere.

The differences between Scottish Parliament elections and UK general

Table 5.8 Constitutional preferences and Nationalist support, 1999–2007

	% voted SNP amongst those favouring		
	Independence	Devolution	No parliament
1999	62	17	5
2001	35	10	3
2003	58	12	4
2005	33	9	3
2007	78	22	6

Source: Scottish Social Attitudes

elections in the pattern of support for the SNP is not, however, confined to national identity. It can also be found when examining the link between SNP support and people's constitutional preferences. As Table 5.8 shows, support for the SNP amongst those who do not think that the Scottish Parliament should exist at all is very low irrespective of the election being contested. SNP support does rise and fall to some degree amongst those who favour having a devolved Scottish Parliament while remaining part of the United Kingdom, but only to a relatively modest degree. In contrast, support for the SNP amongst those in favour of independence differs between the two types of contests by at least 20 points, and sometimes by more. In other words, the SNP apparently find it easier in Scottish Parliament elections to secure the support of those who might be regarded as 'natural' supporters of the party, that is those who would like their country to become independent. In elections to Westminster the SNP struggle to persuade more than one third of this group to back the party. In Scottish Parliament elections, in contrast, over half regularly do so. So as well as providing a forum for the mobilisation of Scottish identity, Scottish Parliament elections are occasions when voters' preferences in respect of Scotland's constitutional future hold greater sway too.

We have, then, acquired some understanding of why the SNP consistently finds it easier to win votes in a Scottish Parliament election. Even so, its performance in the 2007 election, when it won power, still appears to be exceptional. Here too, however, our analysis can shed some further light. A further look at Table 5.8 reveals that although support for the SNP was higher in 2007 amongst those who favoured devolution than it had been at either of the two previous Scottish Parliament elections, the difference was not dramatic. In contrast, support for the SNP among those who favoured independence rose from the three in five or so that pertained in the first two Holyrood elections to over three quarters in 2007. It seems

Table 5.9 Constitutional preference and evaluations of SNP leaders, 2003 and 2007

% giving SNP leader a score of 7/10 or more amongst those who support	2003	2007	Change 2003–7
Independence	14	62	+48
Devolution	6	35	+29
No parliament	3	18	+15

Source Scottish Social Attitudes

that a crucial foundation of the SNP's success in 2007 was that it gathered together under its umbrella for the first time the vast majority of those who favoured independence.[4]

Table 5.9 gives us some idea of why this development might have occurred. It shows for each constitutional preference the proportion of people who, when asked to say how good a First Minister they thought the leader would be, gave the SNP leader a mark of seven or more, first in 2003 and then in 2007. In all cases the proportion who in 2007 gave Alex Salmond such a score was higher than the proportion who did the same when asked about his predecessor, John Swinney, in 2003. But the increase in the proportion doing so was far greater amongst those who favoured independence than it was amongst those who did not. It seems as though in 2007 the SNP were particularly able to exploit the favourable environment afforded it by Holyrood elections because it was able to persuade in particular those who already favoured independence that the party was capable of providing Scotland with good government. Scottish identity, a sense of nationhood and apparent governing capacity evidently came together on this occasion to propel the SNP to power.

CONCLUSION

Devolution has provided the SNP with an unparalleled political opportunity. It has created an environment in which it finds it easier to win votes. And it has introduced an electoral system in which the party is better able to turn votes into seats. In certain circumstances, at least, as the outcome of the 2007 election demonstrated, the party is able to exploit these circumstances such that it can outpoll the Labour party and find itself in government.

Thus Nationalism as a political force now looks stronger than ever. Yet how far this has brought the party closer to its objective of an independent Scotland is open to question. The success of the SNP has not been founded on a rising tide of rising public support for independence. According to the 2007 Scottish Social Attitudes survey only 24% backed independence as the SNP came to power, slightly below the 27% who did so in 1999 (Curtice et al. 2009). Rather, it has been founded on a greater ability to turn existing support for independence into votes, and then those votes into seats.

However, the party is committed to determining Scotland's constitutional future not through electoral success but by holding a referendum on independence. So ultimately the party needs not simply to persuade those who already support independence to back the party, as happened in 2007, but rather to persuade more people to support independence in the first place. Its hope is that a successful period in office will enable that to happen. Yet while such a spell might well leave the party well positioned to profit once again at election time from the favourable circumstances created for it by devolution, the key lesson to be drawn from its Holyrood success to date may well be that those who are most likely to be impressed by the performance of the SNP in government are simply those who are already convinced of the case for independence. The big challenge now facing the party is to demonstrate it can reach out beyond the converted.

NOTES

1. In this respect the character of SNP support is similar to that for the Liberal Party and its successors across the UK for much of the post-war period. See Curtice 1996.
2. Note that similar survey data for the 1992 election shows relatively little difference between Protestants and Catholics in the level of SNP support. On that occasion 20% of Catholics said they had voted SNP and 22% of Protestants. In contrast, just 12% of Catholics but as many as 30% of Protestants voted for the SNP in October 1974.
3. In two regions, Glasgow and the West of Scotland, Labour won more seats than it would have secured if all the seats within them had been allocated by the D'Hondt formula, rather than just the list seats. Overall, this boosted Labour by three seats in two regions, two at the expense of the SNP and one at the Conservatives'. The Liberal Democrats also secured an extra seat at the expense of the SNP in the Highlands and Islands. Such imbalances were also evident in the results of the 1999 and 2003 elections (Curtice 2006a).
4. We can also see from Table 5.7 that in doing that the party also secured increased support in particular from those who regard themselves as exclusively or primarily Scottish.

REFERENCES

Curtice, J. (1996),'Who Votes for the Centre Now?', in McIver, D. (ed.), *The Liberal Democrats*, London, Harvester Wheatsheaf.

Curtice, J. (2006a), 'Forecasting and Evaluating the Consequences of Electoral Change: Scotland and Wales', *Acta Politica: International Journal of Political Science*, Vol. 41, pp. 300–14.

Curtice, J. (2006b), 'Is Holyrood Accountable and Representative?', in Bromley, C., Curtice, J., McCrone, D. and Park, A. (eds), *Has Devolution Delivered?*, Edinburgh, Edinburgh University Press.

Curtice, J. (2009), 'Do Devolved Elections Work?', in Jeffery, C. and Mitchell, J. (eds), *The Scottish Parliament 1999–2009: The First Decade*, Edinburgh, Luath Press for the Hansard Society.

Curtice, J., McCrone, D., McEwen, N., Marsh, M. and Ormston, R. (2009), *Revolution or Evolution? The Scottish Parliamentary and Local Elections of 2007*, Edinburgh, Edinburgh University Press.

Electoral Commission (2007), *Scottish Elections 2007: Electoral Administration Issues arising from the Scottish Parliamentary and Local Government Elections 3 May 2007*, Edinburgh and London, Electoral Commission.

Erikson, R. and Goldthorpe, J. (1992), *The Constant Flux: A Study of Social Mobility in Industrial Societies*, Oxford, Clarendon Press.

Goldthorpe, J. and Heath, A. (1992), *Revised Class Schema 1992*, JUSST/CREST Working Paper No. 13, London and Oxford, SCPR and Nuffield College.

Gudgin, G. and Taylor, P. (1979), *Seats, Votes and the Spatial Organisation of Elections*, London, Pion.

Hassan, G. and Fraser, D. (2004), *The Political Guide to Modern Scotland*, London, Politico's Publishing.

Jeffery, C. and Hough, D. (2003), 'Regional Elections in Multi-Level Systems', *European Urban and Regional Studies*, Vol. 10, pp. 199–212.

Moreno, L. (1988), 'Scotland and Catalonia: The Path to Home Rule', in McCrone, D. and Brown, A. (eds), *The Scottish Government Yearbook 1988*, Edinburgh, Unit for the Study of Government in Scotland.

Paterson, L. (2006), 'Sources of Support for the SNP', in Bromley, C., Curtice, J., McCrone, D. and Park, A. (eds), *Has Devolution Delivered?*, Edinburgh, Edinburgh University Press.

Rallings, C. and Thrasher, M. (2006), *British Electoral Facts 1832–2006*, Aldershot, Ashgate.

Rose, D. and Pevalin, L. (eds) (2003), *A Researcher's Guide to the National Statistics Socio-economic Classification*, London, Sage.

Rosie, M. and Bond, R. (2003), 'Identity Matters: The Personal and Political Significance of Feeling Scottish', in Bromley, C., Curtice, J., Hinds, K. and Park, A. (eds), *Devolution – Scottish Answers to Scottish Questions?*, Edinburgh, Edinburgh University Press.

Seawright, D. and Curtice, J. (1995), 'The Decline of the Scottish Conservative and Unionist Party, 1950–92: Religion, Ideology or Economics', *Contemporary Record*, Vol. 9, pp. 319–42.

CHAPTER 6

Who are the SNP Members?

James Mitchell, Robert Johns and Lynn Bennie

Much of the literature and commentary on the SNP has rested on speculation and assumptions rather than empirical evidence. While we have a
relatively clear idea of the party's leadership's views on a range of matters,
we know little about the ordinary membership. The only data available
were resolutions passed and elections to national office decided by activists attending annual SNP conferences and quarterly National Councils.
In the past, this rough and ready guide to the state of opinion within the
SNP was the basis of informed opinion. However, conferences and councils have increasingly resembled the rallies of other major parties rather
than the decision-making *fora* of the past. And until recently there was no
large-scale survey of party members equivalent to those for other parties
(Seyd and Whiteley 1992; 2002; Whiteley et al. 1994; 2006; Rüdig et al.
1991; 1996; Bennie et al. 1996; Bennie 2004). That has now changed,
however, following a major ESRC-funded membership study.[1] The data
from the survey of party members allows us to explore the SNP in a way
that has never before been possible. In this chapter we have three aims.
First, we offer a socio-demographic overview of SNP members. Second,
we explore some of the key attitudes and identities of the party's members.
Finally, we look at levels of political activity before drawing general
conclusions about the SNP.

WHO ARE THE MEMBERS?

This first section of the chapter offers a profile of the SNP's membership.
We begin with the gender breakdown of party membership, comparing this
with data from previous party membership studies. As Table 6.1 shows,
there is a general tendency for males to predominate in political parties but
this is pronounced in the SNP, with just 31.8% of members being female.
What is unclear is the extent to which this is peculiar to the SNP or a feature

68

Table 6.1 Sex and age of party members

	Women %	Men %	Average age
SNP 2007/2008	31.8	68.2	58.7
Labour 1997	39.0	61.0	52
Labour 1989/1990	39.2	60.8	48
Conservative 1992	52.0	48.0	62
Lib Dem 1998/1999	46.0	54.0	59
Lib Dem 1993	47.0	53.0	56
Scottish Greens 1990	45.3	54.7	39
Scottish Greens 2002	36.8	63.2	47
UK Greens 1990	47.0	53.0	41

of Scottish parties more generally. There is some evidence of the latter given that the equivalent figure from a small sample of Labour members in Scotland in 1997 was 35%. Moreover, traditionally Scottish politics has been dominated by men, even more so than in England (Brown et al. 1996: 163–88). Given this low base of women members, the SNP has achieved a comparatively high proportion of women MSPs: in 2009, women made up 29.8% of SNP MSPs. Nonetheless, by almost any measurement, the SNP appears to have a problem attracting women as members.

SNP members also appear older than those in other parties, at least compared with figures drawn from earlier comparable surveys. The average (mean) age of respondents was 58.7 (and the median member was 61). Only in the study of Conservative members in 1992 was an older average age of member recorded, although it is probable that the average age of Labour members has increased following that party's loss of members since 1997. Less than 8% of SNP members are below the age of 35; and these young members are considerably outnumbered by those over the age of 75. Overall, nearly two thirds of members (64.4%) are aged 55 or above; and nearly 40% are 65 or older, all of which suggests that the party has not been successful in attracting younger people to the party. However, the party's membership has been growing in recent years and this has provided it with more younger members: 20.7% of the survey respondents who joined since 2005 were aged 18–34. The challenge for the SNP, as for all parties, is to continue to renew and refresh its membership.

In common with other political parties, the SNP membership is largely middle class. The type of occupations of party members is predominantly professional: 33% of the members categorise themselves as modern professional (working as teachers, nurses, social workers etc.) and another 26% senior managers or administrators, or as traditional professionals (accountants, solicitors, doctors etc.) Annual incomes also show the party to be middle class: 37% of members have an annual household income of under £20,000, while 20% have a total household annual income over £50,000. The average SNP member has an income of between £20,000 and £30,000. However, four in ten of the members are retired from work. When these are excluded from the analysis, the average household income rises to between £30,000 and £40,000. Nearly half the members – 46% – work (or worked) in the private sector, as against 48% in the public sector.

The SNP's members are also well educated. Just over a third (35%) have a degree, a proportion which rises to 54% in the 18–34 age group. These figures are comparable with the Labour party, but predictably below those of the Scottish Greens, more than three quarters of whom had a degree in 2002.

SNP members are reluctant to assign themselves to a class as compared with members of other parties, perhaps reflecting an emphasis on national rather than class identity. Only 42.7% of survey respondents answered 'yes' when asked 'Do you think of yourself as belonging to a particular social class?' When prompted to choose, 38.1% opted for working class, 44.3% for middle class and 17.7% would still not choose. This indicates that working-class identity is markedly more common among SNP members than among members of the more traditionally middle-class parties, the Conservatives and the Liberal Democrats. One reason for the divergence between subjective and objective class could be the continuing impact of family background: 68.5% of SNP members reported their parents as working class compared to just 25.7% reporting a middle-class background.

Religion has played a significant role in Scottish politics, but early research on SNP support suggested that the party was most able to advance amongst those who were irreligious, non-aligned or weakly aligned to any denomination (Miller 1981: 146). Amongst our respondents, 42.6% reported no affiliation with any religion, a rather larger proportion than in the Scottish public. Among those who do have a religious identity, the breakdown among SNP members broadly reflects that in Scotland as a whole.

A large proportion of members (51%) has lived outside Scotland for six months or more. Most of these (47.2%) had lived in England, though 44.9% had lived somewhere outside the UK or Ireland. In keeping with the civic nationalist image that the SNP leadership projects, the party's membership includes a significant proportion of people born in England: 6.7% of members, not far below the 8.1% recorded in the 2001 census for the population as a whole.

In the next table we show the geographical distribution of SNP

Table 6.2 Think in terms of class, and if yes, which class

	Think of yourself as belonging to a class	'If you HAD to choose . . .?'			
		Middle	Working	None	Other
SNP	42.7	44.3	38.1	–	–
Lib Dem 1999	66.0	53	12	33	2
Labour 1997	65.9	32	58	–	2
Conservative 1992	62.0	76	18	–	4
Scottish Greens 1990	59.1	73	27	–	–

Table 6.3 Religion of those 'belonging to a religion'

	SNP members %	Current religious affiliation, Scottish public (2001 census) %
No religion/religion not stated	42.6	33.0
Church of Scotland	37.4	42.4
Catholic	10.4	15.9
Other Christian	6.9	6.8
Other	2.9	1.6

members, based on the eight Scottish Parliament electoral regions. To put these in context, the middle column shows the percentage of the SNP's list vote and the right-hand column shows the corresponding proportions among the population as a whole. (In order to maintain that comparison, the 3.4% of SNP members living outside Scotland are excluded.) Apart from the Highlands & Islands, each region is broadly similar in size in proportion of the electorate, but regional diversity as a percentage of the SNP's list vote across Scotland is more marked (8.8%–16.6%). However, the relationship between share of vote and share of membership is not straightforward. The most striking difference is found in the South of Scotland, which provides only 4.2% of the SNP's members yet 12.2% of its voters (and was a region in which the party came a close second to Labour in 2007 list voting). In contrast, Glasgow and (especially) Lothians provide large proportions of the SNP's membership, yet this is not reflected by the party's regional vote shares in those predominantly urban areas. Indeed, as the regional breakdown implies, the SNP is quite a rural party, with most members (69%) living in small towns and villages or in the country and only 31% in a big city or suburb.

Table 6.4 Regional distribution of SNP members and Scottish population

Region	% of membership	% of SNP total list vote	% of electorate
North East Scotland	16.7	16.6	13.0
South of Scotland	4.2	12.2	13.2
Lothians	18.3	12.0	13.2
Central Scotland	9.9	14.0	14.2
Glasgow	16.0	8.8	12.3
Highlands & Islands	10.2	10.1	8.6
West of Scotland	13.7	12.0	12.3
Mid Scotland & Fife	10.9	14.2	13.3

Perhaps the most noticeable feature of the results so far is precisely the lack of striking findings. The profile of SNP members in terms of age, social class, education and religion is not markedly dissimilar to the Scottish population, and quite similar to most other parties based on previous membership studies. The biggest contrast tended to be with the Greens, suggesting that, at least in terms of membership, the SNP belongs more among the 'major' parties than among the 'minor' or 'protest' parties. In the absence of comparable data from earlier years, we cannot tell whether this has long been true of the SNP, or whether it is a feature of the party since devolution and becoming a serious contender for government power.

WHAT DO THE MEMBERS THINK?

It might have been expected that all members of the SNP would identify themselves as exclusively Scottish. Using the standard measure of national identity, which asks respondents to locate themselves on a five-point scale running from 'Scottish not British' to 'British not Scottish', we find that 77.4% chose the first of those options. In other words, a significant minority – around one in five – see themselves as being British to some extent. In response to a different question, 20.5% agreed or strongly agreed that 'Sometimes it is more appropriate to say you are British and sometimes it is more appropriate to say you are Scottish'.

When SNP members were asked about which aspects of Scotland were particularly important to them, the single most cited answer was the Scottish people. Scotland's sporting achievements barely received a mention. But the Scottish Parliament and its 'democratic tradition' together constitute a significant element of pride in Scotland. More revealing were responses to a

Table 6.5 National identity

Which best describes how you see yourself?	%
Scottish not British	77.4
More Scottish than British	16.0
Equally Scottish and British	2.6
More British than Scottish	0.2
British not Scottish	0.3
Other	3.5

Table 6.6 First preference among constitutional options

Constitutional option	%
Abolish Scottish Parliament	0.3
Status quo	0.7
More powers	11.9
Independence within EU	65.4
Independence outwith EU	21.8

question about what, if anything, made respondents *less* proud of Scotland. The familiar catalogue of Scotland's social ills, combined with what are perceived to be their causes, emerge. 'Lack of self-confidence' was by some distance the most often-cited response.

As the SNP's main aim is Scottish independence, it might have been expected that all members would subscribe to this objective. And indeed, when asked to choose their first preference among constitutional options, the vast majority (87.2%) opt for independence. However, there are two significant limits to this. First, roughly a quarter of those who favour independence would prefer to see Scotland outside the European Union, in opposition to SNP policy. Second, there remains a minority in the party – 11.9% of SNP members – that does not give independence, either within or outside the EU, as its first preference but instead would prefer that the Scottish Parliament had more powers. Moreover, fully 48% of respondents placed 'more powers' as either first or second preference. In particular, those whose first choice was independence in Europe split almost 50:50 between independence outside the EU and further devolution short of independence as their second preference. Electoral studies have long noted the party's ability to win votes beyond its core of independence supporters (e.g. Miller 1981; Brand et al. 1994; Johns et al. 2009). These results suggest that the same is true of members.

Widespread openness to further devolution leads us to consider which powers the SNP members would most like to see transferred to Holyrood.

Table 6.7 Selected Left–Right and Liberal–Authoritarian attitudes

	Strongly agree %	Agree %	Neither %	Disagree %	Strongly disagree %
There is one law for the rich and one law for the poor	25	40	19	12	3
It is not government's responsibility to provide a job for everyone who wants one	8	39	19	29	6
The government should cut spending in order to cut tax	3	9	16	52	19
The death penalty can never be justified	28	23	11	24	14
In principle, ID cards are a good idea	8	26	11	21	34
The law should always be obeyed, even if a particular law is wrong	7	29	21	36	7

When asked which responsibilities should be prioritised, most respondents (55.7%) opted for economic and taxation powers. This may reflect the emphasis on fiscal autonomy that has been evident amongst SNP leaders since 1999. However, members were less preoccupied by broadcasting, another area that SNP leaders had previously prioritised. Fewer than 5% of SNP members list that as first priority for further devolution. Defence and foreign affairs, though a long way behind economic and taxation powers, comes next (12.6%) and may reflect the SNP's long-standing opposition to nuclear weapons and its strong stance against the Iraq War.

Other political attitudes explored in the survey included the members' positions on traditional left–right and on libertarian–authoritarian issues. On the left–right spectrum, we see a fairly consistent, moderate consensus on the left. Responses on the liberal–authoritarian scale are rarely as coherent as on the left–right spectrum, but SNP members certainly appear more liberal than the electorate as a whole.

PARTY STRATEGY AND IMAGE

Although the willingness of SNP members to countenance alternatives to independence is noteworthy, we should not overstate the case:

Table 6.8 Attitudes regarding pacts, compromises and furthering independence

	Strongly agree	Agree	Neither	Disagree	Strongly disagree
Primary goal is independence; all else is secondary	38.4	32.7	11.0	16.4	1.5
To achieve independence, concentrate on making devolution work	35.7	50.1	9.3	4.1	0.7
To achieve independence, work with other parties	29.7	60.1	7.5	2.4	0.3
Primary goal independence but may need to take second place	13.9	50.8	15.0	16.1	4.2
Devolution makes independence more difficult to achieve	3.9	12.3	16.1	50.2	17.6
Being in coalition in the Scottish Parliament involves compromise on independence	6.6	26.2	23.4	35.7	8.1
SNP should stand by principles even if it loses support	30.1	50.7	11.8	6.6	0.7
SNP should explore pacts with other parties, even if it involves compromises	4.3	43.0	26.4	23.4	3.0

independence remains clearly the most popular option. However, the means of achieving that goal have long been a matter of controversy. In the survey, respondents were asked a variety of questions about party strategy.

There is widespread agreement that the party's goal of independence should be primary and all else secondary. However, there is also strong support for the proposition that the primary goal of independence may need to take second place, and there is a more general willingness to cooperate and to compromise. More formal pacts with other parties were slightly less popular, but favoured on balance, and respondents tended to disagree that coalitions in the Scottish Parliament would obstruct the path to independence. These figures partly reflect the situation prevailing when the survey was conducted. The SNP had formed a minority government with the support of the two Green MSPs. Taken together, these results indicate pragmatism and an acknowledgement of the need for cooperation, albeit with some hesitancy concerning the value of coalition. Above all, there is little evidence of potential for a fundamentalist backlash against devolution. These findings dovetail with the profile of the membership sketched earlier, in that both point to pragmatism and willingness to cooperate with other parties. Little in the results so far suggests a particularly unconventional or radical membership.

Not only do the SNP members appear content with the party's strategic direction, they reveal extremely high levels of satisfaction with the way the party is organised internally. They are overwhelmingly positive about the party leadership and the role played by members: 87% agreed that SNP politicians try to represent the views of ordinary members and only 18% indicated that ordinary party members do not have enough say in determining policy. These findings are probably related to when the survey was conducted, following the party's election to government and a time when the SNP was riding high in the polls. Nevertheless, the level of contentment amongst the SNP membership is remarkable by comparison with the other studies of parties in Britain.

SNP members appear to be the most active of any party. A similar story is told by responses to a question asking respondents how often they attend local party meetings. Around one third of SNP members attend local meetings regularly (and these are more or less the same people who consider themselves very or fairly active). Conversely, most members are inactive. Just over a third (36%) of members never attend meetings and another 17% less often than once a year. Thus, 53% might be categorised as passive, which is consistent with the 57% of members who say they devote no time to party activities in the average month. Roughly speaking, then, a third of members look to be fairly active, a third are completely passive, and the final third may attend the odd meeting but are generally more passive than active. Even accounting for a tendency to exaggerate self-reported activity, these represent fairly high levels of political activity.

CONCLUSIONS

The SNP has often been presented as more a movement than a party, but the data from the membership survey suggests that the party is as much a

Table 6.9 Self-reported level of activity

	Very	Fairly	Not very	Not at all
SNP	11.6	21.3	39.8	27.2
Scottish Greens	5.4	17.1	32.7	44.7
Lib Dems 1999	10.0	20.0	41.0	29.0
Labour 1997	8.0	19.0	42.0	31.0
Conservative 1992	6.0	14.0	36.0	45.0

conventional one as any other. It is united in its core aims and the pragmatic approach which its leaders have adopted, making devolution work,
finds considerable support amongst the membership at all levels. Given
how divisive support for devolution had previously been, this is a remarkable change, although the context in which the survey was conducted,
less than a year after the SNP became Scotland's largest party and at a
time when the party was riding high in the polls, will likely have affected
members' assessments. Two striking socio-demographic features of the
membership are the high proportion of men and the average age. Again,
this is noteworthy because of past expectations – the idea that Nationalism
attracted support amongst women (Dalyell 1977: 224) and that it had a
core of young members – are simply not borne out by the evidence. It is a
largely middle-class party that draws its support fairly evenly from different religious groups though, as it traditionally did in its electoral support,
it draws heavily upon the irreligious and those with weak religious affilia-
tions. Its spread of members is fairly even at regional level, though there
are some intriguing findings such as the relatively low membership in the
South of Scotland compared with its reasonably high share of the vote.
It might have been expected that SNP members would feel exclusively
Scottish, but the party's civic tendencies are in evidence across a number
of measurements of identity.

NOTE

1. A postal survey of the entire SNP membership was fielded in late 2007 and early 2008,
   achieving a total response of 7,112 at a response rate of 53.9%. For more details see
   http://www.strath.ac.uk/government/staff/mitchelljamesprofessor/snp/

REFERENCES

Bennie, L. (2004), *Understanding Political Participation: Green Party Membership in
Scotland*, Aldershot, Ashgate.

Bennie, L., Curtice, J. and Rüdig, W. (1996), 'Party Members', in McIver, D. (ed.) *The Liberal Democrats*, Hemel Hempstead, Harvester Wheatsheaf, pp. 135–54.

Brand, J., Mitchell, J. and Surridge, P. (1994), 'Social Constituency and Ideological Profile: Scottish Nationalism in the 1990s', *Political Studies*, Vol. 42, pp. 616–29.

Brown, A., McCrone, D. and Paterson, L. (1996), *Politics and Society in Scotland*, Basingstoke, Macmillan.

Dalyell, T. (1977), *Devolution: The End of Britain?*, London, Jonathan Cape.

Johns, R., Denver, D., Mitchell, J. and Pattie, C. (2009), 'Valence Politics in Scotland: Towards an Explanation of the 2007 Election', *Political Studies*, 57(1), pp. 207–33.

Miller, W. (1981), *The End of British Politics?*, Oxford, Clarendon Press.

Rüdig, W., Bennie, L. and Franklin, M. (1991), *Green Party Members: A Profile*, Glasgow, Delta Publications.

Rüdig, W., Franklin, M. and Bennie, L. (1996), 'Up and Down with the Greens: Ecology and Politics in Britain 1989–1992', *Electoral Studies*, Vol. 15, No. 1, pp. 1–20.

Seyd, P. and Whiteley, P. (1992), *Labour's Grass Roots: The Politics of Party Membership*, Oxford, Clarendon Press.

Seyd, P. and Whiteley, P. (2002), *New Labour's Grassroots: The Transformation of the Labour Party Membership*, Basingstoke, Palgrave Macmillan.

Whiteley, P., Seyd, P. and Richardson, J. (1994), *True Blues: The Politics of Conservative Party Membership*, Oxford, Clarendon Press.

Whiteley, P., Seyd, P. and Billinghurst, M. (2006), *Third Force Politics: Liberal Democrats at the Grassroots*, Oxford, Oxford University Press.

CHAPTER 7

The SNP and the Scottish Parliament: The Start of a New Sang?

Colin Mackay

INTRODUCTION

Far from killing Nationalism stone dead, devolution breathed new life into the SNP, leaving former Labour Shadow Scottish Secretary George Robertson choking on his prediction. The Scottish Parliament has given the Scottish National Party a political platform and status it could never have otherwise achieved. This chapter assesses how Holyrood has changed the SNP, and considers the party's Scottish Parliamentary performance throughout devolution's first decade. It concludes with the challenges facing the SNP in power and the Scottish government's drive towards an independence referendum.

Contemporary Scottish politics started in 1999. Throughout the last 30 years there has always been a handful of prominent Scots MPs in powerful positions at Westminster. In Tory governments Scots held top jobs such as Defence and Foreign Secretary while Labour in opposition was led by John Smith. Since New Labour swept to power in 1997, Scots have played a significant role in the Cabinet, culminating in Gordon Brown becoming Prime Minister. But they were Scottish MPs playing Westminster politics. Devolution debates aside, Scottish politics has mostly played a minor part in the Westminster system with the SNP enjoying little more than the occasional walk-on part.

Since 1999 the SNP has transformed from a voluntary group of oppositionalists to a professional political party of government. Devolution created the platform for this professionalisation. In terms of elected politicians the SNP has 47 MSPs, 7 MPs, 2 MEPs and 365 councillors, making it the biggest party in devolved and local government in Scotland. Before the Scottish Parliament the SNP employed less than twenty people at the party's Edinburgh headquarters and around the country; now it employs almost 150.

Until the first elections to the Scottish Parliament, the SNP's best electoral performance was in October 1974 when they won more than 30% of the vote, returning eleven MPs to Westminster. In the first devolved election the SNP secured 35 MSPs with just under 30% of the vote – that is as many parliamentarians as the SNP had managed to elect in every UK general election combined up to that point.

Devolution moved Scottish politics from sideshow to centre stage. After decades on the fringe at Westminster and eight years of opposition in Edinburgh, the SNP has grown into a formidable force, winning an election for the first time in 2007 and forming Holyrood's first minority government.

With the professionalisation of the SNP, control has shifted from amateur activists running internal elections to one-member-one-vote elections strengthening the leader's authority and power base within the party, and dispensing with damaging internal power struggles.

SALMOND'S FALTERING START

The first elections to the Scottish Parliament gave the SNP its best ever result. Not in terms of its vote or share of the vote, but in seats. For the first time in its history the SNP was a proper parliamentary force, the main opposition party, with a group of 35 MSPs. Alex Salmond led the SNP into the 1999 election with the campaign slogan 'A Penny for Scotland'. At the time, Labour Chancellor Gordon Brown was proposing a 1p cut in the basic rate of income tax. The 1998 referendum on devolution granted the new Scottish Parliament the power to vary income tax by 3p up or down. In order to raise more cash to pay for other manifesto pledges, the SNP said it would not allow Scots to take the tax cut, instead maintaining the basic rate at 23p in the pound to invest the extra £690 million in better health, education and housing services for Scots voters.

It made the SNP's election campaign distinct, suggesting a left-of-centre social democratic party. But the election did not go as the Nationalists had hoped. The SNP's manifesto received more rigorous scrutiny than ever before from a largely hostile media. In the last weeks of the campaign the SNP abandoned press conferences and launched its own daily newspaper, *Scotland's Voice*. It was an expensive attempt to re-launch a struggling campaign and on polling day the SNP failed to reach the heights of pre-election polling.

Labour won the election with 56 seats, and promptly entered coalition talks with the Lib Dems, who had 17 MSPs, giving the first Scottish Executive a comfortable majority in the 129-member Scottish Parliament.

This meant there was little opportunity for the main opposition party to defeat the Labour–Lib Dem coalition.

Finding its role in the new institution was one of the biggest challenges facing the SNP after the 1999 election. Most of the SNP's leading lights were now MSPs, but they formed an incoherent group with few professional politicians among their ranks. Some 'fundamentalists' were opposed to the whole idea of devolution, even as a stepping stone to independence, while other MSPs appeared unsure of what to do with their new parliamentary positions.

In his opening exchanges in the Scottish Parliament on 13 May 1999, Alex Salmond dedicated the SNP 'to being an innovative and determined opposition . . . every bit as important to a new democracy as the Administration itself' (Scottish Parliament 1999b), and the SNP did engage in the new system. John Swinney and Roseanna Cunningham were excellent committee conveners, Mike Russell and Alex Neil were among the chamber's best debaters, but there were a great many teething troubles.

Alex Salmond was used to a small group of MPs at Westminster, so the new bigger group meetings where everyone wanted a say were a chore. First Minister's Question Time against Donald Dewar did not provide the platform to further the cause he had hoped, with many exchanges dominated by the Holyrood building fiasco and Salmond not always coming out on top.

Just over a year after Winnie Ewing recalled the Scottish Parliament with the famous words 'the Scottish Parliament, which adjourned on 25th March 1707, is hereby reconvened' (Scottish Parliament 1999a), Alex Salmond made the shock announcement that he was standing down as SNP leader. There was much feverish speculation about why he was going, but it seems that after a decade in the job, constantly fighting an uphill battle, he needed a break. Another three years as opposition leader in a parliament being slated daily in the media held no appeal:

> I started to believe that for much of the press corps in Scotland I had become the issue and therefore the SNP couldn't get a fair crack of the whip. So I'd done ten years, time to give somebody else a chance, and I thought the SNP would get a fairer run with somebody else at the helm. (Radio Clyde, 3 May 2009)

Alex Salmond had taken the SNP to a new position in Scottish politics, but his failure to win in 1999 hurt and left him wondering what it would take to win. It was a few years before he found that out.

SWINNEY'S LEADERSHIP WITHOUT POWER

At the SNP's annual conference in Inverness on 23 September 2000 John Swinney took over the leadership. Elected by delegates from across

Scotland, he convincingly beat off the challenge from fellow MSP Alex Neil by 547 votes to 262. But he inherited a party ill at ease with itself and its place in the new political situation facing Scotland. Instead of seizing the opportunities offered by devolution and the new political focus, the SNP turned in on itself.

There were problems with internal dissent and indiscipline among MSPs. John Swinney had loyally served the SNP for many years as National Secretary and then deputy leader to Alex Salmond, but he could not match the charismatic style of his predecessor. He tried to clamp down on internal problems, arguably too hard, in an attempt to show how tough he was.

He had a series of run-ins with his own MSPs. Maverick Glasgow MSP Dorothy-Grace Elder refused to contribute £3,000 from her parliamentary expenses, a requirement from all group members, to help pay for research staff. John Swinney tried to have her removed from the Scottish Parliament's Health Committee and threatened her with suspension from the parliamentary group, but she quit the party first, blaming 'arrogant, bullying behaviour'.

Much of the instability stemmed from insecurity among MSPs worried about list selections. Only seven of the SNP's 35 MSPs elected in 1999 represented constituencies, the other 28 having been elected from party lists. That left many political careers dependent on rankings in the run-up to 2003 and caused almost two years of turmoil in the party and parliamentary group. Like the leadership election, local activists rather than the whole membership decided the outcome of this. This resulted in local deals between candidates and cliques for second preferences causing deep wounds, some of which still smart today.

In 1999 Margo MacDonald topped the Lothian list, but after a few years in the Scottish Parliament regularly criticising the leadership and the direction of the SNP, she found herself slipping down to fifth on the list with little realistic chance of re-election. She blamed dirty tricks by other candidates, announced she would stand as an independent for the Lothian list in the 2003 election and was promptly expelled from the SNP.

She was not the only high-profile casualty of the list rankings. In Central Scotland frontbencher Andrew Wilson slipped down the list after losing the support of local activists who felt he had focused too much on Holyrood at the expense of his own backyard. In the South of Scotland Mike Russell suffered a similar fate, while Christine Grahame, who had maintained strong local campaigning links, overtook him on the regional list, making her and others in a similar position across the country better placed to survive a poor SNP vote.

Between the 1999 and 2003 Scottish Parliament elections, the SNP was uneasy with itself and unsure of its direction. There were constant battles between the old fundamentalist wing, who wanted 'Independence, nothing less', and the gradualists, who sought to use devolution to build towards independence through a referendum. Ironically several leading 'fundies' had been elected to the devolved parliament, rather destroying their own argument. However, by this time the fundie/gradualist split had become little more than an easy way to describe the personality clashes and bitter power struggles still raging within the party.

These problems aside, John Swinney's leadership was always overshadowed by Alex Salmond and throughout the internal strife, calls for Salmond's return rumbled round SNP members, even after he had quit Edinburgh to return to Westminster full-time at the 2001 General Election.

John Swinney also suffered a string of poor parliamentary performances. Throughout Henry McLeish's 'Officegate' troubles, the SNP leader was regularly outgunned at First Minister's Questions by Tory leader David McLetchie. But this low-key opposition was partly a tactical decision. The SNP decided that all-out attack would further damage devolution and the Scottish Parliament, in turn undermining its own position. But to the wider political world it suggested that John Swinney lacked the killer instinct to finish off a political opponent.

The 2003 election saw the SNP take a hammering, down from 35 to 27 seats, with their share of the vote cut to less than 24% of the constituency vote and just under 21% of the regional vote. Labour lost six seats with the rise of the Greens and Scottish Socialists but, scenting blood, the media focused on the SNP and targeted Swinney.

John Swinney knew things were not going well, but he was angered by a formal challenge to his leadership by little-known Glasgow activist Bill Wilson. In the end John Swinney won easily by 577 votes to 111 at the party's autumn 2003 conference in Inverness. However, the result failed to draw a line under the issue and rumblings in the party grew. The leadership difficulties were kept alive among MSPs by West of Scotland list member Campbell Martin, who took every media opportunity to attack his leader, until his suspension from the SNP in April 2004.

In June 2004 John Swinney faced the third electoral test of his leadership, this time the European Election. The depth of his problems was made abundantly clear in an infamous quote by Mike Russell, who had lost his Scottish Parliament seat in the 2003 election. He warned that the 'men in grey kilts' (Russell 2004) would be coming to get John Swinney if the SNP suffered another poor election result. On 10 June the SNP's vote fell below 20%. Twelve days later John Swinney resigned:

> It has become clear to me over the last few days that the constant and relentless speculation over my position is obscuring – and crucially in my judgement, will continue to obscure – the political objectives of the SNP. (SNP 2004)

Despite his problems, John Swinney had changed his party, bringing in 'one member one vote' for leadership elections and list rankings which meant there should be no repeat of the turmoil in the run-up to 2003. He also started the process of turning the SNP into a modern election fighting machine with a centralised membership list giving the leadership and professional staff more control, in particular of fund-raising. And throughout this difficult first term, SNP MSPs engaged in the work of the parliament with Tricia Marwick co-sponsoring the ban on hunting with dogs and Kenny Gibson attempting to ban smoking in public places.

THE EMERGENCE OF NICOLA STURGEON AT HOLYROOD

The leadership election which followed in 2004 looked set to be a close-run affair with Alex Salmond's choice, Nicola Sturgeon, facing a stout challenge from deputy leader Roseanna Cunningham. Mike Russell threw his hat in the ring but was never a serious contender.

Initially Alex Salmond rejected a return to the leadership, quoting US Civil War General Sherman: 'If nominated I'll decline. If drafted I'll defer. And if elected I'll resign' (*North Tonight*, 15 July 2004). But there were some concerns that Roseanna Cunningham might win and pressure mounted on Salmond. Just before nominations were due to close, Nicola Sturgeon switched to the deputy leadership leaving the way clear for Alex Salmond's return. In doing so, he made it clear that his ambition lay beyond just leading the SNP: 'I intend to offer myself as the next First Minister of Scotland and lead the party into government at the next Scottish elections in 2007' (*BBC News*, 15 July 2004).

Alex Salmond easily won the leadership, with 76% of the membership vote, but he was an MP not an MSP, having quit the Scottish Parliament in 2001. Filling the gap as de-facto leader in Edinburgh was left to his deputy, Nicola Sturgeon. The new leadership team took the opportunity of the Scottish Parliament moving out of its temporary home on the Mound to its controversial new home at Holyrood as a chance to move the SNP on.

The difficulties in the first term and start of the second were to be put aside and the SNP would start preparing for the 2007 election. Alex Salmond underwent a transformation from 'smart Alex', the clever point-scoring debater, to 'nice Mr Salmond', unfailingly positive about Scotland's prospects: 'I took off some of the abrasiveness . . . you learn that even when you're convinced you're right sometimes it's best not to rub somebody else's face in it to win the argument' (Radio Clyde, 3 May 2009).

This Hyde-to-Jekyll transformation was assisted by coaching from the Really Effective Development Co., who helped the SNP focus their positive message. The issue was forced by a group including Moray MP Angus Robertson, coordinator of the SNP's 2007 election campaign. 'Part of rearranging the mental furniture for people was saying could they imagine Alex Salmond being First Minister of Scotland? So part of that "Alex Salmond for First Minister" was explaining to people on the doorstep what the election could be about' (Robertson 2008). And it worked.

Unburdened by Holyrood duties, Salmond was left free to lead his party and become more statesmanlike. This left Nicola Sturgeon to focus on the Scottish Parliament. Her first performance in First Minister's Questions against Labour leader Jack McConnell marked a stark contrast from what had gone before. He had talked of the Scottish Parliament raising its game in its new home. Ms Sturgeon asked if he had raised his, particularly on the NHS. The following day in *The Times* Magnus Linklater, a long-term critic of the SNP, wrote:

> It would be stretching things to call this check-mate but Ms Sturgeon had made a useful point, while at the same time avoiding the strident point-scoring that has so frequently marked these exchanges in the past. At least as significant was the almost respectful silence with which her questions were greeted on the Labour benches. (Linklater 2004)

Nicola Sturgeon continued to shine, turning in some of the best opposition performances at First Minister's Questions and she was the most consistent parliamentary performer since the start of devolution. Having been elected to the first Scottish Parliament as a list MSP for Glasgow before the age of 30, Nicola Sturgeon showed just how much she had grown as a politician.

In Holyrood's second term the agenda was dominated by Labour's 'war on neds' attempting to deal with youth crime, as well as First Minister Jack McConnell's campaign against sectarianism, the introduction of proportional voting in local council elections and of course the ban on smoking in public places. The single transferable vote for council elections was SNP policy and it was the SNP that championed the smoking ban with Labour Health Minister Andy Kerr taking up Stewart Maxwell's member's bill, making these policies easy for the SNP to support. The SNP group at Holyrood was smaller and more stable, having lost some of its most disruptive members in the 2003 election. Nationalist MSPs stopped making extravagant spending pledges or demands and seemed like they might be ready to give Labour a run for its money in 2007.

In March 2006, the SNP lost one of its best loved MSPs when Margaret Ewing died. She had held Moray in the Scottish Parliament since 1999 with a substantial majority and had previously held it at Westminster since 1987. The SNP's past record in parliamentary by-elections flatters to deceive with Westminster victories in Motherwell, Hamilton, Govan and Perth long remembered by SNP supporters. The many more by-election defeats are ignored or forgotten.

To contest the by-election, Richard Lochhead had to quit as a North East list MSP. Despite Moray being the SNP's second safest seat, some felt it was a risky strategy with the Tories campaigning hard from second place, but it turned out to be an electoral turning-point for the Nationalists on the road to 2007. The SNP increased its majority and hailed its triumph in the Moray by-election as a springboard to success in the 2007 Holyrood elections. It had been a chance to try out new campaigning techniques including the 'Activate' computer system of identifying voters. Alex Salmond claimed the SNP could win 20 extra seats in the 2007 Holyrood election and form the next government. The result was a great morale boost for SNP members and activists, who started to believe their leader's claims.

A year before the third elections to the Scottish Parliament, this showed how far the SNP had come since devolution. It had moved from a party at war with itself in the first term and transformed during the second term into a party seriously challenging for power in the third term.

SALMOND RETURNS: THE FIRST SNP GOVERNMENT

On Friday, 4 May 2007, Radio Forth broke news of the SNP victory before the final result from the Highland list count had been officially declared. There's no room in this chapter to attempt to explain the 2007 Holyrood election except to say that Labour's campaign was a shambles and the SNP hardly put a foot wrong running the most professional campaign in its history. Alex Salmond had delivered his promise of taking 20 seats including his own in Gordon. That left the SNP with 47 and Labour with 46.

Alex Salmond quickly asserted his right to try to form an administration. He had expected to be able to go into coalition with the Liberal Democrats, but talks quickly broke down over the issue of an independence referendum and because the Lib Dems were too sore after losing to the SNP in Argyll and Gordon. It is SNP policy not to deal with the Tories, leaving the Nationalists with the prospect of leading the first minority administration since devolution. Alex Salmond secured the support of Holyrood's two Green MSPs (with Independent Margo MacDonald abstaining) to become Scotland's fourth First Minister and set out his stall in parliament:

> In this century, there are limits to what governments can achieve, but one thing that any government that I lead will never lack is ambition for Scotland. Today I commit myself to leadership wholly and exclusively in the Scottish national interest. We will appeal for support across the chamber policy by policy. That is the Parliament that the people of Scotland have elected and that is the government that I will be proud to lead. (Scottish Parliament 2007)

He quickly changed the name of his administration from 'Scottish Executive' to 'Scottish Government', a move which Henry McLeish tried in 2001 when he was First Minister but which was quickly quashed by Labour at Westminster. There was some resistance to the move in 2007 from opponents at Westminster and some parts of the media in Scotland, but that has faded. The SNP slimmed down its administration, cutting the Cabinet from eleven during the coalition to six – a bigger name, but a smaller bureaucracy.

The SNP's 'first 100 days in government' seemed like a whirlwind of activity: they scrapped tolls on the Forth and Tay Bridges, saved accident and emergency units from closure, froze the council tax, scrapped student tuition fees and started to phase out prescription charges. Alex Salmond hit the ground running, showing a remarkable turn of pace.

But minority government has changed the nature of the Scottish Parliament. Labour–Lib Dem coalitions focused on legislation, giving MSPs a great deal of work through committees and in the debating chamber. The SNP has no majority to push through tricky legislation, leaving its own backbenchers and opposition MSPs on committees twiddling their thumbs at times. So, just as the SNP is a party changed by the Scottish Parliament, since 2007 it has changed the nature of the institution. Labour and the Lib Dems have struggled to come to terms with this and with finding themselves out of power, but the Tories have grasped the opportunities presented by a minority administration – working closely with the SNP.

On taking power, the SNP government was warned by senior civil servants that the main parliamentary threats they faced were getting a budget through, and a confidence vote. The new minority administration faced its first serious challenge on the funding of a tram system for Edinburgh. Labour, the Tories, Lib Dems and Greens all favoured the scheme, leaving the SNP isolated in its opposition. The government lost the vote but, rather than allowing it to become a confidence issue, agreed to fund it.

The minority SNP government would go on to lose more votes, but so far has avoided allowing them to be turned into confidence issues.

The other threat was the Budget. Every year Holyrood has to pass spending plans for the next twelve months based on the block grant from Westminster. To secure passage of its first Budget the SNP gained Tory support in return for standing by its election pledges to recruit an extra thousand police officers and cut business rates. The Greens and Margo MacDonald were also persuaded to back the Budget and this gave the government 66 votes, one more than it needed for a majority. Nevertheless on the eve of the vote the First Minister could not resist the opportunity to exert his new authority by threatening to resign if the Budget failed.

A year on, in the run-up to the SNP government's second Budget for 2009–10, Finance Secretary John Swinney reiterated the threat just days before the vote:

> If the government was unable to get its Budget through, we would have to leave office and there would have to be either a new administration formed or an election called. Politically the government has to get its Budget through, because without getting its Budget through the government cannot function. (Radio Clyde, 7 January 2009)

Again the SNP secured Tory support with the promise of a £60 million fund for town-centre regeneration. Margo MacDonald pledged her vote in return for a special fund for Edinburgh, and Alex Salmond and John Swinney thought they had the support of the Greens for a £33 million home-insulation package. But there was no deal in writing and at the last minute the Greens voted with Labour and the Lib Dems against the Budget. That tied the vote at 64 each, leaving the Presiding Officer to use his casting vote. By convention, he voted for the status quo. The Budget was defeated, but the government did not resign.

Instead Alex Salmond called a media briefing and warned that he was 'putting the SNP on election footing'. It was a political masterstroke, seizing the next day's headlines and completely wrong-footing the opposition. It was a direct challenge to the opposition in true *Dirty Harry* style, asking: 'Do you feel lucky?' Within a week a new Budget deal had been agreed with the support of both Labour and the Lib Dems. Labour agreed to much the same deal to create new apprentices which they had been offered and refused the week before, and the Lib Dems dropped their demands for a 2p cut in income-tax, offering support in return for a letter to the Calman Commission looking at the future of devolution and backing borrowing powers for the Scottish Parliament.

So despite having just one more MSP than Labour and leading the Scottish Parliament's first minority government, the SNP has had to concede very little to get either of its budgets through and has yet to face a confidence vote.

A QUIET REVOLUTION?
EVOLUTION THROUGH DEVOLUTION

In his review of this book's sister publication on the Scottish Labour Party, the *Sunday Herald*'s Paul Hutcheon concludes that the only cure for Scottish Labour's intellectual inertia is 'the cold blast of defeat' (Hutcheon 2004). In 2007 Labour suffered an icy blast and doesn't seem to have thawed out yet. That has left the way clear for the SNP to dominate the constitutional debate.

Just after the 2007 election Alex Salmond unveiled his Independence White Paper and launched *Choosing Scotland's Future: A National Conversation* (Scottish Executive 2007). It showed how much the SNP has changed since devolution. The old fundamentalism demanding 'Independence, nothing less' has gone. The SNP is a much more pragmatic party. Its commitment to an independence referendum meant that in the 2007 election Alex Salmond could suggest voting SNP to deliver a competent government at Holyrood, with the further option of voting for independence at a later date.

The white paper, published in August 2007, set out plans to hold a referendum, probably on St Andrew's Day 2010, but it was not just a straight choice on independence or the status quo. It made clear the SNP favours independence but supports a multi-option referendum including the choice of 'enhanced devolution'.

In February 2009 the SNP government started the second stage of its National Conversation with Finance Secretary John Swinney launching 'Fiscal Autonomy in Scotland' (Scottish Government 2009). Again it underlines the SNP's support for independence, but outlines what it considers are the options for a more powerful Scottish Parliament remaining part of the United Kingdom. It suggests options including 'enhanced devolution giving Holyrood greater responsibility for raising revenues and more power to spend in areas such as welfare' (Scottish Government 2009). But it also offers the idea of 'devolution max', making Holyrood responsible for 'raising, collecting and administering all revenues and the vast majority of spending in Scotland', while paying its share of central UK services such as defence.

The second stage of the National Conversation followed the Budget deal with the Lib Dems which forced the SNP government to respond to the Calman Commission. This commission was set up by Labour, the Conservatives and Liberal Democrats to look at the case for further devolution of powers ten years after the establishment of the Scottish Parliament. Until the Budget deal the SNP had refused to engage with Calman because the commission refused to consider independence; but the deal gave the SNP a way in without losing face.

It now looks as if the SNP is controlling the constitutional debate not just on independence but increasingly on the future of devolution. For SNP gradualists playing the long political game, a multi-option referendum offering the choice between independence, enhanced devolution or the status quo would guarantee them at least more powers. Not only would it be the first choice of many voters, but also the second choice of most others.

The SNP is unlikely to deliver a referendum in 2010, though. The Tories and Liberal Democrats reject it out of hand. Labour under Wendy Alexander's ill-fated leadership called on the SNP to 'bring it on', but under Iain Gray's more cautious leadership Labour says 'no'. In March 2009 Labour, Tory, Lib Dem and Green MSPs voted against a referendum in 2010: 'The Scottish Parliament . . . calls on the Scottish Government to concentrate its efforts on economic recovery and abandon its divisive plans for a Referendum Bill for the remainder of its term of office' (Scottish Parliament 2009). That leaves the SNP minority unable to push a Referendum Bill through Holyrood, but Ministers say they fully intend to try. The vote killed off any hopes harboured by the SNP leadership that the Lib Dems could be persuaded to back a referendum which included the option of more devolved powers in this parliamentary term. During the debate, Deputy First Minister Nicola Sturgeon quoted opinion poll figures suggesting that 59% of Labour voters, 63% of Lib Dem voters and even 63% of Tory voters support a referendum (YouGov 2008). You can bet the SNP will take its call for a referendum on independence or more devolved powers in to the 2011 Scottish election.

Concluding Remarks

After the painful disputes and divisions of the first few years, the SNP has accepted, and even embraced, devolution. Most within the party see it as a step along the path to independence, rather than a roadblock.

The SNP is a modern professional political party. Membership has grown from a low point of less than 7,000 to stand at 15,335 at the end of March 2009. Funding has soared both from members and from rich business leaders, including half a million pounds from Stagecoach tycoon Brian Souter. This enabled the SNP to outspend its opponents for the first time at the 2007 election. The democratisation of the SNP under John

Swinney's leadership has paved the way for the authority Alex Salmond enjoys within his party today, and Nicola Sturgeon has emerged as his natural successor.

But minority government means compromise and the SNP has been forced to drop plans to scrap the council tax and is struggling to deliver other key election pledges such as cutting class sizes. At the mid-point of the third Scottish Parliament, the SNP claims to have implemented about half its 2007 manifesto, but there is no doubt things are getting tougher with parliamentary votes proving harder to win and budgets getting tighter. If Labour was stronger, the SNP could be facing serious problems.

Confidence in Scotland was high when the SNP took power in 2007 and that has undoubtedly taken a knock with the banking crisis and recession. After winning the Glasgow East Westminster by-election from Labour in July 2008, the SNP bandwagon looked unstoppable, until it came to the Glenrothes Westminster by-election in November 2008 when Labour proved it could still win. In Holyrood the SNP is still the dominant political force. The party has taken full advantage of the opportunities devolution offered. Alex Salmond claims that with a Scottish Parliament and the SNP in government, Scotland is two-thirds of the way to independence (Radio Clyde, 3 May 2009).

To complete the final part, the SNP would have to win the 2011 Holyrood election and agree a referendum deal with another party, then win over the electorate. At the moment, opinion polls suggest there is no majority for independence. But by maintaining its push for independence, the SNP will keep pressure on the unionist parties and the UK government to devolve more powers to the Scottish Parliament. For generations the SNP struggled to keep the constitutional debate on the political agenda. Now it has the power to set Scotland's political agenda, the constitution will remain near the top.

REFERENCES

Hutcheon, P. (2004), 'Scottish Labour under the Microscope . . . Again', *Sunday Herald*, 11 April.

Linklater, M. (2004), Can Scotland's MSPs match this magnificent building?, *The Times*, 8 September.

Robertson, A. (2008), 'Calling Time: Interview with Mandy Rhodes', *Holyrood*, 1 October.

Russell, M. (2004), 'Swinney could face "men in grey kilts"', *Sunday Herald*, 4 April.

Scottish Executive (2007), *Choosing Scotland's Future: A National Conversation*, Edinburgh, Scottish Executive.

Scottish Government (2009), *Fiscal Autonomy in Scotland*, Edinburgh, Scottish Government.

Scottish Parliament (1999a), *Official Report*, Vol. 1, No. 1, 12 May, Edinburgh, Scottish Parliament.

Scottish Parliament (1999b), *Official Report*, Vol. 1, No. 2, 13 May, Edinburgh, Scottish Parliament.

Scottish Parliament (2007), *Official Report*, 16 May, Edinburgh, Scottish Parliament.

Scottish Parliament (2009), *Business Bulletin*, 3 March, Edinburgh, Scottish Parliament.

SNP (2004), 'John Swinney to Step Down', SNP Press Release, 22 June, http://www.snp.org/node/11745

YouGov (2008), *Scottish Political Issues*, April, http://www.yougov.co.uk/corporate/archives/press-archives-pol-Main.asp?dID=2008

CHAPTER 8

The SNP and Westminster

Isobel Lindsay

Nationalists have to learn that it is the winning of a seat that hurts the big parties, not what they can do or say when they reach the Commons. (Billy Wolfe, 1973)

This comment from *The Times* 40 years ago highlights one of the two central questions in relation to the SNP's involvement with Westminster. Apart from proving that there is electoral support and that you can deprive the other parties of seats, is there anything of significance that you can do when you get there? In a broader context this question could be posed of backbench MPs in all parties given their very marginal role in policy-making in the Westminster system.

The other big question is the fundamental one of whether a nationalist movement should act as a conventional party and engage with the institutions of state or whether, even if it contests elections, it should take the Sinn Fein position and refuse on principle to take up seats. This issue was, in effect, decided with the formation of the SNP although the party/movement tensions persisted. In contrast to some other nationalist movements where the 'hard-liners' veer towards non-constitutional protest, in Scotland the fundamentalist position was ironically associated most with an unshakable commitment to contesting Westminster parliamentary elections. The cultural context in Scotland would not have been amenable to either boycotting the Commons or violent protest. But the first question – is there anything useful for a nationalist party to do when they get there? – is still a legitimate one to ask.

The big credibility problem for any smaller party is how to present a convincing road map for change through the electoral process. This has been difficult for the Liberal Democrats and, for any regionally based party, it is even more problematic in theory. Although the official SNP position was that winning a majority of Scottish seats would give the right to negotiate an independence settlement, in practice the assumption was that

93

any electoral success would create a momentum for change. While it was politically necessary to make confident projections, only the more naïve thought that winning even a majority of Scottish seats would produce an early offer of independence. There were three possible Westminster positions with potential to produce change:

- By posing a serious electoral threat to established MPs, there might be sufficient pressure to make them concede a Scottish Parliament. Both the seats won and the number of good second places would be significant. But, of course, this could only affect the 10% of MPs in Scottish seats.
- In the situation of a hung parliament, there could be significant leverage even with a small number of seats. But no one could predict or control the arithmetic of such a situation – it would purely be chance.
- Building voting coalitions with other Westminster parties might deliver some change. But apart from Plaid Cymru and possibly the Liberals, there were no natural allies.

None of these scenarios had any relevance to the SNP until the late 1960s. They were political fantasy. And the most optimistic outcome was that Westminster would agree only to deliver a devolved parliament.

Beyond the Fringe

Throughout the 1950s and into the 1960s the SNP was a tiny fringe party, much less significant than, say, the Communist Party in Scotland at that period; 18.7% in the Bridgeton by-election in 1961 and 23.3% in West Lothian in 1962 hinted at change. The 1964 election saw the party win 64,044 votes standing in 15 seats and save 8 deposits; in 1966 some progress was evident, with 128,474 votes won with 23 seats contested and 16 deposits saved (Kellas 1971). It was only with a good result in the Pollok by-election and the spectacular win in Hamilton in 1967 that engagement with Westminster was seriously on the agenda. Gwynfor Evans's victory for Plaid Cymru had taken place in the previous year, but Winifred Ewing's win was different and was a watershed.

For Labour this could not be dismissed as 'Celtic Fringe' or as the equivalent of the Orpington suburban protest vote. This was a win in one of Labour's safest industrial heartland seats and it was a pointer to the possibility that the predictable two-party system was no longer predictable. It was also accompanied by a substantial expansion of SNP membership, branch formation and media focus on independence. Whoever had won the seat would have been the target for intense hostility and remorseless scrutiny but Winnie presented another challenge to the Westminster club. She was a feisty young woman who had a successful legal career and a family – so this was a double offence.

Gwynfor Evans had not found the House of Commons easy, but he was an older male who could be pigeonholed as part of the Welsh cultural revival rather than the vanguard of a mainstream political movement. He was a man whose ethical qualities were beyond question and he had a very gentle and charming personality. Winnie was more assertive and aggressive and this made other MPs regard her as 'fair game'. She had almost 70 other Scottish MPs intent on scrutinising and criticising everything she did in and out of the Commons. Not quite all of the other Scottish MPs were critics. She received sympathetic support from Emrys Hughes, the highly respected, left-wing South Ayrshire MP, who acted as one of her sponsors when she entered parliament (Harvie 1977: 252). He was Keir Hardie's son-in-law and very much in the Independent Labour Party tradition. He died a year later and his election agent, Sam Purdie, moved from Labour to become the SNP candidate in the by-election. Whether Emrys – had his health been better and had he lived – would have 'come out' as an articulate supporter of a Scottish parliament is one of the historical unknowns, but if this had happened it would have been influential on the left.

The achievements from that by-election win and from over two years in the Commons were considerable. The Wilson government set up the Commission on the Constitution and, while this was a delaying tactic and did not report till 1973, under Lord Kilbrandon's chairmanship it did take the demand for self-government seriously and gave legitimacy to major constitutional reform.

There was a shortage of accessible information on many aspects of the Scottish economy and society and the SNP used the presence of their MP in the Commons to table large numbers of parliamentary questions that were used in the Black Book and other party publications (Wolfe 1973: 112, 119). The Select Committee on Scottish Affairs was established by a government that had to be seen to take initiatives on Scotland. Winnie Ewing's Westminster work highlighted the inadequacy of information and debate on Scottish issues that the Select Committee was intended to address. As a member of that Committee, she produced (with party research input) a minority report on the Scottish economy. So in two and a half years her Westminster presence did produce some results and, while most of this was because of the shock of her win and the 1968 local election gains, her actual presence was a continual challenge and the resources of the Commons were used to the full by a party that was under-resourced.

DRIVING THE WESTMINSTER AGENDA

The period 1974–9 is the only time when the SNP has been a major player at Westminster, although that seemed an unlikely outcome at the start of the decade. The political and media establishment view at London and Scottish levels was that the SNP surge had been seen off and that the one MP, Donald Stewart from the Western Isles, could be comfortably placed not just as 'Celtic Fringe' but as a pleasant 'character' who was acceptable in the Westminster club.

The coincidence of the SNP on a strong upward swing and the chance of the Westminster arithmetic producing a minority government in February 1974, followed in October by a slender majority of three, provided the SNP group of eleven with the potential to influence legislation in the Commons. Harold Wilson was very conscious of this and believed he had to deliver something on devolution and later Jim Callaghan, when he replaced Wilson, reluctantly thought the same. From research on Callaghan's papers, the following sums up the attitudes:

> Callaghan's close advisers, Bernard Donoughue and Tom McNally, argued that Labour had to support devolution to keep Nationalist support in Parliament and sustain the minority Labour government. Donoughue told Callaghan he was 'riding a tiger' in so doing. Another Labour colleague agreed it was necessary to work with the SNP leadership, even though this included 'a lot of mad men in kilts'. (Bangor University 2008)

The presence of the SNP in the Commons pressurised the government to make two serious attempts at devolution legislation which took a major chunk of parliamentary time in a period of serious economic crisis, much to the irritation of other MPs. The intense antagonism that Winnie Ewing faced continued in the post-1974 period, especially from Scottish Labour MPs and some Scottish MPs in English constituencies. A not untypical example of attitudes was the comment of the Aberdeen MP Bob Hughes, who described SNP members in the Commons as 'the kind of people who remind me of Afrikaner Nationalists' (Marr 1992: 151).

But being in (or close to) a balance-of-power situation had its disadvantages, for it put a sharper focus on the policy choices MPs made. This had obvious pitfalls since, although the party had put some work into policy development in the previous years to help build a coherent identity, the Westminster votes do not always fit manifesto pledges. The MPs' constituencies were not typical of Scotland as a whole. Eight out of the eleven seats were gained from the Conservatives. Only two could be described as being from industrial Scotland and one of these, East Dunbartonshire, was Central Belt but very much suburban territory. It was significant that people like Billy Wolfe, Margo MacDonald and Tom McAlpine standing in Labour seats did not get elected. This was particularly important since the 1970s were years of economic crisis and industrial unrest and the SNP needed to position itself on these issues. Because most of the MPs were elected from previous Conservative seats, 'they wrongly assumed they had been elected through a coalition of SNP supporters and Conservative defectors . . . and stood to lose their seats if the SNP became over-identified with the centre-left and trade unions' (Lynch 2002: 140).

In the early 1970s, under Billy Wolfe's leadership, the party in Scotland had allied itself strongly with trade unions in the Upper Clyde sit-in and the miners' strike, but some of the MPs were less enthusiastic with that positioning in the context of their own constituencies. The notorious example that highlighted the tensions between the parliamentary group (or some in it) and the national executive was the vote on the 1976 Aircraft and Shipbuilding Nationalisation Bill and, in particular, the tearing up of the STUC's telegram urging them to support it. The National Executive Committee (NEC) had made their support clear to the unions in Scotland (Bayne 1991: 56). Although the reason given for voting against was lack of Scottish control, discomfort in identifying with nationalisation and trade unions on the part of some MPs was part of that decision. This example was used constantly by Labour opponents in industrial seats and angered many SNP activists in these seats.

The tension between party representatives in and out of legislatures is fairly universal in political systems. The reasons are obvious. They are two rival power centres. The members of a legislature have become professional politicians and, in general, have higher public and media status. In the non-proportional UK voting system, the MPs elected may not be representative of their parties in the way that elected party office-bearers are. In the SNP case there are also geographical factors, given the distance between Westminster and the Edinburgh-based national office-bearers, that makes communication more difficult.

Because the SNP had no history of parliamentary representation but had an established party history that had evolved when the party was small, there was not an elitist leadership tradition. Even with the growth of the SNP in the previous decade, the structures and ethos were more democratic than in the two large parties. Despite the prestige of the parliamentary group, power was still quite firmly in Scotland, not just in the national executive but in the policy role of the National

Council, National Assembly and Annual Conference. The modern trend for Annual Conference to be simply a rally had not started. Although Billy Wolfe was not generally seen by the media and the public as a strong leader, he had a very clear strategy when he took over as Chair to strengthen party democracy and to move in a clear centre-left direction. He firmly believed that while the Westminster group had to be given a respected place, the direction of policy and strategy should remain firmly in the party institutions at home. He and Gordon Wilson MP had a fairly good relationship and were broadly in agreement in this. The policies promoted by the majority in the NEC generally prevailed. In the two significant Westminster votes in which the parliamentary group went against the NEC position – shipbuilding nationalisation and the confidence vote in autumn 1978 – the NEC leadership asserted its authority by ensuring that the media knew this was not the official party position.

Westminster in the 1970s was a stressful place for a small group in a high-profile position. Not only were there tensions between the SNP parliamentary group and the national executive, there were also tensions within both. The core of these intra-group and NEC–parliamentary group problems were tensions endemic in the party as a whole. Of course there were personality issues, but the most divisive issue was the competing strategy of 'devolution as the route to independence' and 'Independence, nothing less'. There was also to a limited extent the conventional left–right dimension, although the range of views fitted more into a centre-to-left spectrum. None of the MPs supported the usual signifiers of right-wing ideology – opposition to a strong public sector and extensive social services, commitment to shifting the balance of rewards towards the more prosperous, support for nuclear weapons and the military–imperial tradition – although some were more uncomfortable with militant trade unionism and criticisms of the private sector than others. There were also divisions on the European Union, but these were cross-cutting in relation to the other divisions and there was an agreed formula for the referendum in 1975 that enabled united support for a 'No' vote without the very public splits in the other parties.

On the devolution issue, party policy and most of the parliamentary group supported the strategy of voting for any devolution bill as a step to independence so long as the proposed assembly was directly elected and was a legislature. But, as with the wider party membership, there were some who always resented supporting any compromise position. In one notorious incident Douglas Henderson, who was one of the 'Independence, nothing less' MPs, made a tub-thumping speech to that effect at the Motherwell conference in 1976, but though it was received enthusiastically by many delegates, this was never translated into votes for a change of policy. The failure of the first devolution bill in 1977 on a guillotine motion, as a result of an alliance between Conservatives, Liberals and Labour anti-devolution rebels, created predictable tensions given that the SNP had supported it despite its very serious flaws. The pro-devolution position was saved by the substantial gains in the following local elections that vindicated the SNP's strategy and also convinced the government that they had to make another attempt to get an improved bill through.

The defection of two Labour MPs, Jim Sillars and John Robertson, at the end of 1975 because of their disappointment at the failure of the government to produce an effective devolution scheme, is one of the 'what-might-have-been' scenarios of Scottish politics. They, along with some other senior Labour activists, chose to set up the Scottish Labour Party, a new party which attracted a fair number of talented members and considerable publicity but collapsed with internal disputes.

Had the MPs and their other supporters moved directly to the SNP, as Jim Sillars, Alex Neil and others did later, what might the impact have been? It would have given the SNP a substantial boost, especially in the Central Belt where it was most needed, and might have altered the political dynamic in the following three years. On the other hand, the personality clashes might have created more problems than benefits. Had the Nationalist MPs done more to build positive relationships with those Labour MPs who were known to favour maximum devolution, a straight move to the SNP might have been considered more seriously as an option. Had Margo MacDonald (who during her short period at Westminster in 1973–4 had developed a friendship with and was later to marry Jim Sillars) been in the parliamentary group, there might have been a bridge to the rebels. This was a missed opportunity.

The pro-devolution line came under stress again after the Cunningham 40% referendum rule amendment, but the clear NEC priority was to get a Scottish legislature delivered or, if not, to avoid being blamed for the failure to deliver. This was the majority view in the party as a whole and among the MPs, but the long, bitter and tedious passage of the Scotland Bill did undermine support. The biggest clash between the NEC and the parliamentary group came in autumn 1978 when the majority in the group wanted to vote against the government in a confidence motion, thinking this would be popular in their constituencies, while the NEC opposed this. There were divisions in the parliamentary group; two of them did not vote with the others and the motion was unsuccessful.

The post-referendum confidence vote was to some extent the reverse of this. Most of the pro-devolutionists in the party as a whole thought that the only chance of salvaging anything out of the Scotland Act was to threaten support for a confidence motion. If there were no significant concessions, there would in any case be no point in sustaining an impotent government for a few more months. Ironically there was now more resistance from some of the parliamentary group, given the prospect of an immediate election. George Reid was one of those expressing this when he commented before a National Council meeting that 'the suicide pilots will be out in force' (Bayne 1991: 48). The government thought that the prospect of an immediate election would be sufficient to ensure that the Nationalists at least abstained, but that National Council vote had united both fundamentalist and devolutionist wings and, when there were no serious concessions, all of the MPs voted together. It is unlikely that, had the election been six months later, the outcome for both Labour and the SNP would have been much different.

Apart from political tensions there were other problems in the parliamentary group that were endemic in all the Westminster parties. The club culture of the place encouraged excessive drinking by those so inclined. Living away from home in an artificial bubble can create behavioural issues. This is hardly unusual at Westminster; it is simply more visible in a small group. These issues had some impact on group morale because it caused some embarrassment to those whose behaviour was impeccable, but this was not visible to the public or most party members. This is a reminder of the massive shift in media culture that has taken place. There was still an implicit protocol that political journalists did not 'clype' on the personal behaviour of our elected representatives unless it was part of some more serious scandal. Where there was a marginal effect was in relation to the party leadership at home who were aware of the gossip and it undermined the confidence in some of those in the parliamentary group.

Were there lessons from the 1970s? It was the high electoral support that resulted in two devolution bills, but it was not just electoral support for the SNP that pushed the government into action. There was also the chance occurrence of the Commons arithmetic that made the votes of a small party important and the fear of losing Scotland at a time when oil was increasingly crucial to the UK economy. Could the parliamentary group have been more effective? Refusing to support the Scotland Bill would have been welcomed by opponents, since they would have been off the hook and could blame the SNP for not delivering change. Even if the parliamentary group had had more skill and inclination to network effectively, the intensity of feelings around the devolution issue and the unaccustomed threat to the two-party hegemony would have made it difficult to do so.

The Sidelining of the Nationalists

After the hurly burly ride of the 1974–9 parliament the SNP only returned two seats after the 1979 and 1983 elections and three in 1987. Jim Sillars's by-election win in 1988 made an impact in Scotland but not much in the Commons. It also appears, for reasons that have never been clear, that this period during which both Sillars and Alex Salmond were MPs resulted in a bitter breakdown in what had been a close political relationship. In the parliaments of the 1980s with large Tory majorities, intense hostility to the Scottish dimension and an absolute determination to secure oil revenues for the UK Treasury, the SNP was powerless and would have been irrelevant even if the party had not lost nine of their seats in 1979. One could also say that the same was true of Scottish backbench Labour MPs. Winning seats was still important for credibility but with a steamroller government, there was little prospect of delivering any modification of the Thatcher agenda unless it had been possible to create a serious extra-parliamentary revolt. That did not prove possible until the poll tax protests in the late 1980s.

What many in the SNP failed to realise was that, although support for independence was rising, the antagonism to Margaret Thatcher was so strong that the votes would go to whomever the electorate thought had the best chance of delivering a quick change of government. The SNP could make a strong case for independence, but not a very credible argument that they could deliver immediate change even if they won a large number of Scottish seats. The best that could be done was to build coalitions to strengthen the prospect for achieving a Scottish legislature when the arithmetic of the Commons changed, but the SNP opted out of that process and was sidelined from any practical input. The various campaigns in Scotland that followed the disappointment of the 1992 election did involve the SNP but, again, there was little of significance that could be done at Westminster.

It was not until the change of government that a specific Scottish focus in the Commons emerged, but this was not a re-run of the 1970s. The core of the Scotland Bill had already been agreed in the Constitutional Convention process and former Labour rebels had either changed their mind or been tied into the proposals in the opposition years. The focus for all the parties in Scotland was on the referendum and then on the run-up to the Scottish Parliament elections.

Westminster after Holyrood

Given that the role of all backbench Scottish MPs is under question because of the major areas of public policy that have been devolved, has the SNP group, now with seven members, been able to develop their role at Westminster? At the most basic level, having Westminster MPs means that there are spokespersons available for immediate comment and some of the Scottish-based media will generally include an SNP contribution when covering stories related to reserved powers. They can occasionally generate some publicity through parliamentary activities, but the scope for this is less than in the past, because so much interest and Scottish media resources have moved to Holyrood. There has been one outstanding exception and that was the 'cash for honours' scandal when it was the Western Isles MP, Angus McNeil, who asked the police to investigate. This was an inspired initiative but not part of the standard political agenda – although the subsequent exposure of expenses abuse in the Commons and lobbying abuses in the Lords, suggests that there was an opening there for the group to campaign for a new Puritan ethic at Westminster. They did support transparency.

There are two things that the current group has achieved which the group in the 1970s did not. They have helped to make the SNP more 'mainstream'. The Nationalist MPs, like the younger people who have emerged in the other parties, increasingly are professional politicians. They are well-educated, competent, disciplined, cautious and schooled in conventional modern politics. Perhaps Angus McNeil has still a touch of the free spirit and the recently elected John Mason, victor in the Glasgow East by-election, has a more overt moral agenda. It would be hard for them ever to be dismissed now as 'madmen in kilts'. The downside of this is that the emphasis on being mainstream can also produce unmemorable, identikit politicians. No heather will be set on fire and there will be no deviation from the party line. But if colour is missing, the advantage is that nothing will shock or surprise the folks back home and little will provide fodder for the Lobby except the carefully crafted statement. Even in the expenses scandal saga, the SNP MPs have ranged from innocent to low to medium in the range of excesses – with nothing shocking or extreme (*The Herald*, 23 May 2009).

The other contribution they have made is to develop relationships with the campaigning and 'good cause' groups operating at the London end. The range is limited because of the party decision since devolution not to vote on issues that solely relate to England, but their voting record has been supportive of peace movement and civil liberties issues (see TheyWorkForYou.com[1]) and they are well regarded by those working in those fields. For example, Angus Robertson is one of the MPs to whom CND will go if they need information through parliamentary questions; and John Mason was congratulated by a welfare charity in a letter to *The*

Guardian (11 May 2009) for an amendment he had tabled to the Welfare Reform Bill. This has helped to generate goodwill among some radical influence-leaders and promote a positive view of the SNP.

However, the area of greatest failure (the same can be said of the leadership at Holyrood) is on the reserved issues of macro-economic policy and economic inequality. Their failings in this respect were more sins of omission than commission. Unlike others on the left, they went along with much of the neo-liberal consensus on the economy, apart from privatisation and private finance initiatives. They maintained a centre-left position on most topics but promoted low business taxes and light-touch regulation of financial services on the Irish model and were silent on excessive remuneration for top executives.

They would criticise the government's failure to take effective action on poverty, but they would not take on the issue of growing inequality arising from excessive rewards for the top 10% of earners. They shared Gordon Brown's fear of antagonising the rich. They did not make an issue of the excessive personal indebtedness promoted by corporate banking. One thinks nostalgically of what the late Donald Stewart's acerbic comments might have been on our bankers' millions and the debt-fuelled economy. Had the group taken a more critical stance on the out-of-control greed culture over the past decade (and they were in the Commons and had legitimate opportunities to develop a profile on corporate and taxation policies), they would have been exposed to media criticism but would have struck a sympathetic chord with the public and been in a very strong position now. But that would have taken them away from the mainstream and, one assumes, undermined the SNP's version of John Smith's prawn cocktail initiative. In all of this they were acting entirely within the context of the policy agenda set by the leadership in Scotland and, in terms of personality and power relationships, it is difficult to envisage the Westminster group deviating in any significant respect.

The Future

Whether there is a more important Westminster role to play in the near future is going to depend on a particular configuration of circumstances. Will the next general election produce minority government or a government with a small or large majority? How will the SNP respond to the challenge of the Calman Commission and will it fuel the appetite for further constitutional change, or assuage it? Will the next government open up the Scotland Act again to implement these changes? Will the SNP return a large enough group to worry the others? If Labour does very badly in the general election, will that alter the attitude of Labour in Scotland to an independence referendum?

What is unlikely to occur again is a power struggle between the Westminster group and the Scottish-based leadership. Even with a much larger number of MPs, authority is now firmly established with the Holyrood leadership. The Scottish Parliament gives access to substantial power when in government and some influence when in opposition. Everyone in the SNP now sees the road to independence either as a staged expansion of Holyrood powers or a negotiated settlement between Holyrood and the UK government after a successful referendum. But a larger Westminster group, even if it is not engaged in a revision of the Scotland Act, will still have a role to play in projecting the core values of the SNP and working with networks beyond Scotland to make friends and influence people.

Note

1. TheyWorkForYou.com is a website with information on MPs' voting records.

References

Bangor University (2008), 'Party Leaders and Devolution, 1979: New Secrets from the Archive', Bangor University Press Release, 20 August, http://www.bangor.ac.uk/news/full.php?Id=620

Bayne, I. (1991), 'The Impact of 1979 on the SNP', in Gallacher, T. (ed.), *Nationalism in the Nineties*, Edinburgh, Polygon, pp. 46–65.

Harvie, C. (1977), *Scotland and Nationalism: Scottish Politics and Society 1707–1977*, London, Allen and Unwin.

Kellas, J. G. (1971), 'Scottish Nationalism', in Butler, D. and Pinto-Duschinsky, M., *The British General Election of 1970*, London, Macmillan, pp. 446–62.

Lynch, P. (2002), *SNP: The History of the Scottish National Party*, Cardiff, Welsh Academic Press.

Marr, A. (1992), *The Battle for Scotland*, London, Penguin.

Wolfe, W. (1973), *Scotland Lives: The Quest for Independence*, Edinburgh, Reprographia.

CHAPTER 9

SNP Economic Strategy: Neo-Liberalism with a Heart

Jim Cuthbert and Margaret Cuthbert

INTRODUCTION

This chapter offers an analysis of SNP economic policy under devolution, with particular emphasis on its performance in the period during which the party has been in office. The task facing the SNP, working towards independence through a process of incremental constitutional change, is not an easy one. In effect, what they face is a triple challenge: first, to persuade the electorate of their competence in exercising those powers which have already been devolved. Second, and at the same time, to persuade the electorate that there are fundamental flaws and constraints with the devolved settlement – so that the electorate is motivated to back further constitutional change. And the third challenge is to articulate a convincing strategic vision of what an independent country would look like, and how it could sustain economic success.

This triple challenge is clearly far greater than that which faces a unionist party. In order to achieve independence, it is not enough for the SNP to establish itself as being at least as capable as Labour in managing the Scottish economy. In assessing the SNP's performance, therefore, the relevant approach is a question of judging it not so much against the performance of the other parties in Scottish politics, but against the sterner discipline of its own independence goals.

What we aim to do in this chapter is examine how the SNP's economic strategy, and how its implementation of that strategy, measure up to the triple challenge. Their task, of course, has been made much more difficult by the onset of global recession. While there have undoubtedly been specific successes, our overall assessment is sobering: namely, that the SNP government is underperforming to a greater or less extent on each leg of the challenge. Ultimately, we will argue, a major reason for this underperformance is that the SNP has espoused a flawed economic model.

105

It is not alone in this. As we will see, the SNP's economic strategy is a variant of the neo-liberal 'Washington' consensus, which has dominated the economic strategy of all major UK parties, and more widely has landed the world economy in such deep trouble. More generally, neo-liberalism has been defined, as 'a theory of political economic practices that proposes that human well-being can best be advanced by liberating individual entrepreneurial freedoms and skills within an institutional framework categorised by strong private property rights, free markets, and free trade. The role of the state is to create and preserve an institutional framework appropriate to such practices' (Harvey 2005: 2).

We will categorise the SNP's variant of the policy as 'neo-liberalism with a heart'. That the SNP is merely following a consensus model provides no excuse: a party which wants to achieve fundamental change cannot afford to be just a follower, but must be well ahead of the pack in the clarity of its analysis. But first, to set the SNP economic policy in context, it is useful to summarise in bullet points the following well documented points about the Scottish economy:

- Scotland has a large service sector, a large public sector and a diminishing manufacturing sector.
- Its major trading partner is the rest of the UK.
- For at least the last 40 years, it has had a relatively low rate of growth in GDP compared to the UK as a whole and to many other EU comparator countries.
- Scotland has a static and ageing population; and has suffered from a chronic drain of its qualified young.
- There has been a long history of regional aid initiatives, many of which have failed to take lasting root.
- There is a low rate of business research and development, compared with the UK as a whole, and even more so with other advanced economies.
- There are relatively few head offices in Scotland: and there is a relatively low proportion of workers in higher-level occupations.

THE SNP GOVERNMENT'S ECONOMIC STRATEGY: PURSUING THE 'ARC OF PROSPERITY'

Our starting-point is an analysis of the economic strategy published by the new SNP government after it took power in the Scottish Parliament in 2007 (Scottish Government 2007).

The first, and in many ways the key, question to be asked about any economic strategy is whether there is an underlying vision. It is very clear from a reading of the SNP economic strategy that there is a vision. The economy is at the very centre of all other priorities: 'Sustainable economic growth is the one central purpose to which all else in government is directed and contributes' (p. v). This economic growth is to be delivered in a regime which is basically low tax and has a light regulatory touch: there should be 'a competitive tax regime which incentivises business growth and attracts mobile factors of production' (p. viii) and there is a need to 'address the streamlining of regulation, reducing unnecessary burdens on business' (p. 35). There is a clear feeling that government action risks interfering with the efficient operation of the market: 'Without addressing significant market failures or legitimate equity concerns, government action risks crowding out private sector activity or creating new sources of inefficiency or inequity' (p. 4). Globalisation is seen as an opportunity, not a threat: the Irish experience demonstrates how 'the opportunity of globalisation can be realised by delivering accelerated rates of growth through developing, attracting, and retaining mobile capital and labour' (p. 6).

To achieve success in this globalised environment, the strategy foresees that it will be necessary to focus on particular sectors and businesses: there should be 'a particular focus on a number of key sectors with high growth potential and the capacity to boost productivity' (p. 29) and there should also be 'focused enterprise support to increase the number of highly successful, competitive businesses' (p. viii). Scotland's human capital is seen as a key resource: 'Scotland has real strength in the most vital factor for modern economies – the human capital offered by our greatest asset – Scotland's people' (p. vii); and an important priority will be to align training and education, at all levels, to the needs of the economy, to 'ensure the supply of education and skills is responsive to, and aligned with, actions to boost demand' (p. 35). Another important enabler is the government's role in providing infrastructure, particularly transport: 'Enhancing Scotland's transport services and infrastructure are key to supporting business and employment opportunities' (p. 30).

Even within the limited powers available under devolution, the strategy envisages that much could be done to boost Scotland's competitiveness and economic growth: 'Scotland can rediscover much more of a competitive edge. It can become an attractive and more tax friendly business environment, with efficient transport and communications as well as a skilled and able workforce' (p. v).

According to the strategy, the upshot would be that Scotland would move into a self-sustaining cycle of high economic growth: 'this will drive up economic growth – and economic growth will, in turn, create a virtuous cycle with multiple positive effects: more opportunities for high quality employment: more successful new companies: and more of our brightest and best working in, and returning to Scotland' (p. v).

Overall, the strategy envisages the economies of other small Northern European countries as providing both a guide and a model, the 'arc of prosperity': the strategy 'draws on the lessons and approaches of the successful small independent economies of Norway, Finland, Iceland, Ireland, and Denmark – hereafter referred to as the 'arc of prosperity countries' – which are similar to Scotland in scale and geographically close' (p. 2). Ireland is seen as a particular exemplar: 'Today we have everything it takes to be a Celtic Lion economy, matching, and then overtaking, the Irish Tiger' (p. v).

So here we have a vision which distrusts the role of government: it favours a low-tax, low-regulation, business-friendly approach and sees opportunities in globalisation and free movement of capital and labour. Do we recognise this? Absolutely – it is an expression of the neo-liberal or Washington consensus. After being driven forward by Margaret Thatcher and Ronald Reagan, neo-liberalism became a new orthodoxy, coming to dominate the economic policies of the Anglo-Saxon world over the next 20 years. Even though it is normally regarded as a right-wing political philosophy, it was enthusiastically embraced across most of the political spectrum in the UK – particularly by New Labour. So in adopting an economic vision with a strong neo-liberal flavour, the SNP are certainly not being radical – at least in the context of pre-credit crunch Britain.

While we have categorised the SNP economic vision as a version of neo-liberalism, it is important to note that it is not the kind of red-in-tooth-and-claw neo-liberalism sometimes encountered elsewhere. This can be seen very clearly in relation to privatisation, and the size of the public sector. The SNP strategy makes no proposals for further privatisation of public services, even though Scottish Water or certain areas of health provision would be natural targets for an outright neo-liberal agenda. On the other hand, the SNP strategy does not envisage radical rolling back of current privatisation: for example, in relation to PFI. What is proposed is a modification, the Scottish Futures Trust, which would still leave the assets in the private sector. And the SNP strategy draws something of a veil over what it sees as the appropriate size of the public sector and the appropriate level of public expenditure: the SNP would 'make the case for Scotland to have fuller, and eventually full, responsibility for tax raising and public spending, utilising this to make Scotland the lowest taxed part of the UK' (p. 29). The likely implication of this philosophy is that there would be downward pressure on the size of the public sector in the long term – but the strategy does not quite bring itself to say so.

Another important aspect of the strategy is the emphasis it places on equity. In a sense, the strategy sees an almost symbiotic relationship between economic growth and improvements in equity. On the one hand, economic growth creates the resources which are required to reduce poverty. On the other hand, increasing equity, particularly improving access to education and training, is key to raising economic participation, which in turn is seen as fundamental in improving economic growth: 'Increased participation and enhanced quality of employment across our cities, towns and rural areas will enhance our performance and deliver a more inclusive Scotland' (p. 37). This is still very much a neo-liberal perspective: economic growth and equity are seen to re-enforce each other, basically through the operation of the market. But this vision of increasing equity linked to economic growth contrasts strongly with the opposing reality in which neo-liberal policies normally produce increasing inequality. It is because of its optimistic view that we have characterised the SNP vision as 'neo-liberalism with a heart'.

One final point which is important to note about the strategy is that it sets out clear targets. For example, the target by 2011 is to raise the Scottish rate of GDP growth to the UK level, and by 2017 to match the GDP growth rate of the small independent EU countries (p. 11). These are not conditional targets – they are targets which the SNP set for itself, without any caveats about, for example, the need for further powers.

It is worth remarking on how much the SNP's economic vision itself has changed within the last ten years. To see this, it is only necessary to go back to the SNP's 1999 manifesto for the first Scottish elections (SNP 1999). At that time, the key element in the party's strategy was to position itself as pro-public expenditure and pro-public services, and to portray Labour as the party of low tax and lower investment in public services. As the manifesto said, 'New Labour has taken on Tory principles. Tax cuts, rather than public services, are New Labour's priority'; and 'Scots have said that they are prepared to invest in public services, if given the choice. The SNP is now giving that choice'. This stance was entirely consistent with the SNP's vision for a post-independence economic strategy, as spelled out in its earlier paper, *Towards a Better Scotland*, which had a traditional left-wing and strong public-sector emphasis, rather than giving weight to business friendly policies – although the latter were by no means excluded (SNP 1995).

The change towards emphasis on clearly pro-business policies was largely the result of the SNP defeat in the 1999 election. The SNP leadership realised that it was regarded by sections of the business community as being anti-business. It set itself to develop a much more business-oriented strategy and to sell this to the business community. The legwork in developing the new approach, and selling it both to the business community and to the party (which may not have been naturally receptive to these ideas), was largely undertaken by Jim Mather. The effects on business opinion were marked. In the 1999 election campaign, in a much publicised open letter, 100 prominent businessmen had come out in support of Labour. By 2003, only 17 of these signatories still endorsed Labour's economic policies.

The SNP in Office

Before considering what the SNP has actually delivered in power, it is important to set the context for what it can, and cannot, deliver. There are, of course, the obvious constraints, in terms of those economic powers reserved to Westminster – like the power to borrow, the fiscal power to set major strategic tax rates such as corporation tax, much of research and innovation policy, employment policy, and control over the structure and level of social security benefits. These last two are crucial levers for influencing economic participation rates. Another major power which the Scottish government does not possess is control over interest rates – and, the other side of the same coin, the ability to make strategic exchange rate decisions. It was, for example, fortunate decisions on exchange rate policy which played a large part in propelling Ireland into its ten-year golden decade in the 1990s.

A further constraint which, in a de facto sense, has inhibited the SNP government has been its failure to control an absolute majority in the Scottish Parliament. This problem has lumbered the government with some important policies which it might well have wished to see the back of (such as the new Edinburgh tram system), as well as blocking some other policies which would have had potentially important economic, as well as social, effects (like the local income tax). Finally, it rapidly became clear that the SNP government would be operating in an environment of public expenditure constraints, and perhaps even real public expenditure cuts quite unlike the rapid public expenditure growth experienced throughout most of the Brown boom years.

Against this background, what has the SNP government actually done, to deliver on its economic strategy and vision? Among some of the most important actions taken by the SNP government in its first two years of office are the following:

- It set up a Council of Economic Advisers and a National Economic Forum.

- It has delivered on a bonus scheme to reduce or remove rates bills for around 150,000 small business properties in Scotland.
- It has successfully negotiated a council tax freeze for (at present) two of the targeted three years. While not directly a tax on business, council tax has important economic effects, because it is part of the context within which wage negotiations take place; and also because it directly forms part of the cost structure of the large number of home-based small businesses.
- It has started the simplification of regulation and planning.
- Scottish Enterprise has been reorganised. Its strategy is now driven by the government's policy of achieving economic growth and is primarily focused on companies with high growth potential. Of its business 80% is now concentrated in the key sectors of energy, financial and business services, food and drink, life sciences, and tourism and creative industries.
- Local regeneration and services to small businesses and start-ups have been passed to local authorities: a new organisation, Skills Development Scotland, has taken over responsibility for careers and skills advice and training.
- A Scottish Futures Trust has been set up in an attempt to reform the private finance initiative (PFI).
- A public-sector contracts portal has been established, with the aim of making it easier for small- and medium-sized firms to bid for work in the public sector.
- There have been initiatives on the transport front – including the abolition of tolls on the Forth and Tay bridges, the trial reduction of ferry fares to certain islands, the commitment to press forward with a new Forth crossing and the announcement of a transport infrastructure strategy.
- It has given approval for the development of significant onshore wind capacity, approving the world's largest wave energy project, and launching the Saltire Prize, with the first challenge focusing on developments in wave- power technology.
- The Scottish Skills Strategy was launched in 2007, and subsequently amended following initial criticism by parliament. The strategy's aim is to make skills training relevant to the needs of the Scottish economy. To this end, there has been extensive consultation with employers, skills councils and the STUC. Individual learning accounts have been refocused and can now be used for workplace learning.
- It has set up a Future Thinking Taskforce, to map out the future direction of the university sector.

- In tourism, a major effort has been put into the Homecoming 2009 initiative. This was inherited from the previous administration, but has been very actively pursued by the SNP government.

As regards the current economic crisis, the Scottish government announced in October 2008 a number of tactical steps to counteract the effects on Scotland. These include a six-point recovery programme concentrating on reshaping spending plans, attempting to ensure that all government activity supports economic development, maximising the benefits of Homecoming 2009, taking action on fuel poverty and energy efficiency, and a making available a range of advice and support measures for individuals and businesses (see Scottish Government 2009).

Assessing What has Happened

So how should we regard the success, or otherwise, of the SNP's strategy in action? Our appraisal is structured round these questions:

- Has the administration tried to do what it said it was going to do?
- Have the administration's actions been successful or ineffective?
- Are there other actions which should have been taken, but which have not been?
- And how valid, in any event, is the underlying vision?

It is clear that the SNP in power has indeed tried to do what it had planned. As shown above, action has been taken, or started, in each of the main priority areas identified in their strategy. Credit is therefore due: the SNP government does do, or at least seeks to do, what it says on the can.

On the question of how effective its actions have been, the position is mixed. On the credit side, there are some definite successes, and evidence of progress. The Federation of Small Businesses in Scotland has hailed the new small-business bonus scheme and credited it with preventing many bankruptcies. The council tax freeze has been delivered, but there is a potential downside in that the reduction in the ring fencing of expenditure, which was part of the price of negotiating this deal, makes it more difficult for central government to ensure its priorities are carried out. There has been progress, albeit relatively slow, in simplifying planning procedures, with a marked increase in the proportion of planning appeals processed within twelve weeks.

The action on skills and training has been generally welcomed and has received the endorsement of the General Secretary of the STUC: 'Overall the guiding principles of the Skills Strategy are very worthy and relevant, and are broadly aligned to the work of the STUC and Scottish Union Learning' (STUC 2008). There remain STUC concerns, however, that many small employers will fail to introduce relevant training in the workplace, and to make best use of skills, without further government intervention. As regards the economic recovery programme for the current crisis, the SNP government already claim tangible successes. The most significant of these is probably the bringing forward in Budget 2009–10 of some £293 million of capital spending: this covers, for example, schools, roads, colleges, universities and infrastructure capital projects. In particular, £120 million of this is for the affordable housing investment programme.

On the debit side there are a number of issues regarding effectiveness. Consider, for example, the case of the Futures Trust – in many ways, one of the SNP's flagship policies. Progress has been, by almost universal consent, disappointingly slow: as of spring 2009, almost two years after the SNP took power, it appears that no projects have yet had contracts signed.

In any event, the new initiative itself appears ill-conceived. The consultative document which was issued on the Futures Trust made it clear that capital assets provided under Futures Trust projects should be 'off the government's books' in national accounting terms. This requirement is redundant: with the imminent introduction of new accounting standards, all PFI or Future Trust-type projects are likely to be reclassified as being on the government's books. Further, to get a project off the books under the existing rules, the provision of the capital asset and the provision of ancillary services have to be bound up together in a single contract. This constraint means that projects which are designed to be off the books tend to be large projects – the provision of a serviced asset, rather than separate contracts for the provision of the asset and of associated services. It was the sheer size of the projects involved which led to many of the problems with PFI: from the exclusion of local firms, who could not match the required scale, to the restriction of the market, which in many cases contributed to excessive costs. The unnecessary restrictions built into the Future Trust proposals means that these problems will persist.

Another initiative which could have been more effective is the public procurement portal. There is first the question of whether this adds significant value: there is an already existing UK-wide public-sector portal, which lists public-sector tenders of value less than £100,000. The Scottish scheme does include larger projects but these are, in any event, also listed in the official journal of the EU. However, the main problem with the Scottish portal is that it has not been accompanied by any attempt to unbundle these contracts into smaller constituent parts: in the absence of unbundling, it is not clear how the benefits of the new portal can be maximised for many small Scottish firms.

In the area of transport there has been widespread criticism that the overall strategy lacks coherence and that the approach to the new Forth crossing has neither pressed forward rapidly enough, nor involved sufficiently radical reappraisal of the plans inherited from the previous administration. The handling of the Network Rail franchise renewal, without going out to tender, also raised widespread concern and must pose questions over value for money.

In higher education, although the Future Thinking Taskforce has made a number of recommendations, arguably these do not go far enough. In particular, the required intra-institution mechanisms have not been put in place which would allow issues such as course rationalisation and institute rationalisation to be pro-actively addressed. In addition, given the lack of top-up fees in Scotland, there is the danger of a chronic funding shortfall which has not been addressed.

Our overall verdict, therefore, on the effectiveness with which the SNP government has delivered its specific policy initiatives is a mixed one. They deserve credit for actions in several areas, but they 'could try harder' in others to achieve substantially greater impact.

Let us now look at whether there are actions, not on the SNP's original agenda, which should have been tackled but have not been. First, doing the best for the Scottish economy means not just using the Scottish Budget in isolation but working effectively with the UK government. There is ample evidence that, like the previous administration, the SNP has not worked effectively with UK government departments responsible for reserved matters. Reserved matters cover much of trade, industry, employment and competition, as well as social security, defence and foreign affairs, including Europe. Working with these departments to ensure that their efforts are indeed relevant to Scotland, and exposing them publicly when this is not the case, should be a high priority for any Scottish government, especially one committed to independence.

Second, there is the question of water charges in Scotland. There is a unique opportunity here. Scotland has a publicly owned water industry – water is the only utility where the responsibility for regulation is devolved to Scotland – and Scotland has in operation an inappropriate pricing model for water. The pricing model leads to a large amount of new capital formation in the water industry being funded direct from customer charges, breaching the normal principles of inter-generational equity. For example, in the strategic review of water charges for 2006–10 the amount of net new capital expenditure projected to be funded from customer charges was over £400 million. In effect, the pricing method used for setting water charges in Scotland sets prices at too high a level. As we have argued at greater length elsewhere (Cuthbert and Cuthbert 2007a), water charges in Scotland could be significantly reduced, in a fully sustainable way. This would have several advantages, including giving industry in Scotland a significant competitive edge and preventing Scottish water becoming a cash cow and eventual privatisation target. Given that there are no apparent downsides to taking action in this area, the SNP government's failure to act appears incomprehensible.

A third area where, in our view, the Scottish government has failed to take appropriate action relates to the European structural funds. Up until 2006, because of the rules associated with the operation of the Barnett formula, Scotland received significantly less funding in relation to the European structural fund than it had to pay out to the final recipients of structural fund grants. Essentially, Scotland had to fund a large part of structural fund spending in Scotland out of its own resources. The amounts involved were large: the shortfall in Scottish funding amounted to almost £1 billion over the period 1995/6 to 2005/6 alone (Cuthbert and Cuthbert 2007b). The Scottish government accepts that Scotland was short-changed in this way and has raised the issue several times with the Treasury – to be met by a complete stonewall. No progress on this issue can be expected as long as it continues to be addressed in closed discussions with the Treasury. It appears that the only lever the Scottish government has is to open the issue up, so arousing public debate. It is difficult to understand why they have not done this.

Our final example is in relation to the current recession and credit crunch. Although, as we have already noted, the SNP government has taken a number of tactical steps to counter the effects of the recession, in a strategic sense it has been badly wrong-footed. One of the main arguments put forward by Unionists has always been the supposed benefit to Scotland of sharing in the perceived strength of the UK economy. On the face of it, therefore, the SNP should have been able to capitalise in a political sense, as recent events have demonstrated the fundamental weakness of the City-based economic model. In the event, as the polls indicate, support for the SNP was weakened, at least temporarily, by the onset of the credit crunch. The credit crunch enabled Scotland to be portrayed as too small to survive on its own in such troubled seas, with the economy being seen as too dependent on the discredited financial services sector, and with several of the 'arc of prosperity countries' suffering badly in their own right. We would argue that the SNP's inability to take greater political advantage from the current situation reflects multiple failings on its part.

There has been failure to see this crisis coming, even though it is clear, from the economic strategy papers produced by the SNP itself in the early 2000s, that they were already well aware of the unstable pressure-cooker nature of an economic model based on the City. There has been a failure to distance the SNP sufficiently from the banking sector, even though the party had been warned of the dangers. And there are basic problems of vision – to which we return below.

So there have indeed been serious failures of omission. But finally, what of the SNP's economic vision itself, as set out in the 2007 Economic Strategy? How valid is this vision? The first point to make is that, even if one were to accept the Washington consensus or something similar as the appropriate vision for Scotland's economy, nevertheless, the realisation of that vision set out in the SNP's economic strategy has not been adequately thought through. Take the question of the appropriate currency and exchange rate policy for an independent Scotland. These are not issues which are explicitly addressed in the 2007 strategy, the implication presumably being that, in line with the SNP's 'Scotland in Europe' policy, membership of the eurozone would be the appropriate strategy for an independent Scotland. But if this is the position then it still leaves huge questions unanswered. For example, would Scotland be in a viable position if it became a member of the eurozone while its largest market and probable closest competitor, namely the rest of the UK, remained outside? Particularly given the magnitude of the swings in the relative values of the pound and the euro which have been observed over the past ten years?

Another issue on which, as we have already noted, the strategy is largely silent, is the question of the optimal size of the public sector. There is, however, an even bigger problem for the SNP economic vision – namely that the Washington consensus itself is now widely recognised as having failed. Rather than spending time arguing this point ourselves, we need do no more than appeal to the words of Gordon Brown himself, the former high priest of neo-liberalism, who on 25 March 2009 told an audience of US bankers that the Washington consensus was dead. Eight days previously, in an interview quoted on ITN, he said, 'Laissez-faire has had its day. People on the centre left and the progressive agenda should be confident enough to say that the old idea that the markets were efficient and could work things out by themselves are gone'.

While the failure of the neo-liberal vision is damaging for the SNP, it is important to stress that this failure is by no means fatal to the cause of independence. As Gordon Brown so frequently points out, the current economic crisis is global. A good case could be made that a small and relatively resource-rich country, like an independent Scotland, would find it easier to adapt to a new economic order than the UK as a whole will do – particularly bearing in mind the inertia of the large UK economy, its over-dependence on the City, and the extent to which its economy was distorted by easy credit and the property boom.

Nor are we arguing that the SNP's response to the failure of the neo-liberal model should be that it should set about saving the whole world, by crafting a completely new world economic order. Gordon Brown's attempt to do just this is being seen increasingly as a doomed diversionary tactic. The appropriate response by the SNP is surely to develop a new economic vision, and a strategy, both of which are robust in the face of current economic uncertainties. It is not for us to prescribe what that strategy should be, but it would be very surprising if any emerging strategy did not embody the following key features:

- Much less reliance on the financial services sector as the dominant driver of the economy.
- Given the failure of the UK's regulatory mechanism for the financial sector, a strong push towards taking control of financial regulation in Scotland.
- Given the vital importance of Scotland rebuilding its industrial and exporting bases, an industrial strategy which has a broader sectoral base and is firmly focused on developing Scotland's comparative advantages into sustainable export industries.
- A continuing strategy of skills and training, which is not only firmly allied to Scotland's industrial strategy, but also has sufficient teeth to ensure widespread implementation.
- Maximum use of the considerable leverage the state possesses to nurture and support indigenous businesses. Even within the context of the rules on state aid, much more could be done.

CONCLUSION

We conclude by returning to the question posed at the beginning of this chapter. How well has the SNP in power responded to the triple challenge of establishing its economic competence, while highlighting the inherent weaknesses of the present constitutional set-up – and presenting a compelling economic vision for an eventually independent Scotland?

Our conclusion is that the SNP has underperformed on each leg of this challenge. On the first part of this challenge, our verdict on its competence is 'could try harder' – while some things have been done well, on other issues there has been slow progress and an insufficiently radical approach, and there are some inexplicable omissions concerning things it clearly should have done but has not attempted.

As regards the second leg of the challenge, the SNP made the grave tactical blunder of setting explicit targets for what an SNP government could achieve. There were two things wrong with this. First of all, given the multiple constraints under devolution on the SNP in power, delivering on many of these specific targets is beyond their reach. Therefore, setting these explicit targets creates huge hostages to fortune for the party. But worse than that, the act of setting a target involves taking responsibility for failure to deliver. It is very difficult, if the targets are not achieved, to then try to pin the blame on fundamental weaknesses in the constitutional settlement. By adopting a target-driven strategy, therefore, the SNP largely surrendered its ability to succeed on the second leg of the challenge.

And finally, the SNP's choice of long-term economic vision has proved damaging. Adopting a version of the consensus neo-liberal model may have seemed a fairly safe choice at the time – even though the inherent flaws in that model were already showing clearly when the 2007 strategy was being written. In the event, the flaws in the neo-liberal model have become more and more apparent, and the SNP has proved extremely slow in trying to distance itself from that model. The paradox is that Gordon Brown has moved faster and further from his light-touch-regulation neo-liberal model than the SNP has. The effect has been that what should have been a political opportunity for the SNP, namely the collapse of the previously dominant UK economic model, has in fact turned out to be a disadvantage. The third leg of the challenge has been comprehensively failed.

The question that then arises is – why has the SNP not performed better? The answers to this question are inevitably complex. But if we were pressed for a single defining weakness, it would be that the approach adopted has been too consensual, and too apparently safe. A party which is committed to an ultimate objective that is effectively revolutionary has to be more willing to challenge along the way to such an objective – to challenge the over-riding economic consensus, to challenge the status of the bankers and square up to the power of existing vested interests like the civil service. A party which is not willing to challenge on issues like these is ultimately not going to succeed in bringing about fundamental change.

References

Cuthbert, J. R. and Cuthbert, M. (2007a), 'Fundamental Flaws in the Current Cost Regulatory Capital Value Method of Utility Pricing', *Fraser of Allander Institute Quarterly Economic Commentary*, Vol. 31, No. 3.

Cuthbert, J. R. and Cuthbert, M. (2007b), 'How Scotland will be Disadvantaged in the Longer Term by Recent Changes in Government Accounting for European Structural Funds', *Fraser of Allander Institute Quarterly Economic Commentary*, Vol. 31, No. 4.

Harvey, D. (2005), *A Brief History of Neoliberalism*, Oxford, Oxford University Press.

Scottish Government (2007), *The Government Economic Strategy*, Edinburgh, Scottish Government.

Scottish Government (2009), *The Scottish Government's Response to the First Annual Report of the Council of Economic Advisers*, Edinburgh, Scottish Government.

SNP (1995), *Towards a Better Scotland*, Edinburgh, SNP.

SNP (1999), *Manifesto for the Scottish Parliament Elections*, Edinburgh, SNP.

STUC (2008), *Statement on Skills Strategy*, Glasgow, STUC.

Chapter 10

Social Justice and the SNP

Stephen Maxwell

The SNP was founded, and remains, a party whose overriding purpose is the achievement of independence for Scotland. That is the source and the target of its strongest impulses. Its second strongest impulse, sourced in the desperate economic conditions of the inter-war years which saw the party's foundation, is the improvement of Scotland's economic performance. Perhaps its third strongest impulse is opposition to the nuclearisation of Scotland, focused with a particular intensity on the use of Scottish territory as a base for the UK's nuclear weapons capacity. Only then comes the impulse for social justice.

This ranking is supported by a 2007 survey of SNP members' first priority for the powers they would like to see transferred to the Scottish Parliament. Economic and taxation powers came first with 55.7%, defence and foreign affairs second with 12.6%, and social security and pensions third with 6.7%. (Aberdeen and Strathclyde Universities 2007). This is consistent with my personal judgement based on several decades of membership and observation of the party. The ranking is offered here in support of the proposition that while independence, economic development and opposition to nuclear weapons are in the SNP's political DNA, a politically relevant sense of social justice has had to be learned.

The Origins of SNP Social Policy Thinking

The leaders of the SNP in the immediate aftermath of the Second World War were drawn mainly from the professions and small business. The first historian of modern Scottish Nationalism, H. J. Hanham, presents them as small-town democrats (Hanham 1969). While their Presbyterian heritage gave them a strong sense of the fundamental equality of all men and women, as well as a robust ethic of social responsibility, it was at best ambiguous towards economic and social equality and distanced from the all-pervasive sense of class which characterised so much of Scotland.

These limitations are evident in the party's 1946 *Statement of Aims and Policy*. It had plenty to say about a Scottish constitution, about local government, planning and economic development, but rather less to say about Scotland's social future. It advised that medical and other health services must be provided 'free, if necessary, by the state where they do not exist or do not reach a reasonable standard', while insisting that state intervention must not transform the medical profession into a state monopoly. While it identified housing as one of Scotland's most urgent problems and called for national building standards and planning, it said nothing about who should fund and own the new stock.

It declared that economic democracy was the basis of political freedom, without any reference to industrial democracy or to the security and welfare of workers. It offered an economic policy aimed at maximising Scotland's economic potential as a precondition of providing a 'decent standard of living and not of a bare subsistence' for those unable to work, to be funded by a contributory social insurance scheme paying benefits 'without recourse to the humiliation of means test'. It stated that there should be no 'great inequalities' in individual wealth or income, but offered no suggestions as to how any redistribution should be effected.

Overall it was a limited and ambivalent response to the social and economic challenges which had generated a political mandate for the creation of the British welfare state (SNP 1946). From this limited base the SNP's sense of social justice has been shaped by three main factors – its electoral rivalry with the Labour Party, the impact of Thatcherism and the creation of the Scottish Parliament.

ELECTORAL RIVALRY

Of these three, electoral rivalry with the Labour Party is the most important and, from the February and October 1974 elections onward, the SNP called itself 'social democratic'. That this was more than a handy piece of camouflage was made clear by the direction of the SNP's policy development. Under Gordon Wilson's leadership the party's 'It's Scotland's Oil' campaign was promoted nationally through posters featuring, documentary style, the faces of four deprived Scots – a pensioner, an unemployed industrial worker, a child in poverty, a harassed housewife – above statistics describing the extent of Scotland's social problems and the punchline, 'It's his oil . . . It's her oil'. This directed the SNP's attack at the heart of Labour's traditional claim to be the champion of social justice for Scotland's working class.

The SNP followed this up by adopting at its 1974 conference a strategy to combat poverty. Where previous SNP conferences had tended to treat poverty through isolated resolutions, the 'War on Poverty' policy took a more comprehensive approach, drawing on the policy packages – raising of tax thresholds, increased child benefits, guaranteed minimum income – publicised by UK campaigning bodies such as the Child Poverty Action Group (SNP 1974). Labour's sensitivity to this new emphasis was displayed by its furious denial of a subsequent SNP claim that 5,000 elderly Scots were dying from hypothermia each year in oil-rich Scotland, a dispute which resolved around the distinction between deaths by hypothermia and deaths from cold-related diseases (Maxwell 1987).

The movement in the SNP's understanding of social justice towards mainstream social democracy was also influenced by increasing reference to Norway and other Scandinavian models. Norway was already popular with SNP activists because it provided the example of a small country successfully pursuing nationally oriented strategies on both oil and fisheries while, in the SNP's eyes, Scotland's oil and fisheries were being sacrificed to UK priorities. But the Scandinavian welfare model was also increasingly recommended as the solution, with the help of oil revenues, to Scotland's intractable social problems.

DISTANCE TRAVELLED

The distance the SNP had travelled from 1946 was measured by its 1978 policy summary, *Return to Nationhood*, which looked confidently forward to the following year's referendum on the Scottish Assembly. Rather than concentrating on the SNP's classic claim for Scottish sovereignty it proclaimed that the party fought elections on its proposals for 'social and economic justice for the people of Scotland'. Based on the Universal Declaration of Human Rights, its policies would eventually eradicate 'society's damaging divisions without resort to the extremes of outdated class politics' (SNP 1978). Those policies included raising the tax threshold for low-income families, the replacement of tax allowances by tax credits guaranteeing a universal minimum income, the replacement of rates with a redistributive local income tax, an uprated universal child benefit, a comprehensive system of allowances for disabled people, opposition to any incomes policy which further eroded living standards, the index linking of main benefits to average earnings, the extension of care 'in the community' rather than in institutions and an assisted home-buying scheme for council house tenants where the public housing stock was equal to the demand.

Of course it is the prerogative of opposition parties – particularly parties as distant from government as the SNP then was – to adopt populist policies without too much regard for their practicality. But the cursory attention SNP policy-decision bodies gave to complex social policy issues reflected some features peculiar to the party. One was the paucity of social policy expertise within the party membership and the lack of any specialist policy staff beyond oil and economic development. What expertise existed within the party's active membership was usually conscripted into the policy committee charged with developing policy and so was likely to be *parti pris* before the wider party membership was engaged. Among the party's MPs only Margaret Bain majored on social policy issues, though Gordon Wilson was a forceful campaigner for a cold-climate allowance in the 1979–87 parliaments. Nor did the SNP have an associated think tank which could make up the deficits. A further factor was the widespread confidence within the party by the mid-1970s that North Sea oil revenues would cover the costs of whatever policy commitment the party chose to make.

THE THATCHER EFFECT

The consolidation of the SNP's left-of-centre position on social issues was completed by Margaret Thatcher. Her imposition of a poll tax in Scotland in 1987 was received as a gross injustice by almost as many of the middle-class Scots who stood to gain from the tax as of the working-class Scots who stood to lose, a sentiment which the SNP enthusiastically encouraged by its campaign of non-payment. But it was the social consequences in Scotland of her flagship policies on the economy and welfare reform – Scottish unemployment and poverty levels both peaked in the later 1980s at more than double the 1979 levels – that had the deepest impact. The offence caused to Scotland's sense of moral identity strengthened the SNP's commitment to social democracy as the Scottish alternative to what was widely seen as Mrs Thatcher's denial of social solidarity and even social compassion.

But while Mrs Thatcher's perceived social ethic was firmly rejected by the SNP, her promotion of a liberalised market as an indispensable source of economic dynamism struck a chord with sections of the party leadership looking for ways of injecting new vitality into the Scottish economy. The SNP's embrace of the single European market through its 'Independence in Europe' policy went part of the way to meeting the need while the emergence of Ireland as Europe's tiger economy provided a model of small-state economic success without the Nordic ambivalence towards the EU.

A NEW TESTING GROUND

The establishment of the Scottish Parliament forced social issues to the forefront of Scottish politics. Scotland's designated First Minister Donald Dewar raised the stakes for the new parliament in 1998 in a preview of its main challenges: 'We have a proud tradition [in Scotland] of working to tackle social division . . . Devolution is an end in itself: but it is a means to other ends, and none more important than the creation of a socially cohesive Scotland' (*The Herald*, 3 February 1998).

While there is room to challenge Dewar's confidence that the parliament had the capacity for effective action on the most important factors behind Scotland's social problems, there is no doubt that the Parliament has made social policy the main front of Scottish politics. The first, Labour-led executive took up the challenge by appointing a Minister for Social Justice committed to Annual Social Justice reports, established a Scottish Social Exclusion (soon amended to Inclusion) Network recruited from civil society as an advisory forum, and part-funded a Centre for Research on Social Justice based at Glasgow University.

The SNP faced a particular challenge. Having built a social democratic platform against poverty which assumed independence, it now confronted the reality that its credibility on social issues would be judged on the more immediate and certainly no less complex social issues devolved to Edinburgh. It would no longer be able simply to counterpoint any Westminster failures on social justice issues with its own pristine commitments to more radical action. While UK issues would continue to exert a strong influence on Scottish electoral preferences, the Scottish Parliament had created a new testing ground for the party's credibility on social policy.

If some opponents of the SNP hoped that the extended social challenge presented by the Scottish Parliament would expose deep tensions and divisions in what they continued to see as a 'one-issue' party, they were disappointed. Building on the devolution referendum's endorsement of a tax-varying power for the parliament, the SNP campaigned in the 1999 elections on the theme of 'A Penny for Scotland'. This was a bold affirmation of its social priorities, detailing the social and educational projects on which the SNP would spend the £670 million additional income generated over three years by a 1p 'tartan' tax supplement.

The struggle with Labour and the challenge of Thatcherism had helped to educate and stabilise the SNP's sense of social justice around a policy platform which proved well matched to the politics of devolved Scotland. In the parliament the SNP was part of a regular parliamentary majority with Labour and the Lib Dems, and later the Greens and the Scottish

Socialists, which embraced free personal care, radical homelessness legislation, abolition of Section 28, charity law reform, social inclusion programmes, new rights for mental health patients, the recognition of civil partnerships, opposition to top-up fees for students, the abolition of poinding and warrant sales, new safeguards for the rights of people with learning difficulties, and a ban on smoking in public places.

The rights agenda was advanced by the extension of freedom of information and the creation of a public services complaints ombudsman and new arm's-length service inspectorates. Supported by large increases in public spending, the expansion of health and education within the public sector also enjoyed majority support, though the SNP became progressively more critical of the use of PFI as a major source of funding. Housing and council tax were other areas where the SNP broke with the consensus, criticising the Glasgow Housing Association (GHA) model as the vehicle for the transfer of Glasgow's housing stock and opposing the council tax as an inflexible and regressive form of local taxation.

PUBLIC AND PARTY OPINION

In its adoption of a pragmatic left-of-centre position on social policy the parliament was in tune with Scottish public opinion. Successive opinion surveys have shown Scottish public opinion as being to the left of English opinion on a range of attitude tests. Election Surveys from 1979 to 1997 show the proportion of Scots favouring more redistribution of income and wealth varying from between 14% and 6% higher than English voters. The Scottish Parliament Election Survey 1999 indicated a 25% gap, with 61% of Scots respondents in favour as against 36% of English respondents. The differences on other indicators were much smaller. More Scots than English agreed that income inequality in Britain was too high, fewer Scots believed that benefits were too high, and more Scots agreed that government was mainly responsible for providing health care, support to retired people, disabled people and low-income parents, and residential care. The only measure on which Scots were to the right of the English respondents, albeit narrowly, was rather perversely on whether government should increase taxes to spend more on health and other support (Paterson et al. 2001: 126–7).

Evidence from the 2005 British Social Attitudes Survey shows more mixed results, with 51 % of Scots agreeing with the proposition that benefits were too generous compared to 50% of English respondents (Sinclair et al. 2009). On the other hand, a 2008 poll revealed that 61% of Scots said that they would be more inclined to support a political party that took serious measures against poverty, compared to an average of 51% across Great Britain (Maxwell 2009).

The 2007 survey of SNP members suggests that in its social values, if not its constitutional aims, the party membership is aligned with the values of the country. Forty five per cent agreed that there is one law for the rich and one for the poor against 15% who disagreed, while no less than 71% disagreed with the proposition that the government should cut spending in order to cut tax. On the more challenging proposition that it is not government's responsibility to provide a job for everyone who wants one, 47% agreed against 35% who disagreed (Aberdeen and Strathclyde Universities 2007).

Most commentators maintain that these differences in surveyed social values between England and Scotland are too small and variable to serve by themselves as the political foundation for a distinctive Scottish social politics (Paterson et al. 2001; Sinclair et al. 2009). This of course leaves the leftist bias of the parliament's actual social record to be explained. One explanation is that the values of the elected MSPs are to the left of the Scottish voters while remaining within the voters' margin of tolerance.

A more structured explanation looks to the particular conditions of the Scottish constitutional settlement – the devolution of spending power, principally social spending, to a legislature elected by a form of proportional representation but without any substantial tax-raising power. While the lack of fiscal responsibility biases the parliament towards populist spending, the electoral system ensures that the party most disposed to challenge the bias, the Conservative Party, struggles to escape from its minority status in the parliament.

This explanation is at best partial. While the electoral system does indeed make it difficult for a single party to achieve an overall majority by comparison with the Westminster system, by the same token it provides more opportunity to other parties critical of the parliament's bias in favour of spending to gain representation. The more representative a voting system, the less credible it is to dismiss the role of voters' preferences.

The Challenge of Government

If the arrival of the Scottish Parliament created a new testing-ground for SNP social policy, the party's move into government following the 2007 election added a new dimension to the challenge. The inclusion in the party's election manifesto of ambitious targets for raising Scotland's rate of sustainable economic growth was entirely expected, as were commitments to reducing Scotland's levels of poverty and welfare dependence. Rather less expected was the focus on inequality. The manifesto identified Scotland as having one of the highest levels of income inequality in Europe, attributing it to 'serious political and economic failure'. The SNP's response was a promise that as part of its economic growth strategy it would set specific targets to increase the proportion of national wealth held by *each of the* lowest *six income deciles* of the population.

This must be one of the most radical commitments to redistribution made by any UK political party since the founding of the welfare state. To increase significantly the share of national income of each of the six lowest deciles would require a major transfer of income from the top 40% of Scottish earners, going well beyond a common-sense interpretation of the warrant provided by the margin of Scottish over English support for redistribution in opinion surveys. A cynic might claim that its inclusion in the manifesto was a symptom of the rather casual way in which the SNP's policy-making process treated social issues. It is not surprising that the SNP government's subsequent social strategy papers have carried a much reduced, though still significant, commitment to reduce income inequality.

In government the SNP has strengthened rather than diluted its commitment to social democracy. While the major economic policy strategy paper, *The Government Economic Strategy* (GES), defined the government's single overriding purpose as being 'to increase sustainable economic growth – to which all else in government is directed and contributes' (Scottish Government 2007), for a statement of economic strategy it has an unusual amount to say about the social dimensions of economic growth. Its economic objectives are to be consistent with three 'golden rules' ranking solidarity and cohesion alongside sustainability. While cohesion is presented as equity between geographical area, solidarity is presented in terms of equity between income groups, with Scotland's inequality levels compared unfavourably, though with minimal differentiation, with those in the 'arc of prosperity countries' (Ireland and selected Nordic countries). The radical manifesto commitment to reducing income inequality between each of the six lowest deciles and the top four is replaced by a more sober, but still challenging, commitment to increase the share of the *three* lowest deciles as a *group*. At the same time Ireland is commended for using the 'opportunity of globalisation' to achieve high rates of economic growth through large-scale infrastructure investment and low corporation tax with only the most fleeting reference to its poor record on poverty and inequality.

The GES was followed by *Taking Forward the Government Economic Strategy: A Discussion Paper on tackling Poverty, Inequality and Disadvantage in Scotland* (Scottish Government 2008a). In contrast to the GES, *Taking*

Forward is clear about the lack of any automatic transfer from economic growth to reductions in poverty and inequality. It carries a table showing that Ireland's high growth rate had been accompanied by rates of poverty and inequality among the worst in the developed world alongside the US and UK. The table also showed that even the Nordic countries with their long commitment to egalitarian welfare had not been able to prevent some increase in poverty during the 1995–2005 period, albeit from levels half or more lower than in Ireland, the US and UK. As a discussion paper it was focused more on questions and issues than solutions and so left many loose ends, but it stretched the horizons of the Scottish policy debate farther than they had been pushed before under either Westminster or devolution.

The Scottish government's record of executive decisions during its first two years in office reveals the politically pragmatic side of the party's convergence on social democracy. Among the government's earliest actions was the decision to halt the closure of the A&E departments at hospitals in Ayr and Airdrie, which had been the target of vigorous local opposition. It abolished some hospital car-parking fees and began the phased abolition of prescription charges. It announced that the £850 million bill for the new Southern General Hospital in Glasgow would be funded publicly and not through PPP. While it retreated from its election promise to write off student debt, it went ahead with its promise to abolish the graduate endowment and to establish a fund for the support of part-time learners. It piloted free school meals and committed to rolling them out across primary and secondary schools. It abolished the right to buy for new social housing and made £25 million available for the building of new council houses for rent. It uprated payments for residential care and continued to meet the rising bill for free social care.

Some of these measures have invited charges of populism and opportunism from the SNP's political opponents. But they fit into a consistent trend in SNP policy of challenging some of the more controversial Labour Party policies introduced by the Blair and Brown administrations and adopted with varying degrees of enthusiasm by their Scottish colleagues.

A New Dawn?

The impression of a party comfortable in presenting itself as a champion of a pre-Blairite, if not 'Old Labour', understanding of social democracy is reinforced by the Scottish government's latest social policy statements: *Equally Well* (Scottish Government 2008b), presenting the government's proposals to tackle Scotland's health inequalities; *Achieving our Potential: A Framework to Tackle Poverty and Income Inequality in Scotland*

(Scottish Government 2008c); and *The Early Years Framework* (Scottish Government 2009).

Early Years, the most recent of the three, claims that taken together the statements represent 'a new dawn in social policy' for Scotland. If the claim can be justified it is less because of their shared promise of a 'coordinated approach to early years, health inequalities and poverty at national and local levels' than because of the consistency of the focus on inequality. *Achieving our Potential* firmly identifies inequality as a cause and not just a symptom of poverty. It restates *Taking Forward*'s modification of the manifesto's commitment to reduce income inequality as a commitment to increase the share of national income enjoyed by the three lowest deciles as a group.

The excision of any references to Ireland and Iceland gives a monopoly to the core Nordic countries, though no analysis is offered of the reasons for their superior record on poverty and inequality. Alongside reminders of actions already taken, it reaffirms its commitment to a fairer and more redistributive system of local taxation and extends its strategic horizons by promising a study of the scope for action on public pay, as well as a joint campaign with the STUC and the voluntary sector to raise awareness of workers rights' on pay and leave entitlements. It also reaffirms its intention to engage with the UK government on the interaction of the benefits system with employability programmes, as well as on the case for devolving benefits along with tax to the Scottish Parliament.

The claims of the health and early years documents to be social policy pathbreakers rest principally on three elements. One is their emphasis on the need to combat the effects of generational inequality by shifting the focus of services from crisis intervention to prevention by 'anticipatory' intervention. The government's approach is described as being to provide a high level of universal services with additional support provided at the earliest possible opportunity to the most vulnerable, to prevent their vulnerabilities developing into major social or health problems. The third element is a focus on the 'engagement and empowerment of children, families and communities' in the services they receive. Though no attribution is offered, these three elements – early intervention to support and engage the most vulnerable from a baseline of high-quality universal services – could serve as a summary of the best practice in the Nordic welfare states.

Omissions and Limitations

How coherent and how adequate to the challenges facing Scotland is the understanding of social justice at which the SNP has now arrived? First, the gaps should be noted. There are very few references in either party or government documents to inequality of wealth as a cause of poverty and other social ills and, notoriously, the SNP's proposals for a local income tax excluded unearned income (Mooney and Wright 2009). After three decades of increasing inequality of wealth, the paucity of reference seems significant.

Second, the government fails to provide targets for reducing income inequality, or to specify which of the many policies described in its policy documents it expects to do the heavy lifting in achieving the desired reduction. It gives no indication of what share of national income the three lowest deciles should enjoy, nor how that share should be distributed between them. The relative roles of paid employment, fiscal redistribution and public services in achieving the reduction are never explained. The government seems to be relying on a higher rate of economic growth and the better coordination of public services though council-led Community Planning Partnerships to make a major contribution in defiance of recent experience and medium-term prospects.

Another neglected area is sexual equality. While the importance of the equalities agenda in general is acknowledged, the SNP seems content with the rather modest role of women in Scottish public life beyond the economy. Despite Norway's favoured status as a model, there is no public evidence of SNP interest in Scotland emulating Norway's highly effective initiatives on boosting the role of women in Norway's business and political life. This indifference may reflect the complacency with which SNP appears to regard the modest representation of women among the party's elected representatives, its members, and even in recent years among its voters (Aberdeen and Strathclyde Universities 2007).

The implementation of the SNP's 2007 manifesto commitment to engage and empower individuals and communities has been selective. While the government has extended the discretionary spending power of councils by reducing ring-fencing, the freezing of council tax has increased councils' financial dependence on central government, an effect which would have been reinforced had its local income tax proposals been implemented. Direct elections to health boards have been provided for and the intention to legislate for patients' rights reaffirmed, but promises to pilot measures directly empowering local communities have been ignored, perhaps as the price of securing the concordat with local councils, and little has been done to fulfil commitments to promote direct payments.

POLICY DUALISM: THE ECONOMIC HEAD AND THE SOCIAL HEART

While some of these omissions may be attributable to the inevitable attrition of government and others to tactical compromises on a longer road to a social democracy, some – notably the exclusion of wealth from the strategy to reduce inequality, the absence of targets for the reduction and the vagueness about the main policy instruments – may reveal a persisting ambivalence about the social democratic model itself. Over the last decade as the SNP's social heart has become more attached to social democracy, its economic head has inclined to neo-liberalism. The dualism is most evident in the SNP government's social policy documents. *Taking Forward* compares the poverty records of neo-liberal Ireland and the social democratic Nordic countries statistically, much to the former's disadvantage, but even though it is presented as 'taking forward the government's economic strategy' to tackle Scotland's poverty and inequality, it ignores the conflict between its preferred social model and the government's preferred economic model. In some political parties such tensions would be the stuff of major debate if not ideological division – but the SNP has always shied away from ideological contention. *Achieving our Potential* and its two companion statements continue the Nelsonian strategy.

That the tension has not created division or significant debate within the party may be due in part to the way the dualism seems to run through SNP leaders rather than between them. Alex Salmond has been the chief cheerleader for the Irish low-tax model even while claiming it, by virtue of its high level of investment in education and infrastructure and its social partnership, as an example of social democracy (Salmond 2004). In one of only two published attempts by any SNP leader to resolve the tension, Kenny MacAskill (currently Justice Minister) acknowledges strengths in both the Irish and the Scandinavian models on his way to asserting that 'competitive business taxation is not inconsistent with social justice and quality public services'. But his supporting argument swings wildly between recommending the Scandinavian model for Scotland and declaring that the Swedish social welfare model is no longer an option in an interdependent global economy, while completely ignoring Ireland's poor social record and the fact that after 2000 low taxation in Ireland spread from the corporations to personal incomes (MacAskill 2004).

Minister for Culture, External Affairs and the Constitution Michael Russell's recent assessment of Scotland's options aspires to be more radical, but is not much more coherent. He proposes cutting Scotland's public spending/GDP ratio by half to the Irish level and abolishing universalism in public service provision. Yet at the same time he acknowledges the economic (though not the social) success of the Nordic countries, even with their much higher public expenditure/GDP ratios, and warns against losing any of the 'guarantees of essential services which are the hallmark of a modern and civilised society'. Like MacAskill, he omits any reference to Ireland's social record (MacLeod and Russell 2006).

Further symptoms of dualism may be found in the SNP's response to the impact on Scotland of the crisis in financial services and of the global recession. On the one hand, the Scottish government has campaigned for a sustained public expenditure-led response to the economic crisis. On the other hand, it has offered no policy response to the collapse of the greater part of the Scottish banking system. None of its economic spokespersons – neither Salmond, Finance Secretary John Swinney or Industry Minster Jim Mather – has made any public statement about the lessons to be drawn for the future shape and regulation of Scotland's financial services, except for vague murmurings that it must be consistent with reform of the international system. This may be a tactical silence intended to avoid drawing public attention to a general Scottish embarrassment or to the First Minster's connections to leading figures in Scotland's financial sector. Or it may derive from a strategic judgement that SNP talk of tighter regulation would frighten off potential supporters in the financial and business world in the run-up to an independence referendum and a Westminster general election. Or again it may be because the SNP leadership, or at least the sections of it in charge of economic strategy, continue to favour light-touch regulation as an essential ingredient along with low corporation tax and low wealth taxes for a dynamic Scottish economy under independence capable of achieving the government's single overriding purpose of a higher rate of sustainable economic growth.

RESOLUTION

It is difficult to be sure how, or whether, this dualism will be resolved. The SNP has a strong aversion to ideological debate, as the left-wing 79 Group discovered between 1979 and 1981. The establishment of the Scottish Parliament shifted policy initiative further from the party's elected policy-making bodies – the National Council and the Annual Conference – to the leadership in the parliament and its paid staff. The SNP's move into government has centralised policy initiative even further. SNP members are in any case traditionally loyal to the party's leadership and the party's recent electoral record and its move into government have cemented that. If the tension between the party's social heart and its economic head is to find resolution, the initiative will have to come from within the party's leadership, or at least from within the ranks of its MSPs and MPs.

It is tempting to assume that the ministers responsible for the 'new dawn' in social policy – Health and Wellbeing Ministers Nicola Sturgeon and Shona Robison, and Early Years Minister Adam Ingram – will be most sensitive to the tension between their social democratic strategy and the neo-liberalism underpinning their party's economic strategy, and that their perspective would be shared by the two ministers publicly identified as of the left, Housing Minister Alex Neil and Environment Minister Roseanna Cunningham. It might also be supposed that MPs and MSPs with a demonstrated interest in social issues, for example Glasgow East MP John Mason (the first SNP MP to serve on a Westminster Bill committee for a welfare reform issue) and MSP John Wilson, a former director of the Scottish Low Pay Unit, would be alert to the tension. But given the absence of public comment by any of the ministers or backbenchers and the general opacity of the party's policy process, this remains supposition.

As always it is external pressures which will force change, in this case the exceptional pressures generated by the multi-layered global crisis. Neo-liberalism was the first victim of the global financial and economic crisis, although its demise has so far been acknowledged by the SNP only by its prompt exclusion of Ireland from its list of small-state exemplars. The cost of the crisis to Scotland is not just the destruction of what remained of a Scottish-led banking sector, but increased levels of unemployment and poverty and an intensification of the chronic social problems which the government's new social policies were designed to combat. The third wave of the crisis, the public-spending crunch, will condemn many of those policies to survive only as paper promises.

What price the government's commitment to universalism in public services caught between the relentless rise in public demand and a reducing public budget? The signs so far are that SNP will try to persevere with the policy pragmatism which has brought, or at least accompanied, the relative electoral success the party has enjoyed over the last two decades, in the hope that things will return eventually to pre-recession normality. But overshadowing these dire medium-term economic prospects is the fundamental challenge of environmental degradation with its own imperatives of radical economic and social adaptation. The inescapable challenge for the SNP is to integrate its case for Scottish independence with the transformational social and economic policies which our multiple global crisis demands.

REFERENCES

Aberdeen and Strathclyde Universities (2007), *Results of the ESRC SNP Membership Survey Study*, Aberdeen and Glasgow.

Hanham, H. J. (1969), *Scottish Nationalism*, London, Faber and Faber.

MacAskill, K. (2004), *Building a Nation: Post-Devolution Nationalism*, Edinburgh: Luath Press.

MacLeod, D. and Russell, M. (2006), *Grasping the Thistle: How Scotland must React to the Three Key Challenges of the Twenty First Century*, Glendaruel, Argyll Publishing.

Maxwell, S. (1987), 'The Politics of Poverty in Scotland', in McCrone, D. (ed.), *The Scottish Government Yearbook 1987* , Edinburgh, Unit for the Study of Government in Scotland, pp. 81–98.

Maxwell, S. (2009), 'Principles and Absences: A Critique of the Scottish Government's Approach to Combating Scotland's Problem of Poverty and Inequality', *Scottish Affairs*, No. 67, pp. 57–69.

Mooney, G. and Wright, S. (2009), 'Wealthier and Fairer? Reflecting on SNP Proposals for Tackling Poverty, Inequality and Disadvantage in Scotland', *Scottish Affairs*, No. 67, pp. 49–56.

Paterson, L., Brown, A., Curtice, J., Hinds, K., McCrone, D., Park, A., Sproston, K. and Surridge, P. (2001), *New Scotland, New Politics?*, Edinburgh, Edinburgh University Press.

Salmond, A. (2004), 'Salmond pledges a revitalised social democracy for Scotland', Edinburgh, SNP, 4 September, http://www.snp.org/node/10890

Scottish Government (2007), *The Government Economic Strategy*, Edinburgh, Scottish Government.

Scottish Government (2008a), *Taking Forward the Government Economic Strategy: A Discussion Paper on tackling Poverty, Inequality and Disadvantage in Scotland*, Edinburgh, Scottish Government.

Scottish Government (2008b), *Equally Well: Report of the Ministerial Task Force on Health Inequalities*, Edinburgh, Scottish Government.

Scottish Government (2008c), *Achieving our Potential: A Framework to Tackle Poverty and Income Inequality in Scotland*, Edinburgh, Scottish Government.

Scottish Government (2009), *The Early Years Framework*, Edinburgh, Scottish Government.

Sinclair, S., McKendrick, J. and Kelly, P. (2009), 'Taking the High Road? Media and Public Attitudes Towards Poverty in Scotland', *Scottish Affairs*, No. 67, pp. 70–91.

SNP (1946), *Statement of Aims and Policy*, Edinburgh, SNP.

SNP (1974), *War on Poverty*, Edinburgh, SNP.

SNP (1978), *Return to Nationhood*, Edinburgh, SNP.

CHAPTER 11

The SNP, Cultural Policy and the Idea of the 'Creative Economy'

Philip Schlesinger

INTRODUCTION

Since coming to power in May 2007, the SNP government has taken significant initiatives in broadcasting and cultural policy. In doing so, it has been deeply influenced by current thinking about the key role of the 'creative industries' and the 'creative economy' in conditions of global competition. Such ideas first came into focus in the UK with the advent of New Labour to power in 1997 and were rapidly adopted in Scotland under the Labour–Lib Dem coalitions that ruled in the Scottish Parliament from 1999 to 2007.

The creative economy has moved increasingly to the centre of policy thinking in the UK, latterly crystallised by *Creative Britain* (Dept for Culture, Media and Sport 2008), a government report endorsed by Prime Minister Gordon Brown. At the heart of the official vision of creativity are the harnessing of culture to the growth of the national economy and a grandiose post-imperial design to make the UK the 'world's creative hub'. 'Creativity' has become a doctrine, continually modified in government discourse and sustained by sympathetic think-tankery (Schlesinger 2007; 2009). The New Labour government has defined creative industries as involving individual effort productive of intellectual property and demonstrable of entrepreneurship. The idea of creativity as such has widespread ideological resonance, and accords with aspirations to seek fulfilment in work. But while it is often officially presented as inclusive and democratic, creative economy policy is focused on a small minority's cultural labour and its successful commodification for the sake of 'UK plc' (Heartfield 2008; Mulholland 2008). As the Nationalists have drunk deeply from the same cup, the impact of such thinking is evident in their approach to broadcasting and culture.

Shortly after coming to power, First Minister Alex Salmond set up the Scottish Broadcasting Commission (SBC), prompted by the need to address Scotland's 'deficit' in the volume and value of television production for the UK networks. The Scottish government's intervention in broadcasting policy broke with the reticence and backstairs lobbying of previous administrations. The SBC's work illustrates the decisive intervention that can be made in a policy field formally reserved to Westminster and will be the first of the two cases examined here.

The move to address broadcasting policy issues directly has posed an interesting (if still minor) challenge to the established UK framework. Broadcasting is a 'reserved' power under the Scotland Act 1998 and falls under the purview of UK ministers and the Westminster Parliament. In practice, therefore, broadcasting policy is in the hands of the Secretary of State for Culture, Media and Sport while Ofcom (the Office of Communications) regulates broadcasting on a UK-wide basis. Scotland is not represented on the Ofcom Board although it does have national members on the Ofcom Content Board and the advisory Consumer Communications Panel. The regulator has offices in each of the nations: Ofcom Scotland is based in Glasgow. BBC Scotland, long headquartered in Glasgow, is the corporation's Scottish arm. The BBC is regulated by the BBC Trust, which has a territorial member – currently the economist Jeremy Peat – who represents the Scottish interest.

By contrast with broadcasting, culture is an area of 'devolved' policy. If the SNP has intervened decisively to try to shape broadcasting in Scotland, the field of culture demonstrates instead the profound continuity of policy ideas in Scotland, and indeed, their deep dependency on thinking fashioned in London. The continuing saga of Creative Scotland offers an apt illustration, as will be illustrated below.

The Scottish Arts Council (SAC) was established in 1994 but has worked autonomously under a Royal Charter since 1967. A Non-Departmental Public Body (NDPB) operating at 'arm's length' from government, it has long been formally accountable to Scottish ministers whether, as originally, under the Scottish Office or, as now, under the Scottish government and Scottish Parliament. Scottish Screen was set up in 1997 as a company limited by guarantee to operate as the national development body for the screen industries. Also an NDPB, it reports directly to Scottish ministers. On present government plans, these two agencies are to disappear in 2010. The SNP has inherited a key plank of Labour–Lib Dem creative industries policy. This involves setting up a new public body, Creative Scotland, intended to provide strategic leadership in the 'creative economy'. The complexities engendered by this reform are my second main theme.

Each case, it is apparent, stands in a distinct relation to the Scottish and UK political systems. One traverses the devolved/reserved powers distinction, raising questions about its renegotiation. The other sits wholly within the devolved order. Taken together, they neatly demonstrate Scotland's asymmetrical institutional framework and policy capacity across the interlinked fields of broadcasting and culture.

WHY BROADCASTING MATTERS TO SCOTLAND

Television broadcasting is of prime importance to the competitive functioning of the creative economy north of the border. Glasgow is a long-established broadcasting production centre in the 'nations and regions' of the UK. It is Scotland's audiovisual media capital: Pacific Quay is home to BBC Scotland and the Channel 3 incumbent, STV, and Channel 4 also has a small presence in the city. Glasgow is the base for key independent television producers.

Given the centrality of media to the culture, economy and polity, the recent precipitous decline in the volume and value of indigenous television production has become an increasingly hot political issue. Public service broadcasting (PSB) channels have obligations to spend varying proportions of their programme-making budgets outside London. Part of this 'quota' is commissioned in Scotland and crucial to sustaining the country's production capacity. In May 2007, Ofcom's report on the communications market in Scotland showed that the country's share of UK network production had fallen from 6% in 2004 to a mere 3% in 2006 (Ofcom 2007a: 83, fig. 29). The fall provoked debate about Scotland's 'deficit', namely the gap between the country's share of the UK population (and consequent contribution to the BBC licence fee) and its share of UK network production.

The BBC's target for network production from the three devolved nations is 17%. Channel 4 is obliged to commission 30% of its programmes from outside the M25 area. Ofcom requires ITV to source 8% of its programmes from the nations, whereas Five has a 10% obligation to seek out-of-London commissions. In 2006 and 2007, and this was 'a matter of concern' to the regulator, *total* Scottish production was under 3% by value and under 2% by volume of UK network production (Ofcom 2008b: 45).

The bad news for Scottish broadcasters and producers in 2007 coincided with the election of the Nationalist government. Prior to taking office, the SNP had challenged the broadcasting status quo. The party's 2007 election manifesto called for a 'dedicated news service and more quality programming made in Scotland'. The Nationalists said they would 'push for the devolution of broadcasting powers to the Scottish Parliament' and wanted the BBC 'to retain more of the licence fee raised in Scotland'

(SNP 2007). Aside from that, however, policy remained very sketchy. The reported fall in television production, therefore, was welcome new grist to the political mill and the First Minister's intervention gave a decided fillip to a desultory and intermittent debate.

In August 2007, Alex Salmond set up the Scottish Broadcasting Commission (SBC) under the chairmanship of Blair Jenkins, a former BBC Scotland and STV executive. The Commission's membership was carefully balanced to represent the main political parties, as well as having its requisite quota of the great and good. At the SBC's launch event, Salmond – in a conversation with this author – said that not only had he been influenced by Ofcom's report but had also taken serious note of the recently published Work Foundation (2007) study of the 'creative economy'. He had been impressed by the dynamism and growth potential of the sector. Reports by a UK regulator and a London-based think tank therefore played influentially into Scottish policy making.

The SBC went through a lengthy process of taking evidence on the economic, cultural and democratic aspects of broadcasting before finally reporting in September 2008. The First Minister's initiative undoubtedly rattled the cage. The Commission was taken seriously in London. It took evidence from all the leading players in British television, focused Ofcom's attention and secured an early assurance in September 2007 from the BBC's Director-General Mark Thompson, that the corporation would enable BBC Scotland to increase its network production figures substantially.

The SBC's final report, *Platform for Success*, was wide ranging. Here, we shall note two crucial recommendations. First, and least surprising given the driving economic interest behind it, that there should be a major increase in 'the value and volume of production for the UK television networks' (Scottish Broadcasting Commission 2008: 8). This was linked to securing a shift of commissioning power from London (by moving a national channel to Glasgow). The SBC also emphasised the need for a quota to ensure that programme supply continue to be UK wide. The BBC was asked to ensure that 8.6% of network production would come from Scotland by the end of 2012, a similar commitment also being requested from Channel 4, given its PSB status.

The second key recommendation was much more challenging: the creation of a new Scottish network, a digital public service television channel and an extensive and innovative online platform. The network should be funded out of the new UK settlement for PSB plurality and should be licensed and given full regulatory support by Ofcom (Scottish Broadcasting Commission 2008: 5). The Commission estimated that the new venture would cost between £50 million and £75 million and proposed that the Scottish Network 'should include a commitment to high-quality information and entertainment, including news and current affairs covering Scottish and international issues, and innovative and ambitious cultural content' (ibid.).

The SBC's report received unanimous support in the Scottish Parliament on 8 October 2008. Of the two key policy recommendations, the upscaling of production by BBC Scotland is presently in train. The BBC's decision to increase output will have the largest single immediate impact on the broadcast economy north of the border. The corporation has forecast a rise in network income to between 5% and 6% in 2009, identified a number of programme strands for transfer to Scotland and initiated a modest shift in commissioning power (in daytime, entertainment and factual) to Pacific Quay.

However, it remains an open question whether the far-reaching proposal to set up a Scottish digital network will be funded. The decision rests with the UK government. If funding is refused, financial stringencies during the present economic crisis will be the prime reason cited, although some will suspect that political motives lie just beneath the surface. To understand this better we need to consider the wider context.

TURMOIL IN BRITISH TELEVISION

The SBC's recommendation came at a time of great volatility in television. In April 2008 Ofcom, reflecting the fact that the UK terrestrial broadcasting system was in crisis, set out several 'models' for the future. Taking devolution into account, these were adjusted to reflect the specific realities of the 'nations', Scotland, Wales and Northern Ireland (Ofcom 2008a). Which model might be secured north of the border?

In a worsening economic climate, the regulator has sought to ensure 'plurality' in television defined as 'based on a limited number of TV channels' (Ofcom 2007b: 5). Crucial to the idea of plurality is a diverse supply of news. The trigger for Ofcom's PSB inquiry in 2008 was the financial crisis faced by all the terrestrial broadcasters – ITV, Channel 4, Five – apart from the BBC, whose foreseeable income will come from the licence fee. The issue has risen up the agenda of the UK government, as is evident from its interim *Digital Britain* report (BERR 2009: 45–50). In a response to *Digital Britain*, the Scottish government welcomed 'the clear recognition of the need to secure adequate provision of public service broadcasting content for Scotland – something that we think is best achieved through the establishment of a new digital network for Scotland' (Scottish Government 2009: 1).

Scotland still has a plurality of supply in public service broadcasting. First, Scottish viewers can access the range of programming offered on the platforms commonly available to other UK viewers. Second, there are distinctive sources of supply in Scotland.

The only nation-wide broadcaster, BBC Scotland, produces and distributes its own television, radio and online services. The BBC's major investment north of the border has been the £188 million spent on BBC Scotland's state-of-the-art digital HQ at Pacific Quay, opened in September 2007. The BBC has given a commitment to produce 8.6% of its output in Scotland by the end of the current Charter (in 2016). As noted, it may achieve this goal in advance of that date.

STV group plc is the Scottish commercial PSB. It holds the Central Scotland and North East Scotland franchises, covering most of the national territory. In March 2007, after an extremely volatile period, a new management team opted to consolidate the STV brand and concentrate on television production. Although STV is a broadcaster, it would like its production division to be classified as an independent producer to compete for the 25% of commissions available to 'indies'. It has played adeptly on its incumbent status and brand recognition in Scotland to argue for a public subsidy for its news service, offering this as a solution to the question of plurality.

ITV Border serves a small segment of the Scottish audience in the South of Scotland but its news operation is based in ITV Tyne Tees. The downgrading of local news coverage has been a sore point with viewers north of the border and it is likely that they will be brought into a pan-Scottish commercial broadcasting framework when present Channel 3 licences are reviewed.

The latest addition to the scene is the Gaelic digital television channel. Badged as BBC Alba, it is run in partnership by BBC Scotland and the Gaelic media service, MG Alba. The channel received the go-ahead in January 2008 after much delay and began broadcasting in November that year. The BBC Trust's reservations over the service's 'public value' kept it off Freeview. It is an open question whether such access will be afforded soon. Presently, BBC Alba is distributed on cable, satellite and broadband. Its impact both on the 60,000 strong Gaelic language community and the wider Scottish public will be reviewed by 2010.

Future policy will play out in this landscape. BBC Scotland will remain the linchpin of the broadcasting economy. It remains to be seen whether the Scottish digital network will become its PSB competitor. Reshaped relations between traditional media and the internet and new uses of spectrum may open innovative possibilities. In 2011, Scotland will face increased UK-wide competition in out-of-London production from BBC North – and the developing cluster of media companies – located at Media City UK in Salford Quays, Greater Manchester.

DEVOLUTION AND THE POLITICS OF BROADCASTING

The demand for 'broadcasting devolution' has been deeply entangled with control over the news agenda in Scotland (Schlesinger et al. 2001: Ch. 2). A hugely symbolic row in 1998 concerned the so-called 'Scottish Six': should BBC Scotland be allowed to broadcast its own 6–7pm hour of news and current affairs on BBC1? This would have entailed an opt-out from London's network news to follow Glasgow's own agenda, just like BBC Radio Scotland. John Birt, the BBC's Director-General, Prime Minister Tony Blair, and senior Cabinet ministers found this possibility likely to encourage separatism. Such attitudes evidently persist in the Brown government. The BBC Executive decided against launching a 'Scottish Six' and the debate over news never fully subsided.

Alex Salmond (2007: 1) invoked the 'Scottish Six' when arguing for 'the devolution of powers to the Scottish Parliament . . . to ensure the principle of editorial and creative control being exercised in Scotland on behalf of Scottish audiences'. Earlier, in 2005, the Cultural Commission, set up by Labour First Minister Jack McConnell to address questions of cultural policy, asked Scottish ministers to introduce 'an element of devolution of broadcasting' and to recognise 'a strong case for the establishment of at least one channel based in Scotland', which might become Holyrood's responsibility (Cultural Commission 2005, Annex G: 5). The Labour–Lib Dem government gave this challenge to the constitutional status short shrift (Scottish Executive 2006a: 43). Subsequently, the SBC (2008: 53) while not advocating broadcasting devolution, has recommended 'an active role for the Scottish Parliament'. The Calman Commission on Scottish Devolution, noting the debate over broadcasting devolution, presented a detailed report on reforming devolution and the union (Commission on Scottish Devolution 2008: par. 5.30; Commission on Scottish Devolution 2009: pars 5.63–5.70). Broadcasting devolution will be debated as part of the Scottish government's National Conversation (Scottish Government 2007: par. 2.44), the preamble to a proposed referendum on independence.

Devolved broadcasting opens up a range of institutional and regulatory issues, still to be aired. How would parliamentary control over broadcasting operate? Which models would be drawn on? How might devolved control relate to UK regulation? What powers might be sought to raise and spend the present BBC licence fee (or a proportion of it) in Scotland?

CREATIVE SCOTLAND'S BUMPY RIDE

In its current *Digital Britain* review, the UK government has character-ised broadcasting as part of the 'digital economy'. But since 1998, the Department for Culture, Media and Sport (DCMS) has designated broad-casting (and film) as creative industries, as at the core of the 'creative economy'. This terminology, rooted in neo-liberal assumptions about indi-vidual talent, entrepreneurship and intellectual property, has exercised a profound influence north of the border, irrespective of the government in power. In fact, the UK's creativity agenda has informed the rationale and scope of Creative Scotland, the new agency to be launched in 2010.

A Draft Culture (Scotland) Bill to set up the new agency was first pub-lished on 14 December 2006 by the Labour–Liberal coalition (Scottish Executive 2006b). A joint board, comprising members of both the Scottish Arts Council and Scottish Screen boards, was set up under the chairmanship of the theologian Richard Holloway. However, no Culture Act was passed before the parliamentary elections of May 2007. Then the coalition fell and the SNP formed the new Scottish government. Once in power, Linda Fabiani, the Minister for Europe, External Affairs and Culture (based in the First Minister's office), adopted the establishment of Creative Scotland as an objective.

In November 2007, the Creative Scotland joint board appointed the arts consultant Anne Bonnar as 'transition director', to lead a 'fast-track' process, with a new CEO and board to be appointed by April 2009. To outsiders, the situation looked increasingly confusing. Who was in charge? The transition director worked alongside the CEO of Scottish Screen, Ken Hay, and the acting CEO of the SAC, Jim Tough, each of whom had a body to run but over whose heads an organisational sword of Damocles was now suspended.

In March 2008, the Scottish government launched the Creative Scotland Bill (Scottish Parliament 2008). After scrutiny, this was defeated in the Scottish Parliament on 18 June 2008. MSPs rejected the bill's financial memorandum. There were also uncertainties in the culture min-ister's account of whether or not funds would be transferred from Scottish Enterprise to the new body. Under Holyrood rules no new bill could be introduced for six months. To try to break the logjam, in September 2008 the Scottish government announced the setting up of a limited company, Creative Scotland 2009 Ltd, chaired by the financier Ewan Brown, to advance the evidently stalled 'transition' process. The aim was still to have a new CEO and board in place by April 2009, with a statutory body established by February 2010. Meantime, during the autumn and winter of

2008, Anne Bonnar's transition project attracted increasing criticism from artists, opposition politicians and the press for failing to deliver value for money and a clear vision (McCracken 2008; Macaskill 2008).

Linda Fabiani was sacked in a reshuffle in February 2009. Her last act was to produce a so-called 'core script' (Scottish Government 2009). Based on the DCMS's 1998 definition of the creative industries, this set out the 'roles and responsibilities' of the Scottish government and various 'delivery agencies' (Creative Scotland, the Enterprise agencies, local authorities, the Business Gateway), all of which were to offer a 'genuine joined up approach'. The blueprint drew on a report produced the previous May for the minister by an ad hoc Creative Industries Working Group (2008) whose conceptual framework came from the DCMS and the innovation body and think tank, NESTA. By insisting on the 'joined-upness' of the effort required, both documents testified to the difficulties encountered by the minister in aligning Scottish Enterprise with the 'creativity' agenda and also the failure to prise money away from that body to boost Creative Scotland's coffers.

THE ENDGAME?

Mike Russell, titled Minister for Culture, External Affairs and the Constitution, replaced Linda Fabiani on 10 February 2009. He rapidly sought to disarm the critics. In a speech in Edinburgh to invited members of the arts community delivered on 18 February 2009, Russell said the new organisation would be central to sustainable economic growth, falling in line with the Scottish government's principal objectives. He asked the cultural community for partnership, dialogue and debate and underlined the crucial importance of artists' support for government policies.

Russell followed up this appeal with an upbeat speech at another conference in Edinburgh organised by *Holyrood* magazine on 28 April 2009. The debate was now in its 'endgame', he stated. The minister affirmed Creative Scotland's role in leading arts strategy. It would need to 'discover the creative reconciliation of the entrepreneurial and the cultural'. Clearly recognising that creative industries policy to date has subordinated culture to the economy, Russell sought to sidestep this line of criticism by arguing that both culture and the economy were important and should be seen as on a 'continuum or spectrum' rather than as in contradiction. It is doubtful that the inherent tensions between economic and cultural purposes and values can simply be wished away. It remains to be seen how the Scottish government's key objective of sustainable growth – to which the creative industries are meant to contribute – will play out against the stated desire to put artists 'at the heart of our cultural policy', in Russell's words.

In a further shift of the timetable, at the same Edinburgh conference, the chairman of Creative Scotland 2009 Ltd, Ewan Brown, announced that a new transition director, Richard Smith, had been appointed and that a new CEO and board would be in place by March 2010, although – he acknowledged – by then Creative Scotland would still not be in 'final form'. These aspirations depend on the successful passage through the Scottish Parliament of the Public Services Reform Bill 2008, the legislative means by which to establish Creative Scotland.

The new body is the unloved child of two ill-matched parents: bureaucracy and intellectual dependency. Creative Scotland originated in the so-called bonfire of the quangos, back in 2003, when the then culture minister, Mike Watson, proposed one cultural agency to replace two. This *idée fixe* has been in the bureaucratic bloodstream of the Scottish Executive ever since and never seriously questioned. Why *Creative Scotland*? Creativity was then in the air as it is now, and similarly propounded as a key strand of economic development. Scottish Labour imported New Labour policy and terminology, without altering a comma or full stop. The paternity suit, therefore, needs to be filed against the coalition Scottish Executive.

But now the mother of this invention will be the present Scottish government. Why did the Nationalists not think again? Like the Labour–Lib Dem coalition, the Nationalist cabinet has taken up and adopted policy made in London. The opening lines of Linda Fabiani's 'core script' for Creative Scotland reiterate word-for-word New Labour's conception of creative industries, 1998 style – not even the reframed creative economy thinking developed by the Work Foundation (2007). The neo-liberal assumptions embedded in the New Labour project live on in the SNP's proposed cultural lead body, just as they have been challenged by our profound financial and economic crisis.

CONCLUSIONS

In broadcasting, where it has least formal room for manoeuvre, the SNP in government has made some significant running. Even before the SBC reported, its very creation changed the climate for demanding that increased television production be located in Scotland; this intervention has produced a positive response from the BBC. So far as a new digital network is concerned, the Nationalists have underlined their commitment to the SBC's idea both for creative economy and cultural policy reasons. At this time of writing, it seems likely that the UK government will argue that there are other more pressing priorities, as UK television faces its deepest crisis ever. In the swirl of rumour and non-attribution surrounding broadcasting policy, it appears that the Scottish government does not expect to win the case, although it will continue to press for the new network to be set up and make a political issue of any outright refusal. For its part, the Labour government appears to be reluctant to yield any control over broadcasting developments in Scotland.

Meanwhile, in cultural policy, where the Scottish government has most scope for autonomous action, it has – astonishingly – boxed itself in with the Creative Scotland legacy. Since the start of 2009 – after a long period of confusion – the process has acquired more clarity and purpose although, according to the minister, a financial standstill for public funding of the arts and creative industries is the most optimistic scenario on offer.

Much now hangs on whether a workable structure emerges from Creative Scotland's long and unsettling gestation period. Its architects face some major challenges. First, to establish credible leadership for Creative Scotland in the line-up of partnerships now decreed. Second, to handle convincingly the competing funding priorities (and value systems) of the arts and the creative industries. Third, to demonstrate to the public that some real advantages derive from this new model.

ACKNOWLEDGEMENT

I have drawn on research conducted for an AHRC-funded project on 'Creativity: Policy and Practice', ID No: 112152. Although I presently chair Ofcom's Advisory Committee for Scotland, this chapter is written purely in a professional and personal capacity.

REFERENCES

BERR (2009), *Digital Britain Interim Report*, http://www.culture.gov.uk/images/publications/digital_britain_interimreportjan09.pdf

Creative Industries Working Group (2008), *Public Support for Creative Industries: Report to the Scottish Government Minister for Europe, External Affairs and Culture*, Creative Scotland Transition Project, May 2008.

Commission on Scottish Devolution (2008), *The Future of Scottish Devolution within the Union: A First Report*, http://www.commissiononscottishdevolution.org.uk/uploads/2008-12-01-vol-1-final--bm.pdf

Commission on Scottish Devolution (2009), *Serving Scotland Better: Scotland and the United Kingdom in the 21st Century*, http:// www.commissiononscottishdevolution.org.uk/

Cultural Commission (2005), *Final Report of the Cultural Commission*, June 2005, Edinburgh, Scottish Executive.

Dept for Culture, Media and Sport (2008), *Creative Britain: New Talents for the New Economy*, London, DCMS.

Heartfield, J. (2008), 'Creativity as ideology', *Renewal*, 16(2), pp. 28–34.

Macaskill, M. (2008), 'Arts body spends £120,000 on three page document', *Sunday Times*, 16 November, p. 7.

McCracken, E. (2008), 'Frustration leads to alliance for arts groups', *Sunday Herald*, 7 December, p. 21.

Mulholland, N. (2008), 'The Cultural Economy', *Renewal*, 16(2), pp. 35–44.

Ofcom (2007a), *The Communications Market Report: Nations and Regions*, London, Ofcom.

Ofcom (2007b), *New News, Future News: The Challenges for Television News after Digital Switchover: A Discussion Document*, London, Ofcom.

Ofcom (2008a), *Ofcom's Second Public Service Broadcasting Review, Phase One: The Digital Opportunity*, London, Ofcom.

Ofcom (2008b), *The Communications Market Report: Nations and Regions Scotland*, London, Ofcom.

Salmond, A. (2007), 'The Case for Devolution of Broadcasting Powers', National Museum of Scotland, Edinburgh, 8 August, http://www.scotland,gov.uk/News/This-Week/Speeches/broadcasting

Schlesinger, P. (2007), 'Creativity: from discourse to doctrine?', *Screen*, 48(3), pp. 413–26.

Schlesinger, P. (2009), 'Creativity and the experts: New Labour, think tanks and the policy process', *International Journal of Press/Politics*, 14 (3), pp. 3–20.

Schlesinger, P., Miller, D. and Dinan, W. (2001), *Open Scotland? Journalists, Spin Doctors and Lobbyists*, Edinburgh, Polygon.

Scottish Broadcasting Commission (2008), *Platform for Success: Final Report of the Scottish Broadcasting Commission*, Edinburgh, Scottish Government.

Scottish Executive (2006a), *Scotland's Culture*, Edinburgh, Scottish Executive.

Scottish Executive (2006b), *Draft Culture (Scotland) Bill Consultation Document*, Edinburgh, Scottish Executive Education Department.

Scottish Executive (2007), *Choosing Scotland's Future: A National Conversation*, Edinburgh, Scottish Executive.

Scottish Government (2009), 'Support for Creative Industries: Roles and Responsibilities' – Core Script, 5 February, http://www.scotland.gov.uk/Resource/Doc/244097/0077349.pdf

Scottish Parliament (2008), Creative Scotland Bill, www.scottish.parliament.uk/s3/bills/07-CreativeScotland/b7s3-introd.pdf

SNP (2007), 'Supporting Culture and Creativity', www.snp.org/policies

The Work Foundation (2007), *Staying Ahead: The Economic Performance of the UK's Creative Industries*, London, The Work Foundation.

CHAPTER 12

The Auld Enemies:
Scottish Nationalism and Scottish Labour

Gerry Hassan

Some might wonder why he as a perfervid Scot was not also a perfervid Nationalist. The reason was that the nationalism which he saw expressed in Scotland at present was not real nationalism: it was petty and parochial, and, he was sorry to say it, had signs of a kind of latent hatred. It had a sort of chip-on-the-shoulder hatred that could create very considerable trouble if it were not recognised as such and opposed. (Willie Ross, 1968[1])

The key argument is that if we remove all Scottish political control and influence over what all accept is a single economic entity in the United Kingdom, then we are left inevitably to be controlled by that total economy. Consequently, we would have less say than we have now over our own fate. Paradoxically, total separatism means less independence. (Norman Buchan, 1971[2])

The one country the Labour left can help liberate, by direct action, and without diplomatic, political or trading inhibitions is Scotland. (Jim Sillars, 1986[3])

Scottish Nationalism and Scottish Labour have had a long, tempestuous and difficult relationship, characterised by differences and disagreements over philosophy and party competition.

The party story is a complex and nuanced one, influenced by a range of factors from the role of ideology to party identity and positioning, competition and relationship to the external environment. This chapter will focus on the Labour–SNP dynamic, examining the way each has tried to negatively define the other, use case studies to explore attitudes, and offer some tentative conclusions on what this tells us about the two parties and their inter-relationship.

There is subtlety and evolution around this subject. Some Labour politicians who are anti-Nationalist were once members of the SNP, while some SNP politicians were once in Labour. Several of Labour's anti-Nationalists politically over the last few decades have been cultural nationalists, Norman Buchan and Brian Wilson being two examples. Buchan was a leading light in the 'folk music movement' of the 1950s and

1960s with people such as Hamish Henderson, and celebrated Scotland's cultural life and nationhood, but saw Scottish Nationalism's fixation on statehood as its 'Ark of the Covenant' (Buchan 1971: 87).

THE POWER OF THE 'TARTAN TORY' BOGEYMAN

Labour dislike of the SNP has seen the party develop a lexicon of phrases. Most originated or were given added impetus by Harold Wilson's Secretary of State for Scotland (1964–70 and 1974–6), Willie Ross: 'narks'; 'phoney party'; 'SNP: Still No Policies'; and the most effective of all, 'tartan Tories'.

Where did 'tartan Tories' originate? Fascinatingly, for such a powerful phrase with such a rich lineage, this is never examined in the literature. The phrase took on its modern meaning in the 1967–8 period as Labour faced an unprecedented challenge from the SNP. In the immediate aftermath of the SNP's sensational victory in the Hamilton by-election in November 1967, Labour reacted in a number of different ways. Politicians such as J. P. Mackintosh and Richard Crossman wanted to understand the alienation people felt from the political system. Willie Ross and most of the Scottish Labour establishment had a very different take: furious at the sheer impertinence of the SNP in daring to encroach onto Labour's territory.

At the March 1968 Scottish Labour conference, according to Harvie and Jones, Ross laid into the SNP and 'fulminated against the "tartan Tory" Nationalists' (2000: 89). Will Marshall, Secretary of Scottish Labour, showed a revealing mixture of pique and being out of touch, complaining that the Scottish National Party 'created interest among young people by hammering away at nothing else but idealism' (*The Herald*, 23 March 1968). Robin King, of Labour Students, believed that the solution to Scottish concerns could only be found at a British level, not by entrenching Scotland behind a border 'which is there only because it was the easiest position to defend for a 14th century Tory king' (*The Scotsman*, 25 March 1968).

Both Wilson and Ross launched into detailed accounts of the government's achievements – with Ross itemising increased public spending and new factories brought to Scotland. This caused even the usually reserved *Scotsman* to reflect: 'Mr. Ross's harangue was, equally, as unappetising as a plateful of vitamin pills and protein tablets set down to a starving man – designed to sustain, but hardly to make the mouth water' (25 March 1968).

At the subsequent STUC, pro-devolution and anti-devolution motions were debated and remitted, with Willie Ross warning delegates not to become 'the Scottish Trades Union Congrouse' or to take refuge 'in the quicksands of nationalism' (STUC 1968: 415).

Labour's 1968 UK conference saw a rare debate, with an air of bewilder-ment, about the advance of Scottish and Welsh nationalism. Tom Clarke, later to be a Labour MP, argued that the Scottish people should be clearly told 'the facts' of what Labour had achieved to stop the SNP 'bandwagon' and asked: 'Are we to agree that the Scottish National Party which has offered no real policy, no real alternative beyond perhaps Scottish police-men wearing kilts, be accepted into an aura of respectability by the British Labour Party?' (Labour Party 1968: 181). James Hamilton stated that if the party had an 'implicit faith in the Scottish people, they will once again rally back to the Labour Party' (Labour Party 1968: 178).

'Tartan Tory' found its modern meaning at a time when Labour was struggling to find a credible and relevant message in response to the SNP's attack. The first recorded use of the term in the Commons was by William Small, Labour MP for Glasgow Scotstoun, in June 1966 in a debate on Selective Employment Tax, towards the Scots Tory MP Fitzroy Maclean (Hansard 1966). It quickly came to have an association with the Nationalists alone and in a November 1969 adjournment debate Winnie Ewing was continually put down and ridiculed by a range of insults includ-ing 'tartan Tory'. Willie Hamilton interrupted and shouted at Ewing, 'The Hon. Lady is a tartan Tory. She voted for the Tories', to be followed by Archie Manuel stating, 'The Hon. Lady is a Tory in disguise'. Manuel followed up by calling Ewing 'a parasite', while Hamilton intervened to comment, 'The Hon. Lady should be on the London Palladium' (Hansard 1969). Ewing had clearly ruffled feathers and revealed an unattractive, bullying side of Scottish Labour (Ewing 2004: 71–2).

This was uncomfortable for Ewing, but Labour knew something was changing. Labour was still wedded to a centralist philosophy and the party saw Scottish Nationalism as anti-Labour, hostile to progress, reactionary and helpful to the Tories. Some of these attitudes went back to the Attlee government when the Tories railed against 'London centralisation' and there was co-operation between home rule supporters and the Tories which saw Arthur Woodburn, Secretary of State for Scotland from 1947 to 1950, call the pro-home rule Convention a 'Tory plot' (Knox 1984: 288). This crystallised in the 1948 Paisley by-election where home rule campaigner John MacCormick stood as a 'National' candidate with Tory and Liberal support.

Paisley gave Labour an excuse to see home rule as an anti-Labour cause and also legitimise its own tribal ethos of everyone else ganging up on them. This anti-home rule sentiment increased in the 1950s and early 1960s and was the Labour position when returned to office in 1964. When the SNP polled significantly in the Glasgow Pollok 1967 by-election, aiding the Tories to gain the seat from Labour, this only added to Labour dislike of the Scottish Nationalists.

This continued in the SNP surge of the 1970s with the party's gains in the February and October 1974 elections – eight seats from the Conservatives and two from Labour – contributing to the image of the 'tartan Tories'. It became a widespread assumption outside the party that the SNP vote in these seats came from the Tories and that its strength in rural Scotland and absence in most of urban Scotland made it a party of the centre-right. The SNP itself debated the nature of its support, with some in the party seeing itself as 'centrist', while others saw themselves as the inheritors of the anti-Conservative vote in rural Scotland.

'Tartan Tory' was the phrase which had the most power and resonance from the 1960s onward. It gained momentum through a number of factors: the creeping anti-Toryism of Scotland, the increased use of the term 'Tory' in politics and popular culture as an insult, and the fall of the 1979 Labour government and the role of the SNP in this (examined later in this chapter). 'Tartan Tory' conveyed invective in both words, of an out-of-date, musky, sentimental, pre- or anti-modern Scotland in an age long before 'tartan' was reinvented and reimagined.

It is no mere coincidence that 'tartan Tory' arose not only in the period where the SNP appeared as an electoral force, but also when the Scottish Conservatives began to decline and disappear as a serious threat to Labour. It was easier for Labour, having defeated one opponent which was 'Tory', to pin the same label to the new upstart. Tam Dalyell wrote of Willie Ross:

> For a quarter of a century he was the 'hammer of the Nats' – though in retrospect it is clear that some of the epithets which flowed from his biting tongue, such as 'Tartan Tories', were counter-productive in terms of Scottish support for the Labour Party. (Dalyell 1977: 74)

'Tartan Tory' served Labour as an assault phrase as it struggled to come to terms with the SNP, something it has never fully managed. Once the SNP politicians began to establish themselves as a permanent feature on the Scottish political scene, the phrase began to lose its sting, but Labour has never found a better one, and nor has it really managed to accept the Nationalists, thus, finding itself in the worst of both worlds.

THE 'LONDON LABOUR' ESTABLISHMENT

What has the SNP had, to challenge the 'tartan Tory' attack? There has been a range of approaches, such as emphasising the decency and integrity of the grassroots Labour Party as compared to the out-of-touch, selling-Scotland-short, parliamentary party. A host of phrases emerged over the years, talking of Labour as 'London Labour' and 'British Labour', denying the existence of a separate Scottish Labour Party, seeing it as a branch-line operation, and talking of the 'English' or 'unionist parties'.

SNP attacks on Labour had to have a certain deftness of touch, given it was the largest party in Scotland. An over-general attack on Scottish Labour could be seen as an attack on thousands of Scots men and women, and thus hundreds of thousands of Labour voters. Winnie Ewing's election in 1967 shocked the Labour establishment, but there is evidence that her attacks on Labour post-Hamilton were counter-productive. Jim Sillars reflects in *Scotland: The Case for Optimism* on hearing Ewing speak in Ayr after the by-election:

> We bristled, as she listed our 'crimes' against the Scottish people and as she sneered at our efforts over generations. It was an ignorant attack against men and women we knew to have fought a great struggle against Toryism and who had broken the landed gentry's grip upon the working people. (Sillars 1986: 24)

Looking back 20 years later, Sillars commented that the SNP had still to learn that certain kinds of attack on Labour could be 'counter-productive':

> Generalised attacks upon the Labour Party when the target should be the Parliamentary Labour Party (by far the least popular element and the most open to indictment) can too easily be taken as denigration of the whole Labour movement and its history. (1986: 25–6)

For decades the SNP has had to navigate this difficult balancing act, damning the representatives of Labour while not dismissing the grassroots or wider values of 'the movement'. The Nationalists were given more room for manoeuvre by the arrival of New Labour, whom the SNP could criticise as a denigration of everything about Labour, and by the wider social trends under Margaret Thatcher and Tony Blair which have under-mined the basis and strength of the 'Labour movement'.

In the world of New Labour post-1997, with Blair et al.'s focus on 'Middle England', floating voters and Westminster, the phrase 'London Labour' began to carry more weight. In the 1999 Scottish Parliament elections the SNP used as one of their central themes, 'London Labour or Scotland's Party: It's Your Choice on May 6th' (SNP 1999). This identi-fied Scottish Labour as being fixated on and subservient to the needs of the British political system. It carried with it a popular signalling of where power lay in the UK and Labour, and the marginalisation of Scottish Labour in this.

There was an element of subtlety in this in the way Sillars had identified all those years ago. By explicitly creating a 'London Labour' entity which the SNP saw it as its role to challenge, it left the mass of Scottish Labour members and voters acknowledging that they were different and thus open to persuasion to coming over to the SNP side.

While 'London Labour' had some success in making Scottish Labour Westminster politicians such as Gordon Brown and Douglas Alexander uneasy, it could not fully deal with the popular sense that voters saw 'Scottish Labour' as an entity and different from 'British Labour', as repeated survey evidence from the Scottish Election Survey has shown (Paterson et al. 2001: 58–9). 'London Labour' was a little too much of a broad-brush attack to be as effective as the SNP hoped. While it captured some Scots anxieties about the direction of Blair's New Labour, it palpably weakened with the arrival of Gordon Brown as Prime Minister (despite his role as co-author of New Labour). It seems likely that this will become a much-diluted phrase in the future, with the possible election of a UK Conservative government.

THE FALL OF THE 1979 LABOUR GOVERNMENT

One of the most significant periods of politics – which gave impetus to the Labour–SNP conflict, Labour's charge of the SNP being 'tartan Tories' and the SNP's distrust in Labour believing in and delivering devolution – was the period of the 1974–9 Labour government. From November 1976 to May 1979 Labour governed without a Commons majority and the SNP's eleven MPs were crucial across a range of votes as well as high profile. No vote, though, was as crucial and controversial than the one which brought down the Labour government on 28 March 1979 and led to the election of Margaret Thatcher.

The Labour government fell in a vote of no confidence by one vote after the 1979 devolution referendum. To understand why this happened it is crucial to appreciate the background. First, in December 1976, the government announced that the creation of Scottish and Welsh Assemblies would be subject to referendums despite no such pledge being in Labour's October 1974 manifesto. Then, on 25 January 1978, the 40% rule was proposed by George Cunningham, Labour MP for Islington North with Tory support and that of five Scottish Labour MPs: Robin Cook, Tam Dalyell, Bob Hughes, William Hamilton and Peter Doig (Wood 1989: 116). The first was motivated by using the referendum device to paper over Labour divisions as the party had done with the European referendum, while the 40% rule can only be seen as a wrecking amendment from Labour anti-devolutionists. Neither proposal strengthened the Scottish and Welsh legislation.

Moreover, the timing of the Scottish and Welsh referendums at the fag end of an unpopular Labour government shaped the debate and outcome.

There was a high degree of Labour disunity and lack of enthusiasm for devolution, and this was magnified by 'the winter of discontent', which hit Labour's poll ratings across the UK and in Scotland.

The Scots vote resulted in 52:48 support for a Scottish assembly, but it was way short of 40% of the electorate. Given the terms of the legislation, this left the government in the situation where, without a majority, it had either to table the Repeal Order of the Scotland Act or face a vote of no confidence. The former would bring the Liberals and Nationalists on board, but expose Labour divisions; the latter would unite Labour, but not win over the Liberals or Nationalists and therefore be lost. Jim Sillars attempted to build bridges between Labour and the SNP, despite having left Labour. The crucial issue was 'whether the Labour MPs from England and some from Wales would put the life of their government before their hatred for a Scottish Assembly'. He believed the Scottish Nationalists were 'unhinged' and large parts of Labour had a 'death wish', and recalls asking Neil Kinnock if he worried about his actions leading to the fall of his government – replying, 'So be it then' (Sillars 1986: 72).

The rest is history. The SNP moved a motion of no confidence in Labour, superseded by the Tory motion as the official opposition. In the debate on 28 March 1979 Labour lost by one vote, 311:310 with the 311 made up of 279 Conservatives, 13 Liberals, 11 SNP and 8 Ulster Unionists alongside two Irish abstentions. Yet Labour anger in 1979 and afterwards was directed towards the SNP. It became routine down the years to get an easy cheer at a Scottish Labour conference to talk of the SNP bringing down the last Labour government and attempt to saddle them with the entire responsibility for the Thatcher era. Little mention is made of the fact there were 32 non-Tory votes with the Tories in the division lobby. Little anger has down the years been directed the way of David Steel, whom Labour was happy to work with in the Constitutional Convention, or towards other Liberal MPs.

The SNP had consistently supported the Labour government in 1974–9 on devolution and proposals which were ill thought out and commanded little genuine enthusiasm. While the SNP gave consistent support, the same could not be said of Labour backbench MPs, many of whom (like Neil Kinnock and Robin Cook) subsequently rose to the top of their party. The no-confidence motion and its consequences have to be seen in the context of what happened in the 1974–9 parliament on devolution and other measures.

The dominant voices in Scottish Labour despised the Nationalists and this clouded Labour's judgement over devolution and the referendum. Helen Liddell's memorandum banning 'collaboration' with other parties in the

1979 vote is striking for the gut, instinctual prejudice it displayed. Labour, in her words, was 'the only party in Scotland which believes in devolution for its own sake'. She went on in triumphalist tones that 'the achievement of an Assembly for Scotland will be ours' and that since the main argument of the 'No' vote would be that devolution could lead to independence, therefore, 'to associate with the separatists would be to provide our opponents with a major propaganda weapon' (Macartney 1981: 17).

It was not surprising, with such force of dislike and venom, that the entire devolution experience of the 1970s ended in tears, particularly when combined with SNP ineptitude in those dark days of 1979. However, Labour chose to use the actions of the Nationalists to validate the feelings of animosity they had, and to deflect any responsibility for the state of affairs from themselves, maybe even in their own inner feelings. The events of 1979 could have turned out differently, but they happened because of the distrust and febrile nature of political relations at the end of the Labour government. For years, some on the Labour side could not let go of the ammunition they thought it gave them, while many on the SNP side were scared and would not trust Labour to deliver devolution.

THE SNP AND THE CONSTITUTIONAL CONVENTION

The idea of a Constitutional Convention began to emerge post-1979 as a way to map out how to bring together a pro-home rule consensus. The first significant politician to suggest such a route was Gordon Wilson, MP for Dundee East, who proposed the Government of Scotland (Scottish Convention) Bill in March 1980, which was later taken up by the SNP and Campaign for a Scottish Assembly (CSA).

Support for a Convention grew after 'the Doomsday Scenario' of the 1987 election, with the CSA commissioning a Constitutional Steering Group who produced 'A Claim of Right for Scotland'. This recommended the creation of a Scottish Constitutional Convention (CSA 1989). Pre-Govan, Labour were nervous about the idea of a Convention, but moved towards it under Donald Dewar's declaration to 'live a little dangerously' after an internal consultation had shown support for party involvement (McLean 2005: 112). When Jim Sillars won Govan from Labour in November 1988, the SNP's success seemed to go to its head and the party refused to join the Convention in January 1989. The outcome of these few months was that 'Labour had out-manoeuvred the SNP, recaptured the mantle of "Scotland's national party" lost only three months before, exploited divisions within the SNP and was able to present the Nationalists as sectarian to the public' (Mitchell 1996: 129).

There were many reasons why such a turnaround of events happened. The SNP had a number of reservations about the proposed Convention. It had come to be seen as a Labour-dominated body with the SNP having 8% representation, when post-Govan it was on 32% in the polls. The SNP had previously supported an 'elected' Convention which emphasised unambiguously the will of the Scots on sovereignty and power. There was the bigger concern of the SNP about whether a Convention would be able to freely debate Scotland's different constitutional options and have these put to the people in a referendum, and not be a vehicle for devolution, with the SNP yet again trapped into supporting Labour's proposals.

The SNP leadership justified its actions, talking of 'Labour's rigged Convention' (*The Scotsman*, 31 January 1989), while Margaret Ewing said staying outside was 'a demonstration of political astuteness' (*The Herald*, 6 March 1989). Chris McLean pointed to the Claim of Right's confused thinking on sovereignty: 'Either you are a nationalist and accept the sovereignty of the Scottish people, or you are a unionist and accept the sovereignty of the British people' (1989: 112).

These opinions touched on much deeper attitudes about the SNP's fear of co-operation and its own fragile sense of its own uniqueness, bordering on what some see as 'sectarianism' (Nairn 1989). The SNP felt it owned 'Scottish nationalism', hence McLean's use of 'nationalism' with a small 'n' and labelling all those who disagreed with it as 'unionists'. Post-1987, the party showed its suspicions of cross-party, civic Scotland by refusing to participate in the STUC Festival for Democracy and their 'Say No to the Poll Tax' campaign – a tendency that was present in the SNP pre-Govan.

The party's refusal to take part in the Constitutional Convention was a watershed in Scottish politics and seen by large parts of civic Scotland and cross-party groups as a body blow to building a home rule consensus. The SNP post-1979 saw the reality of 'civic Scotland' as a smokescreen disguising the brutal face of Labour domination and well-meaning people who were used by Labour. Large parts of the SNP could not recognise that Labour was changing on devolution and instead believed that 'what was on offer in 1989 was the same as in 1974', a complete misreading of the situation (Pittock 2008: 77).

LABOUR AND THE SNP: SIMILAR AND DIFFERENT

Both Labour and SNP claim to be social democratic parties. It is the received wisdom amongst commentators and observers to acknowledge the similarities between the two: that both are on the centre-left, appealing to the same voters and, less explored, that both are compromised by their embrace of neo-liberalism.

However, there is a profound difference between Labour and SNP, their *raisons d'être* and ethos. Labour's ethos sprang from what has been called a 'labourist culture' which saw the world in terms of 'haves' and 'have nots' (Marquand 1991), and which on occasion articulated itself as 'social democratic'. The SNP's ethos is first and foremost 'Scottish nationalist', and 'social democratic' only at a secondary level.

These differences matter, while allowing for similarities and overlap. Both parties are informed by a centre-left social democratic politics which, since the 1980s, has been characterised by the intertwining of this and the national question, but with each party starting from different places. They have similar geographies of support, with the transition of the SNP into a centre-left party going after Labour's Central Belt vote. This has produced an even more adversarial politics between Labour and SNP in by-elections and national contests.

There is also a significant similarity in some of the personnel in each party. In its breakthrough years many of the SNP's activists and prominent people came from Labour backgrounds. Winnie Ewing, for example, grew up reading *Forward!*, was steeped in the Independent Labour Party and was even related to Arthur Woodburn. This reinforced a Labour sense that such people were betraying the values of Labour and one thing the party has long detested is the idea of a 'traitor'.

Then there was the influence of 'the new left' and CND. This could be seen in the rising support for nuclear disarmament in Scotland after Harold Macmillan's agreement with President Eisenhower in 1960 to locate Polaris nuclear weapons in the Holy Loch. This became an effective mobilising issue for the Nationalists after Labour leader Hugh Gaitskell defeated the unilateral disarmers in 1961. It wove together a wide coalition of students, church campaigners and parts of the folk music movement. It also contributed to the form of the SNP's modern symbol: a combination of the St Andrew's Cross and thistle in a CND-like symbol, which originated in William Wolfe's West Lothian party (Wolfe 1973: 46–7).

The cause of nuclear disarmament brought the politics of direct action and peace camps to Scotland and served to underline to many how unradical Labour was despite its protestations. Some senior Labour politicians had in their younger selves been attracted to the SNP over the issue, including some who in later life became very right wing; George Robertson is one example. Others who have followed the rightward march of Labour under Blair and Brown sit uncomfortably defending weapons of mass destruction and the post-Trident military escalation on account of the local jobs provided, and they despise the SNP for reminding them of what they or their Labour colleagues said in days when CND membership was *de rigueur* in Labour.

Many of the SNP's activists post-1979 were the sorts of people who in previous times would have automatically joined Labour as the main anti-Tory force in the country. Politicians such as Roseanna Cunningham, Nicola Sturgeon and Kenny MacAskill were the kind of talents who would have easily made it in any party and certainly in Scottish Labour. Instead, they were repulsed by the political establishment that Labour in Scotland had become, and found in the SNP a vehicle to nurture a very different politics.

Post-devolution Labour's lack of understanding of the Nationalist cause has not gone away. It reached its apotheosis under Wendy Alexander's short-lived and ill-fated leadership where she appeared to be fixated with what she saw as the SNP's obsession with the constitution. Alexander's speech to the 2008 Scottish Labour conference saw her attempt to draw a set of defining lines between the two parties:

> Scotland is a country I love to the core of my being. However 'Scotland' is not a political philosophy. 'Scotland' can just as easily be Adam Smith as it can be John Smith. The world over, politics comes down to a choice: right versus left, conservatives versus progressives, nationalists versus internationalists. (Alexander 2008)

'Red Wendy' did not seem very plausible, given her role in the New Labour project, but what it showed was the tribal power by which Labour thought it could still claim issues as its own and define itself and the SNP: 'Cutting poverty against cutting taxes. Rewarding hard work versus unearned wealth. Socialist versus Nationalist' (ibid.). Scottish politics had moved on, and Labour's attempts to brand the SNP as 'right wing' fell on deaf ears, no matter how the *Daily Record* used the speech to drag up 'the Tartan Tories' taunt (28 March 2008).

The Nationalists have at a leadership level developed a more thought-through and balanced approach which is more adept at challenging political opponents while accepting their legitimacy. Labour, across a swathe of opinion, often seem to have the propensity to see the Nationalists as an illegitimate force in Scottish politics, a group which has somehow confused the natural order and usurped Labour's divine right to rule.

The contest between Labour and SNP in the first Scottish Parliament election saw Labour frame it as a 'battle between social justice and separatism' (Brown and Alexander 1997: 46). Labour presented its case for devolution and against independence invoking the language of 'stronger together, weaker apart' and the politics of fear, instability and uncertainty in relation to independence. This stressed the supposed unique success story of the multi-cultural, multi-national nature of the Union that is the UK (Brown and Alexander 2007). There was an element of vagueness in this, selective memory and a Whig-like sense of history as the forward march of British progress (Hassan 2009).

In finding ammunition to attack the SNP, Labour tried to paint the Nationalists in the same colours as the Conservatives, invoking memories of 'the tartan Tories' by arguing that:

> In their attitudes to Britain in the 1990s, the SNP threaten to be the mirror image of Mrs Thatcher's attitude to Scotland in the 1980s. If the threat then was a Britain intolerant to much that is Scottish, the risk now is a Scotland intolerant to much that is British. There is no idealism in moving from the narrow nationalism of Mrs Thatcher to that narrow nationalism of the SNP. (Brown and Alexander 1997: 37–8)

This was a new kind of toxic pass-the-parcel: trying to taint your opponents by association with Mrs Thatcher. Not only did Labour attempt to do this with the SNP, but the SNP was also trying to do the same thing in branding New Labour as the direct inheritor of Mrs Thatcher. The paradox here was that while both parties demonised Thatcherism, both chose to accept large parts of her legacy – and in significant places sought to extend it (Torrance 2009).

Will the Labour–SNP story of animosity diminish overtime? The old reference points of 1967, 1979 and 1989 are now fading and coming to be remembered for more historic events, from the 'Summer of Love' to Thatcher and the fall of the Berlin Wall; and many of the key players who were bruised in such debates have now long left the stage.

Labour has become a hollowed-out party at both a Scottish and British level. For decades its main rationale north of the border was that it was the political establishment of this nation, a clientist party of patronage and preferment which ran Scotland through a web of networks at local and national level. In just over a decade it has become a central part of the British political system which is corrupted, broken and seen as such by voters. This all-encompassing crisis does leave Scottish Labour wondering what its purpose is, given its old role as a British 'bridge-building' project: selling Westminster's benefits to Scotland, and acting as Scotland's voice in Westminster, is no longer viable.

The SNP has seen transformation by being the Scottish government, along with holding an influential position as the leading party in councils across local government. This throws down numerous challenges about how the party can develop a sustainable policy prospectus in a devolved settlement which advances Scottish independence. It asks questions of the depth of the SNP's commitment to a social democratic politics. What happens to governing when you run out of populist measures which may sometime have the easiest hits but might not be the wisest decisions – such as abolishing tolls on the Tay and Forth road bridges? Does the party have a political strategy for dismantling the Labour state? And what happens if it finds itself trapped in the devolution settlement, unable to advance to independence?

A significant contributory factor in the Labour–SNP struggle will be the battle for and fate of Scottish social democracy. Both parties believe this tradition is safest in their respective hands, but both have compromised and diluted it by colluding with neo-liberalism and a big-business agenda. Neither party has had much to say of interest about the wider crisis of social democracy: a predicament increased by the global economic crises of 2008–9.

The struggle between these two parties and traditions will go on and enter a new phase with new issues, shaped less by past folklore and more by the challenges of Scottish politics after the economic and political crash, the crisis of social democracy and the demise of the neo-liberal order, along with the prospect of a UK Conservative government. This is a story with a long and bitter past and, if nothing else, an undoubtedly fascinating future.

NOTES

1. STUC 1968: 417
2. Buchan 1971: 90
3. Sillars 1986: 98

ACKNOWLEDGEMENT

Many thanks to Carole McCallum of Glasgow Caledonian University Archive for her assistance and interest, and to the staff at the Mitchell Library Archive.

REFERENCES

Alexander, W. (2008), Speech to Scottish Labour Conference, 28 March, http://www.wendyalexander.co.uk/2008/03/28/speech-to-labour-party-scottish-conf erence-by-wendy-alexander/

Brown, G. and Alexander, D. (1997), *New Scotland, New Britain*, London, Smith Institute.

Brown, G. and Alexander, D. (2007), *Stronger Together: The 21st Century Case for Scotland and Britain*, London, Fabian Society.

Buchan, N. (1971), 'Politics I', in Glen, D. (ed.), *Whither Scotland? A Prejudiced Look at the Future of Scotland*, London, Victor Gollancz, pp. 86–93.

CSA (1989), 'A Claim of Right for Scotland', in Dudley Edwards, O. (ed.), *A Claim of Right for Scotland*, Edinburgh, Polygon, pp. 9–53.

Dalyell, T. (1977), *Devolution: The End of Britain?*, London, Jonathan Cape.

Ewing, W. (2004), *Stop the World: The Autobiography of Winnie Ewing*, Edinburgh, Birlinn.

Hansard (1966), Vol. 730 cc 1250–548, 27 June, http://hansard.millbank systems.com/commons/1966/jun/27/clause-42-selective-employment-tax#S5CV0730P0_19660627_HOC_844

Hansard (1969), Vol. 790 cc 787–800, 3 November, http://hansard.millbank systems.com/commons/1969/nov/03/scotland-statistical-information#S5CV0790P0_19691103_HOC_402

Harvie, C. and Jones, P. (2000), *The Road to Home Rule: Images of Scotland's Cause*, Edinburgh, Polygon at Edinburgh.

Hassan, G. (2009), 'Don't Mess with the Missionary Man: Brown, Moral Compasses and the Road to Britishness', in Gamble, A. and Wright, T. (eds), *Britishness: Perspectives on the British Question, Political Quarterly Special Issue*, Oxford, Blackwell.

Knox, W. (ed.) (1984), *Scottish Labour Leaders 1918–1939*, Edinburgh, Mainstream.

Labour Party (1968), *Report of Annual Conference*, London, Labour Party.

Macartney, A. (1981), 'The Protagonists', in Bochel, J., Denver, D. and Macartney, A. (eds), *The Referendum Experience: Scotland 1979*, Aberdeen, Aberdeen University Press, pp. 12–42.

McLean, B. (2005), *Getting it Together: The History of the Campaign for a Scottish Assembly/Parliament 1980–1999*, Edinburgh, Luath Press.

McLean, C. (1989), 'Claim of Right or Cap in Hand?', in Dudley Edwards, O. (ed.), *A Claim of Right for Scotland*, Edinburgh, Polygon, pp. 110–18.

Marquand, D. (1991), *The Progressive Dilemma: From Lloyd George to Kinnock*, London, Heinemann.

Mitchell, J. (1996), *Strategies for Self-Government: The Campaigns for a Scottish Parliament*, Edinburgh, Polygon.

Nairn, T. (1989), 'The Timeless Grin', in Dudley Edwards, O. (ed.), *A Claim of Right for Scotland*, Edinburgh, Polygon, pp. 163–78.

Paterson, L., Brown, A., Curtice, J., Hinds, K., McCrone, D., Park, A., Sproston, K. and Surridge, P. (2001), *New Scotland, New Politics?*, Edinburgh, Polygon at Edinburgh.

Pittock, M. (2008), *The Road to Independence? Scotland since the Sixties*, London, Reaktion Books.

STUC (1968), *71st Annual Report*, Glasgow, STUC.

Sillars, J. (1986), *Scotland: The Case for Optimism*, Edinburgh, Polygon.

SNP (1999), http://gdl.cdlr.strath.ac.uk/aspect/snp/a99snpggo.htm

Torrance, D. (2009), *'We in Scotland': Thatcherism in a Cold Climate*, Edinburgh, Birlinn.

Wolfe, W. (1973), *Scotland Lives: The Quest for Independence*, Edinburgh, Reprographia.

Wood, F. (1989), 'Scottish Labour in Government and Opposition 1964–1979', in Donnachie, I., Harvie, C. and Wood, I. S. (eds), *Forward! Labour Politics in Scotland 1888–1988*, Edinburgh, Polygon, pp. 99–129.

CHAPTER 13

The Journey from the 79 Group
to the Modern SNP

David Torrance

In its initial impact on the SNP the total 1979 experience was tantamount to a death in the family – or even a nervous breakdown. As can happen in the best families faced with such trying circumstances, existing internal tensions and petty jealousies, coupled with mutual recriminations, rapidly surfaced; and the temptation to seek 'scapegoats' – both in personnel and specific policies and strategies – was inadequately resisted. (Ian O. Bayne, 1991)

We want to transform the SNP from a motley collection of people both political and non-political, into a truly political party which sees its electoral struggle and the struggle for independence, in a wider ideological framework. (Roseanna Cunningham, 1981)

I was always getting into trouble before I became leader. And then my troubles stopped! I got expelled from the SNP in 1982 as a rather brash young man. I've often reflected that there was a considerable amount of fault on my side. (Alex Salmond, 2008)

March 1979 was not a fruitful time to be a Scottish Nationalist. Although less than five years had passed since the heady days of October 1974 when the SNP returned eleven MPs to the UK Parliament, the party was performing badly in the polls. The devolution referendum of 1 March was a psychological blow, an uncomfortable indication that a large majority of Scots were not clamouring for more control of their own affairs. So even before the Callaghan government fell and took its case to the country, Nationalists began searching for explanations. The conclusions they reached would shape the party's direction for the next three, often unhappily tumultuous, years.

It was Roseanna Cunningham, in 1979 the SNP's assistant research officer, together with her brother Chris, who first floated the idea for what became the '79 Group' – thus named after the year of its formation – during the February referendum campaign. On the Saturday following the referendum 'defeat', Margo MacDonald, the party's deputy leader, also made an influential speech at a meeting of the party's National Council.

MacDonald's analysis was simple: while working-class Scots had voted 'Yes' in the referendum, Scotland's middle classes had voted 'No'. The SNP, therefore, had to look to the former in order to build future support. This meant that instead of the party maintaining its 'all things to all men' approach of old, it had to become more political and therefore more left wing. The trouble was, as Ian O. Bayne later pointed out, MacDonald's prognosis 'was based on a deeply flawed analysis of the . . . referendum results and on an equally flawed set of assumptions about the nature of the traditional Labour vote' (1991: 57). Closer scrutiny of the referendum results revealed that many middle-class Scots – and even some Tory voters – had actually voted 'Yes', while the notion that Labour voters were motivated by socialist passion rather than essentially conservative sectional interests was also misplaced.

Nevertheless, eight Nationalists sympathetic to MacDonald's viewpoint met in Edinburgh on 10 March, and between 30 and 35 people attended a second meeting at the city's Belford Hotel on 31 May. There, the clumsily named 'Interim Committee for Political Discussion' became the 79 Group. Decisions were also taken to print membership cards and have elected officers. Three spokesmen were appointed: Margo MacDonald, Andrew Currie and Alex Salmond. Although not the group's leader as such, the former Lothian Regional councillor Stephen Maxwell quickly became an influential figure.

When the SNP lost nine MPs and sank to 17% of the vote in the general election of 1979, therefore, internal critics such as Salmond felt vindicated, although the dramatic reversal of fortunes (compared with 1974) was profoundly shocking for the party as a whole. The SNP, observed Jack Brand (later to become a member of the 79 Group himself), was left 'in total, snarling, self-destructive disarray' (1990). Maxwell (1979), however, was soon outlining the 79 Group's thinking in an article for The Scotsman: 'a serious Nationalist movement,' he concluded, 'must give a social and economic content to its demands for political independence.' But when the Group fielded a 'slate' of candidates for election to the party's National Executive Committee, its nominees – Maxwell for chairman and Margo MacDonald for senior vice-chairman (a position she already held) – were soundly defeated by Gordon Wilson and Douglas Henderson respectively, while Billy Wolfe was beaten by Robert McIntyre for the post of party president.

It seemed clear that the 79 Group's aim of transforming the party's image was going to be a long, difficult one. Its three guiding principles were nationalism, socialism and republicanism, the last owing largely

163

to the influence of the Cunninghams (based on their experience of republicanism in Australia), the academic Gavin Kennedy and a busload of students from the Glasgow University Scottish Nationalist Association (GUSNA) who had attended the Belford Hotel meeting (Robertson 2009). Nobody in the SNP quarrelled with the first aim; sympathy for the second extended beyond the 79 Group; while the third was to cause persistent problems. As James Mitchell (2001) recalled of a conversation with Alex Salmond, 'he agreed with certainly one of the three objectives of the 79 Group – independence; [had] some sympathy with the second – socialism; but not a lot of sympathy with the third – republicanism.'

Surveying the composition of the 79 Group in a reflective piece for the magazine *Cencrastus*, Stephen Maxwell (1985) divided its members into three groups. 'One group was composed of Nationalists who had joined the Party in the 1960s and by the 1970s held elected posts at national and constituency levels. Margo MacDonald, Rob Gibson, Andrew Currie and myself were prominent in this group.' A second, smaller group comprised academics who had joined the SNP in the 1970s, such as the Edinburgh University historian Owen Dudley Edwards, the economist and defence specialist Gavin Kennedy and Jack Brand, the political scientist and former chairman of Glasgow City Labour Party. The third, much younger group, however, were the most influential. These included student Nationalists and most of the staff at SNP headquarters in Edinburgh, including Robert Crawford, Roseanna Cunningham, the press officer Duncan Maclaren, and the trade union officer Steve Butler. 'It was this generation', observed Maxwell, 'which created the 79 Group and largely determined its tactics' (ibid.: 11).

To that last group Maxwell could have added Alex Salmond, a civil servant and economist, and Kenny MacAskill, a radical young lawyer whom Salmond persuaded to join the SNP following years of intermittent activism. 'I saw the 79 Group as a way into the SNP,' MacAskill (2009) later recalled, 'it made it respectable in left-wing circles.' Maxwell called this contingent the 'West Lothian Left' and later described Salmond and MacAskill as the two 'discoveries' of the 79 Group.

Salmond, born and raised in Linlithgow, had made his mark at St Andrews University, founding and editing the *Free Student Press*, a left-wing alternative to the NUS-aligned campus paper. In his view (1979), the SNP's recent problems were structural as well as ideological. He was especially critical of the 'haphazard process' by which elections for party office were held: 'The result is to favour seniority and notoriety regardless of politics and, one suspects, merit.' In terms of the Group's prospects, he added,

A lot will depend now on how we organise ourselves within the Party and how other interests respond to our presence. I would have thought that the role of the '79 Group' includes organising backing for specific people and motions within the Party's councils, and some thought should be given as to how this can be best achieved.

THE RADICAL APPROACH?

For a grouping whose critique of the party hierarchy hinged upon its vague notion of political identity, setting out its own beliefs was a natural priority. As Steve Butler (1981) wrote in *Crann Tara*, Labour's lack of action and the Tories' neglect opened 'the door for the Scottish National Party to deliver its message to those Scots who have chosen to ignore it until now'. But to categorise that message as 'socialist' would be simplistic. Rather, as Jack Brand (1990) observed, although it 'might not be socialist in the terms of Karl Marx . . . it certainly meant that the Nationalists could not but identify with the Scottish working class if they wanted to appear to be against the government'.

Importantly, whatever the 79 Group's brand of socialism, what it believed was never systematically spelled out. To be fair, members of the group usually couched criticism of what they called the 'soggy centrist ideals' of the SNP in tactical, rather than ideological, terms and not without reason. In a 'Long-term Strategy Discussion Paper' (1981) written by Jim Lynch (not a 79 Group member), for example, he declared that the 'day of detailed Party policy is past, if it ever arrived'. 'While accepting that there is a need for well-thought-out policies,' Lynch argued, 'we have never managed to get them over to our own members, never mind the electorate.'

The 79 Group, however, not only believed in communicating party policy to party members, but revelled in exploring its detail. This manifested itself most clearly in seven publications called, rather ostentatiously, the 'SNP 79 Group Papers'.[1] These varied in quality but two, *The Case for Left-Wing Nationalism* (No. 6) and *The Scottish Industrial Resistance* (No. 7), came closest to fleshing out the bones of the Group's thinking. The former, written by Stephen Maxwell in 1981, proclaimed that 'the SNP must look to the urban working class to . . . establish itself as the radical Scottish alternative to the Labour Party' (Maxwell 1981: 22).

The Scottish Industrial Resistance, meanwhile, attempted to explain just how. Kenny MacAskill's account of the Plessey dispute, in which he made his name with some creative legal advice, was preceded by an introduction from Alex Salmond (1982). The SNP's track record on industrial politics, he lamented, had not 'been a distinguished one', with no attempt to preach 'nationalism on the shop floor as well as on the doorstep'. As a result of 79 Group agitation, Salmond argued, the 1981 SNP conference had recognised 'that a real Scottish resistance and defence of jobs demands direct action up to and including political strikes and civil disobedience on a mass scale' (Salmond 1982: 2). In addition to the Plessey dispute, the SNP became involved with campaigns to save the Robb Caledon shipyard in Dundee and the Lee Jeans factory in Greenock. Although this sort of engagement was not new (Billy Wolfe's Association of Scottish National Trade Unionists had been established in the 1960s and revived in the 1970s), the 79 Group took it to a more public level.

The driving force behind the 'Scottish Resistance' and 'civil disobedience' campaigns was Jim Sillars, who joined the SNP (and the 79 Group) just days before the 1980 SNP conference. Formerly the Labour MP for South Ayrshire, Sillars came to the party via his own breakaway grouping, the pro-devolution Scottish Labour Party. Although close to members like Salmond and Margo MacDonald (whom he later married), he was not exactly welcomed with open arms. 'I can testify to the nervousness of group members that the membership of such a well-known personality,' recalled Stewart Buchanan (1982), 'ran the risk of reversing the group's deliberate attempt to promote ideas and not personalities within the SNP.' Others feared that both campaigns would distract from wider goals but Sillars, as Stephen Maxwell later recalled, 'won them over' (Maxwell 1985: 14). But although endorsed by conference, the twin campaigns enjoyed a fleeting ascendancy. They ran for only a few months, by Salmond's own admission, 'before being overtaken by public opposition in the party leadership and then the onset of a parliamentary by-election in Hillhead' (1982: 2).

The Scottish Industrial Resistance was published just as the 79 Group was in its death throes. At the 1981 conference, however, it appeared to be on a roll. Andrew Currie was elected vice-chairman for organisation and Sillars vice-chairman for policy. These were influential positions, while the 79 Group and its allies also secured a small majority on the NEC, including a place for Alex Salmond. The *79 Group News* boasted that the Aberdeen conference 'marked a watershed in the SNP's history', adding triumphantly that it was 'clear that the SNP has indeed adopted a more radical, left-wing position' (*79 Group News*, July–August 1981). This hubris was understandable, yet also misplaced. Although 79 Group-inspired motions advocating civil disobedience (for which Gordon Wilson shrewdly made Jim Sillars personally responsible), withdrawal from the European Economic Community (EEC) and NATO had been endorsed by delegates, others – such as one emphasising the role of a greatly extended public sector in Scotland's industrial regeneration – were defeated, while even those that got through could not, as some 79 Group members later admitted, be explained solely by growing left-wing support (Mitchell 1990).

The European issue, for example, divided even 79 Group members, with Sillars as strongly pro as Stephen Maxwell was anti. Social issues also caused tension. At a meeting in February 1980 Roseanna Cunningham proposed 'that the 79 Group opposes the [John] Corrie Abortion Bill in all its provisions as detrimental to women's rights in society'. That this was backed by a majority vote did not prevent Salmond querying 'the political relevance to the Group of this issue' (79 Group minutes 8/2/1980).

Finally, there was the national question. Although the party had enthusiastically endorsed the hardline 'Independence, nothing less' position in 1979, its chairman, the Dundee East MP Gordon Wilson, was determined to nudge the party back to a more realistic position. In March 1980 he introduced a ten-minute rule Bill at Westminster to establish a Scottish Convention which would decide the constitutional future of Scotland, be it devolution, independence or the status quo. Whatever the case, it marked a move away from fundamentalism and was supported by most of the 79 Group. Indeed, the first 79 Group Paper envisaged self-government being 'achieved in a number of stages', even though Andrew Currie rejected the 'gradualist' tag. 'A lasting Scottish constitutional settlement may come in a single leap or as a consequence of a number of steps spread over a period of years,' he reasoned. 'In either event, it is extremely unlikely the . . . SNP will alone determine that settlement' (Currie 1979: 9). To the old guard, however, this was seen as a watering down of the party's *raison d'être*. Not only were the 79 Group extremist and left wing, opponents like Winnie Ewing claimed, they were 'trimmers' to boot.

However, despite undeniable energy, not to mention the eloquence of some of its spokesmen (and women), the 79 Group failed to articulate a convincing alternative to Thatcherism. 'We see ourselves on the left of the political spectrum,' declared one 79 Group paper, 'but we totally reject the state-controlled paternalism of today's centralist Labour Party' (*79 Group Paper No. 1*). In the absence of 'state-controlled paternalism', however, it was difficult to envisage how – having achieved a left-wing position – the SNP would counteract deindustrialisation. 'We claim to be decentralist socialists,' observed Roseanna Cunningham (1981), 'let us start defining what we mean by this'.

PROTEST AND SURVIVE:
THE POLITICS OF CIVIL DISOBEDIENCE

On 16 October 1981 Jim Sillars and five other members of the 79 Group – Chris McLean (later the SNP's press officer), Douglas Robertson (later its secretary), Steve Butler, Ian Moore (the SNP's fundraiser) and Graeme Purves – broke into Edinburgh's old Royal High School building. As an act of 'civil disobedience' the symbolism was obvious, but tactically disastrous. At the abandoned site of the ill-fated Scottish Assembly, Sillars et al. were protesting, in the most direct possible way, about Scotland's 'democratic deficit', although as Roger Levy has observed, it 'was as much a protest against the manoeuvrings of the incumbent leadership of the SNP as it was against the absence of a Scottish Assembly in the building' (1990: 103).

Although Sillars was found guilty and fined, he deployed clever (and constitutional) arguments to demonstrate why the conviction under a recent Criminal Justice (Scotland) Act was not valid. The sextet's actions, however, confirmed the old guard's suspicion of both the 79 Group and the policy of civil disobedience, which was, of course, not just 79 Group policy, but that of the SNP as a whole. Three NEC members dissociated themselves publicly from the break-in and refused to join a rally supporting the occupation, as did Western Isles MP Donald Stewart, on 24 October.

Another event which coincided with the Royal High School break-in – and proved almost as damaging, at least in media terms – was the prospect of links between Provisional Sinn Fein (PSF) and the 79 Group. The SNP's National Council had passed a motion of non co-operation with Sinn Fein in 1980 but the 79 Group established a Northern Ireland committee to discuss common issues like unemployment, and discussed a request from PSF to send a speaker to its annual conference. The 79 Group's executive, however, knew a political hot potato when it smelled one: 'In response to the PSF letter, Alex Salmond, seconded by Chris Maclean [sic] moved that we do not grant the PSF request,' recorded minutes from a meeting on 15 August 1981. Margo MacDonald suggested a compromise whereby speakers from a range of Nationalist parties in Ireland were invited to speak rather than just one. Unfortunately for the 79 Group, the minutes of this meeting were then leaked to the *Glasgow Herald* via William Houston, vice-chairman of the SNP's Craigton branch, who was in the midst of a vigorous one-man campaign against the 79 Group. Houston wrote to every constituency chairman and secretary in Scotland, claiming that 'the executive of the 79 Group proposed investigating setting up a working party with the Provisional Sinn Fein on recruitment/unemployment' and should therefore be proscribed, or in other words expelled from the party (Anon. 1981). There was obvious tension when the leak was discussed at the next NEC meeting. While Alex Salmond 'said the minutes had not been ratified and contained several inaccuracies', Winnie Ewing claimed she 'had been contacted by Mr [Chris] McLean, Chairman of the 79 Group and he was satisfied that these minutes were substantially correct' (NEC minutes, 9 October 1981). At the height of the Troubles in Northern Ireland, and with controversy surrounding the republican agenda of the 79 Group, this was not exactly helpful coverage.

THE BATTLE OF AYR

Indeed, when the Campaign for Nationalism in Scotland (CNS) launched itself at the June 1982 SNP conference in Ayr, it pointed to the PSF incident, recent regional council elections (in which the SNP managed just 13.5% of the vote) and, predominantly, the Royal High School break-in as irrefutable proof that the 79 Group was destroying the party. 'I am now fighting back for the survival of my party,' cried Winnie Ewing (Baur 1982d) melodramatically at a CNS fringe meeting, '. . . for the triumph of evil, it just takes good men to do nothing.' Ewing painted the group as pro-IRA, anti-Catholic and 'a naked and open conspiracy, a plot' to take over the party's executive and pre-empt its policy discussions.

The 'civil disobedience' policy, meanwhile, was being laid to rest. After an ill-judged speech from Sillars, the normally placid Andrew Welsh (Baur 1982d) angrily retorted that after '25 years in this party I don't need Jim Sillars to tell me what its fundamental aims are', while Margaret Bain (later Ewing) and Gordon Wilson argued that the policy had lost public support and had to go. Defending it, Stephen Maxwell pointed to the suffragettes as an example of direct action which had furthered democratic goals, while Alex Salmond (Baur 1982d) warned that the SNP would be adopting 'a defeatist and cringeing mentality' if it forswore the use of civil disobedience on matters of principle. Later, writing in *The Scottish Industrial Resistance*, Salmond (1982) called the decision 'perverse'. 'The Scottish character flaw that enables us to face difficult or even hopeless challenges bravely but proceed then to fluff the short putts in an agony of self doubt is a major psychological phenomenon,' he mused. 'Nothing is more terrifying than the prospect of success' (ibid.: 3).

Then, on 4 June, three-year-old internal tensions came to a head. Despite the absence of any formal motion to proscribe the 79 Group on the conference agenda, in the midst of his keynote speech Gordon Wilson (Baur 1982a) said he was 'now convinced that the party will not

169

recover its unity until all organised groups are banned'. 'Those of us who put Scotland and the party above narrow personal or political obsession,' he added, 'cannot and will not tolerate behaviour which is divisive and harmful'. With that, dozens of delegates rose to their feet to clap and cheer, while a few dozen members of the 79 Group left the hall in protest. The archive television footage clearly shows Kenny MacAskill, Stewart Stevenson, Rob Gibson and Andrew Currie among them, while Margaret Bain and Winnie Ewing applaud energetically on the conference platform. 'My campaign has been so successful it is beyond my wildest dreams,' remarked Ewing (Baur 1982a); 'I believe this is the end of the 79 Group'. Significantly, the walkout overshadowed the main thrust of Wilson's speech, what the *79 Group News* described as 'an innovative strategy for a Scottish Elected Convention to draw up proposals for self-government' (*79 Group News*, August 1982). Personalities, more than policies, had brought the 79 Group to its knees.

Wilson had deliberately polarised the debate and, in doing so, cleverly outmanoeuvred the 79 Group. He not only forced delegates to vote for or against the 79 Group, but by implication also for or against his leadership of the party, a decisive move which earned him much positive media coverage. But the majority for proscription – 308 votes to 188 – was decisive without being overwhelming. So, not without justification, Ron Wyllie (Baur 1982b) accused Wilson of having 'held a pistol to the party's head'. However, while Wyllie (together with Stephen Maxwell) maintained his place on the party's NEC at elections held two weeks after the proscription vote (he had described himself as a Nationalist first and 79 Group member second), Alex Salmond, Rob Gibson, Kenny MacAskill, Roseanna Cunningham and Owen Dudley Edwards did not maintain theirs. The party's old guard, including the new NEC members Dr Robert McIntyre, Arthur Donaldson and James Halliday, now held sway and were determined not to give the 79 Groupers any room for manoeuvre.

For the next few months the SNP's internal battles were played out in the letters pages of *The Scotsman*, as well as in party meetings. In a long letter published on 24 June, Alex Salmond accused certain SNP members of 'running away from political reality'. The party, he added,

> could position itself to be a real alternative to Labour – not by borrowing voters as in the past, but by winning activists, shop stewards and stable political support to the Leftist nationalist programme which meets the aspirations of the majority of the Scottish people . . . In these circumstances only a party willing and able to call for civil disobedience, primarily through organised labour, will be able to effectively back a democratic Scottish majority for a Parliament. (Salmond 1982)

Although Gordon Wilson had publicly declared the SNP as 'moderate Left of Centre', wrote Salmond, 'while he has correctly defined the SNP policy position over a considerable period, most people in Scotland remain unaware of it and he seems hardly in any position now to strengthen the party's radical image'.

Members of the 79 Group, meanwhile, had agreed to await the result of the Coatbridge & Airdrie by-election before deciding whether or not to disband by the 5 September deadline (after which its members faced expulsion). The by-election result, in which Ron Wyllie lost his deposit, offered scant comfort. The 79 Group then toyed with challenging Wilson's ruling on the grounds that it was unconstitutional, while pursuing a last-ditch attempt to win branch support to uphold its 'democratic right to argue the Socialist case within the SNP' (Crainey 1982). But when more than 100 members of the Group met in Edinburgh's North British Hotel on 28 August, a motion was passed disbanding the group as of 30 August. Crucially, that meeting also took the decision to simultaneously re-form under the same name, but with a wider membership drawn from other political parties (this subsequently called itself the 'Scottish Socialist Society', or SSS). In response Wilson (Baur 1982e) warned that members of the new society were 'following a high-risk policy which could place in jeopardy their continuing membership of the SNP'.

This spirited attempt to avoid expulsion, however, descended into undignified abuse in mid-September. Jim Sillars accused Wilson of permitting the creation of 'a Stalinist party'; Margo MacDonald resigned in protest at a 'witch-hunt against the Left-wing'; while calls for a compromise were dismissed by Wilson (Baur 1982c). 'It is intolerable that a tiny elite can cause so much distress to SNP members in general,' he declared. On 20 September seven members were expelled: Stephen Maxwell, Chris Cunningham, Douglas Robertson, Alex Salmond, Brenda Carson, Kenny MacAskill and Andrew Doig. Roseanna Cunningham escaped the same fate only by declaring herself not to be a member of the SSS executive. Some supporters, inevitably, over-reacted. 'The Scottish National Party,' stormed Owen Dudley Edwards (1982) in *The Scotsman*, 'by expelling Mr Stephen Maxwell, Mr Alex Salmond and their five associates, have committed intellectual suicide'.

THE PARTY OF RADICAL SCOTLAND?

The 79 Group's downfall was played out against a backdrop of events which appeared to vindicate its fate. There had just been a royal birth following a popular royal wedding; the Falklands conflict had muted Scottish Nationalist sentiment; while Margaret Thatcher, if not Thatcherism, was in the ascendency. The Coatbridge & Airdrie by-election, meanwhile, appeared to have demonstrated that the 79 Group's campaigning prowess, if not its civil disobedience campaign, did not bear electoral fruit.

The expulsion of the seven 79 Groupers was confirmed at the SNP's National Council on 5 December and upheld on appeal at another meeting in April 1983. 'The 79 Group then disappeared,' observed Peter Lynch in his history of the SNP, 'though it had a considerable legacy in terms of personalities and the ideological outlook' (2002: 174). This was especially the case in terms of personalities. Alex Salmond, for example, was readmitted the following year and elected vice-chairman for publicity in 1985, MP for Banff & Buchan in 1987, deputy leader in 1988 and finally leader in 1990 – at which point he still declared himself to be a 'socialist'. 'His view that the SNP required to project a clear position on socio-economic matters,' as James Mitchell has written, 'did not lead to the party changing its policies so much as presenting them more coherently' (1988: 476).

Indeed, after the 1983 general election – in which the SNP slipped from 17.3% to 11.8% of the vote – Gordon Wilson had laid much of the groundwork in this respect. As he told a journalist (Wills 1982) immediately after the 1982 split, 'We have always had a radical, left of centre bias.' Wilson worked hard to reverse the party's anti-NATO policy (albeit without success), persuade it to support EEC membership and, more successfully, soften its 'Independence, nothing less' stance. Of course, whether the 79 Group slowed or hastened this shift is central to any assessment of their influence. Considering that Wilson was in substantial agreement with the 79 Group in policy terms, he could perhaps have made these changes more quickly and less painfully without the distraction of infighting provoked, at least in part, by the 79 Group. Ironically, as James Mitchell has noted, opposition to Wilson's leadership post-1983 came from fundamentalists and those concerned about his uncharismatic performances, rather than from left wingers. In the short term, however, Wilson's standing in the party was boosted by his handling of the 79 Group. 'Nobody in their right sense should have voted SNP in 1981–82,' Wilson (2008) later reflected. 'The party was split; vicious internecine stuff; no credibility; no clout; its own policies had taken it away from the political mainstream. The party was looking inwards, and it wasn't until the 1983 conference that I managed to turn that around and bring it back.'

Wilson was further vindicated at the 1987 general election, when the SNP gained three seats from the Conservatives (including Banff & Buchan, won by Alex Salmond) having targeted predominantly Tory constituencies instead of concentrating on Labour as a 79 Group analysis would have dictated. An important gain from Labour followed, of course, a year later when Jim Sillars – who had remained on the NEC throughout the 1980s – won the Govan by-election. Sillars' 'Independence in Europe' slogan was also born that year and proved equally palatable to former 79 Groupers and fundamentalists, while even the republicanism of Roseanna Cunningham did not prevent the burghers of Perth endorsing her in another by-election in May 1995.

In terms of the party's ideological outlook, the 79 Group's influence was harder to detect. Republicanism, beyond Roseanna Cunningham's personal views, was quietly forgotten about as the SNP embraced preservation of the Union of the Crowns but not the Treaty of Union. Socialism (at least the 79 Group's version of it), meanwhile, hardly flourished in the SNP. Although the Scottish right appeared to be in terminal decline, the radical agenda of Thatcherism made left-wing Nationalism an increasingly hard sell. The SNP's response was not so different from Labour's: an increasing tendency towards the middle ground in economic if not social terms, although another legacy of the 79 Group was continuing SNP engagement with shop stewards, most notably over the closure of Gartcosh and at the Dalzell Plate Mill. Policies of unequivocal support for the miners' strike of 1984–5 and a campaign of poll tax non-payment in 1989–90 (initiated by Kenny MacAskill) also sprang from a 79 Group analysis, although both failed to attract substantial Labour support.

Salmond (2008), however, never made much of his involvement with the 79 Group, dismissing his expulsion as the result of being a 'brash young man', while Stewart Stevenson (2002) simply reflected that the 79 Group had 'got too big for [its] boots'. Ideological remnants of the Group still remained, although not in predictable forms. MacAskill, for example, spoke in favour of ditching opposition to NATO, while Cunningham – who strongly opposed any move towards privatisation of the Forestry Commission on becoming Environment Minister – advocated the status quo. As MacAskill (2009) put it, 'The attitudes of Alex Salmond and I have changed because we live in a different society. Left-wing nationalism needed to have a voice, now it's got a government.'

Despite much discussion of social and economic policies, however, the 79 Group failed to define its socialist and republican aims, displaying precisely (and ironically) the sort of ideological incoherence it criticised in the party's leadership. 'Significantly, in three years' existence, the Group was to offer no elaboration of the brief outline of republicanism and socialist principles adopted at its launch,' judged Stephen Maxwell. 'The Group failed to achieve its most ambitious aim, to convert the SNP into a socialist party. It is doubtful whether it achieved its more realistic ambition of strengthening the left-wing voice within the SNP' (Maxwell 1985: 15).

Likewise, MacAskill (2009) concluded that the 79 Group 'had a single dominating ethos but found it difficult to articulate its left-wing policies'. Some in the 79 Group, for example Rob Gibson and Douglas Robertson, believed this would have come with time, and that the 79 Group was distracted from doing so 'because it was constantly fighting against getting expelled'. 'We wanted a left-wing agenda but not Labour state centralisation,' reflected Robertson (2009), 'but we never managed to articulate a third way, which was in itself quite a challenging thing to do'.

There was also 'naivety', as Jim Sillars (2009) has reflected, 'in the 79 Group that they could change things quickly', although Maxwell claims the Group 'never suffered from the delusion that the raising of the banner of socialism – let alone the banner of republicanism – by the SNP would bring the Scottish working class flocking to the Party's side' (1985: 13). Members, added Maxwell, saw the 'long march' as realistically taking at least five years, so 'in the event it was the Group's patience rather than its stamina that was tested and found wanting' (ibid.: 14).

Its patience was also tried by internal feuding, mainly over republicanism. As Margo MacDonald (2009) recalled, 'Alex Salmond and Jim [Sillars] argued against it, while Gavin Kennedy and Roseanna Cunningham ratcheted it up. If there was a single issue that killed it [the 79 Group], it was that'. To Douglas Robertson (2009), on the other hand, that 'single issue' was Europe, a division so deep that it deprived Stephen Maxwell of a likely place in the Scottish Parliament post-1999. Always small in number – there were never more than 100 active members – the 79 Group's whiff of student politics also resulted in tactical naivety, most notably over civil disobedience, which dictated a correspondingly short shelf life.

But, on the other hand, Roseanna Cunningham's (1981) stated aim of transforming 'the SNP from a motley collection of people both political and non-political, into a truly political party which sees its electoral struggle and the struggle for independence, in a wider ideological framework' was largely achieved, although that 'ideological framework' naturally altered with time, not least as Salmond et al. embraced the very neo-liberal economic consensus they had previously opposed. There is a similarity in the direction of travel by both the SNP and Labour post-1979, as both became engulfed in bitter infighting, and taking this further, there are parallels between the agendas of the 79 Group and the Bennite left in Labour: both were expressions of the emerging 'new left' and rising 'polyocracy' in centre-left parties. Yet, both the SNP and Labour in their long journey to acknowledge the remaking of the political terrain of Thatcherism, ended up invoking social democracy, while often acting in a way which consolidated Thatcherism and her legacy.

The 'alleged' influence of the 79 Group, therefore, has to be judged in an electoral, as well as an ideological, context. The SNP in the 1960s was certainly centre-left; in the 1970s it identified mainly with social democracy. In the decade that followed, Gordon Wilson correctly asserted that the party had always had 'a radical, left of centre bias', while in 2007 the SNP's manifesto made repeated references to the party's 'social democratic contract with Scotland'. In those terms the 79 Group can be seen as both central and peripheral to the party's mainstream, but an enduring influence – at least in terms of personalities – nevertheless.

NOTE

1. The SNP 79 Group Papers suffered from numerical confusion but included in the series are: *The 79 Group: Its Principles and Aims* (No. 1), *Local Government Elections* (probably No. 2), *Scotland and the British Crisis* (No. 4), *Has the Scottish Private Sector a Future?* (No. 5), *The Case for Left-Wing Nationalism* (No. 6), *The Scottish Industrial Resistance* (No. 7) and at least one other.

REFERENCES

Anon. (1981), 'Pressure mounts for ban on SNP group', *Glasgow Herald*, 20 October.

Baur, C. (1982a), 'Decision-day for SNP's future', *The Scotsman*, 5 June.

Baur, C. (1982b), '79 Group delay decision on future', *The Scotsman*, 7 June.

Baur, C. (1982c), 'SNP Left fail in appeal to Wilson', *The Scotsman*, 18 June.

Baur, C. (1982d), 'SNP Left suffer major defeat', *The Scotsman*, 4 June.

Baur, C. (1982e), 'Warning over 79 Group "ploy"', *The Scotsman*, 30 June.

Bayne, I. O. (1991), 'The Impact of 1979 on the SNP', in Gallagher, T. (ed.), *Nationalism in the Nineties*, Edinburgh, Polygon. pp. 46–65.

Brand, J. (1990), 'Defeat and Renewal: The Scottish National Party in the Eighties', *Strathclyde University Working Paper 23*.

Buchanan, S. (1982), 'How the 79 Group were left in the lurch', *The Scotsman*, 19 June.

Butler, S. (1981), 'A Disobedient SNP', *Crann Tara*, 15.

Crainey, T. (1982), '79 Group to wage campaign against ban', *The Scotsman*, 28 June.

Cunningham, R. (1981), 'The 79 Group – 1980–1981', Gavin Kennedy Acc 11565/23 (National Library of Scotland), 12 September.

Currie, A. (1979), 'Which way forward?', in *SNP 79 Group Paper No. 1: The 79 Group: Its Principles and Aims*, Edinburgh.

Dudley Edwards, O. (1982), 'SNP indulge in the justice of Culloden', *The Scotsman*, 27 September.

Levy, R. (1990), *Scottish Nationalism at the Crossroads*, Edinburgh, Scottish Academic Press.

Lynch, J. (1981), 'Long-term Strategy Discussion Paper', SNP Acc 11987 (National Library of Scotland), 6 February.

Lynch, P. (2002), *SNP: The History of the Scottish National Party*, Cardiff, Welsh Academic Press.

MacAskill, K. (2009), interview with author, 30 January.

MacDonald, M. (2009), interview with author, 10 February.

Maxwell, S. (1979), 'Radical strategy for an SNP revival', *The Scotsman*, 15 June.

Maxwell, S. (1981), *SNP 79 Group Paper No. 6: The Case for Left-Wing Nationalism*, Hamilton, Aberdeen People's Press.

Maxwell, S. (1985), 'The 79 Group: A Critical Retrospect', *Cencrastus*, 21, pp. 11–16.

Mitchell, J. (1988), 'Recent Developments in the Scottish National Party', *Political Quarterly*, 59(4), pp. 473–7.

Mitchell, J. (1990), 'Factions, Tendencies and Consensus in the SNP in the 1980s', in Brown, A. and Parry, R. (eds), *The Scottish Government Yearbook 1990*, Edinburgh, Unit for the Study of Government in Scotland, pp. 49–61.

Mitchell, J. (2001), *The Salmond Years* (STV), 18 February.

National Executive Committee (NEC) minutes, SNP Acc 11987 (National Library of Scotland).

Robertson, D. (2009), interview with author, 30 March.

Salmond, A. (1979), 'Democracy and politics within the SNP', Gavin Kennedy Acc 11565/23 (National Library of Scotland), 12 August.

Salmond, A. (1982), '"Thanks" to the SNP's industrious letter-writers', *The Scotsman*, 24 June.

Salmond, A. (1982), 'Introduction', in *SNP 79 Group Paper No. 7: The Scottish Industrial Resistance*, Aberdeen, Aberdeen People's Press.

Salmond, A. (2008), 'In Conversation with Alex Salmond', *Total Politics*, September.

79 Group minutes, Gavin Kennedy Acc 11565/23 (National Library of Scotland).

Sillars, J. (2009), interview with author, 19 February.

Stevenson, S. (2002), *The Week In Politics* (STV), 5 September.

Wills, J. (1982), 'SNP, surviving the split – at a price', *The Times*, 21 September.

Wilson, G. (2008), interview with author, 16 May.

CHAPTER 14

The SNP and UK Relations

Alex Wright

When the SNP became the governing party after the 2007 election, it appeared that relations between London and Edinburgh would be fractious at best. Initially, that held true but a year later the relationship between the two governments was on a relatively sound footing, not least because it was in the SNP's interest to have a constructive relationship with the UK government. Nonetheless, the potential for tension remains in a number of respects. Firstly, the current devolved arrangements are not constitutionally entrenched and that has consequences; much can depend on the attitude of the government in London towards Scotland. In addition, financial matters and the issue of Holyrood's future powers have already sown discord between them. Consequently, the conduct of inter-governmental relations remains something of a challenge for the SNP. If it respects 'the rules of the game', it could secure concessions from London behind the scenes. But on the other hand it is expected to fight for Scotland's interests if the concessions on offer are inadequate, even if that may involve confrontation with London, as was the case in 1961.

When the UK government submitted its first application to join the EU in 1961, the SNP's response was that it encroached on 'certain Scottish rights' and breached 'limitations on the constitutional powers of the UK parliament'. Its office bearers therefore wrote a letter to Harold Macmillan (the Prime Minister) with the following request:

Sir,
The Writers are citizens of Scotland and office-bearers of the Scottish National Party. In view of the negotiations now in progress for the admission of the United Kingdom to the European Economic Community we wish to draw your attention to the existence of certain Scottish rights, and of limitations on the constitutional powers of the United Kingdom parliament. To remove sovereignty over wide fields from the United Kingdom parliament to what is in effect a European parliament obviously alters the whole basis of the Union

of 1707, and consequently this is a step which the parliament of Great Britain has no power to take as far as Scotland is concerned. The correct procedure, if the Government wish to alter the system of Government set up in the Treaty of Union, must be to call the Scottish and English parliaments separately to negotiate a new basis of association appropriate to the present circumstances, both between themselves and in respect of the European Economic Community. It is obvious that one of the first things a Scottish Parliament would insist on is full Scottish representation on the institutions of the EEC, including a seat on the Council. Since these rights have been accorded to the Grand Duchy of Luxembourg we cannot believe that the nations of the European Economic Community would withhold them from Scotland. (Scottish Office 1961: File 519/ Pt A/ SOE 10/73)

The Prime Minister declined the offer but a civil servant at the Foreign Office was sufficiently concerned about the matter to warn the Lord Privy Seal who was about to visit Scotland that he should avoid getting sucked into debate on this. He advised:

If, however, he is unable to avoid saying more, the opportunities for endless argument which this subject provide to those so inclined make it desirable for any further comments to be as anodyne as possible. As you may already appreciate, the whole question of the position of the Treaty of Union in the constitutional law of the United Kingdom is a very difficult one, affording material to those so inclined for endless argument. (Scottish Office 1961: File 519/ Pt A/ SOE 10/73)

It is surprising that the official was so concerned, given Scotland's status in the UK at the time. Scotland's incorporation within the UK originates not only from the 1707 Treaty of Union but also the Union of Crowns in 1603.

Degrees of Ambiguity

Prior to constitutional change in 1999, the UK could be described as a unitary state. It was unitary inasmuch as supreme authority resided at Westminster. Even so, authority was not wholly concentrated in London (Bulpitt 1983). Northern Ireland had executive devolution, until the imposition of direct rule by Westminster in 1972. For their part, Scotland (Mitchell 2003) and to a lesser extent Wales had 'administrative devolution'. Scotland was administered primarily by the Scottish Office, itself a territorial branch of the UK government. The Secretary of State for Scotland, who was a member of the UK Cabinet, and his ministerial team were appointees of the UK Prime Minister. Whilst a degree of political authority resided in Scotland, however, there was no consensus over the extent to which Scotland enjoyed meaningful autonomy within the UK (see e.g. Kellas 1989; Midwinter et al. 1991; Paterson 1994).

European integration further complicated inter-governmental relations, not least because decisions that affected Scotland would no longer necessarily be taken in London but Brussels. When the UK joined the EEC in 1973 the SNP had reservations about the cost of membership as well as the transfer of political authority to Brussels. In the run up to the referendum on whether the UK should remain within the EEC, senior figures within the party were in the 'no' group. But during the mid-1980s the party's attitude underwent a remarkable transformation. By this time Jim Sillars had joined the SNP after briefly forming a breakaway Scottish Labour Party. In spite of his hostility towards the EEC in 1975, he became one of the leading advocates of the SNP's campaign for 'Scottish independence in Europe' (Sillars 1986). Independence in Europe had its attractions, not least because it acted as a vehicle for promoting constitutional change in the UK. The SNP claimed that it would be an 'equal partnership' (SNP 1994: 19), whereas, the existing union within the UK was 'unequal', thereby rendering Scotland 'a powerless nation' (ibid.: 3). Whether the relationship is more equal now Scotland has its own parliament is a moot point.

Under the current settlement political authority is devolved from Westminster to the Scottish Parliament. Westminster continues to remain 'sovereign' in that this is where supreme authority is held to reside within the UK. It has been suggested that the current framework is tantamount to 'quasi-federalism' with respect to Wales and to Scotland (Bognador 1999). That is debatable. A federal UK remains elusive not least because it would be dominated by England (Sewel 2007: 77). However, although the powers of the respective devolved institutions across the UK have not been constitutionally entrenched, their continuing autonomy would in part be 'guaranteed' by the will of their peoples (Trench 2005: 154–5). Nonetheless, the existing constitutional arrangements cultivate a degree of ambiguity, not just in relation to the delineation of authority between Westminster and the devolved governments (Wright 2005), but also with regard to how they conduct their relations.

On the one hand there is a formal side to this, inasmuch as inter-governmental relations in the UK are currently underpinned by a number of mechanisms, the apex of which is a Memorandum of Understanding (MoU). It sets out the principles which are supposed to guide the conduct of relations between the two levels of government. The key elements that lie at the centre of this arrangement are good communication and consultation, co-operation, the exchange of information, statistics and research, and the need for confidentiality.[1] The other two mechanisms are the Joint Ministerial Committees (one of which is supposed to be chaired by the Prime Minister) and the Concordats. If needs be, the secretariat of the Joint Ministerial Committee (JMC) could act as an arbitrator, although it is a 'consultative rather then an executive body' (Bulmer et al. 2002:52). The Concordats essentially set out in detail how inter-governmental relations should be conducted in relation to specific areas (for instance European matters or fisheries). In theory they are subject to review but it is unclear what exactly would trigger such an event. It could be claimed that the above arrangement is inherently informal on the basis that it does not have any substantive legal standing. At the time of their conception, however, it was claimed that the Concordats did 'create a legitimate expectation of consultation' which, if unfulfilled by one administration, might be 'challenged by way of judicial review'.[2] To date that is yet to happen and with the exception of European committee, the JMCs largely fell into disuse during the period of the Labour–Liberal Democrat coalition in Scotland.

Their demise aroused relatively little controversy, as far as Wales and Scotland were concerned, either because both tiers of government were Labour or because Labour was the dominant partner, albeit that some commentators were critical of the ad hoc nature of inter-governmental relations (Trench 2003: 165). For the most part, formal mechanisms were used infrequently and there was greater reliance on links within the Labour party to resolve potentially divisive issues (Keating 2005: 138). It was therefore argued by officials at Downing Street that relations between the UK government and the devolved administrations could be conducted better on an ad hoc and informal basis, bilaterally rather than via more formal settings such as the JMC. Whilst this might have enabled devolution to bed-in 'smoothly' – in contrast to the experience of other territories elsewhere in the world (ibid.) – it was partially contingent on the same or like-minded parties being in power at both levels of government. If that were to change then it followed that more formal mechanisms would be desirable (Keating 2005: 127; Trench 2005: 153). However, doubts were raised about the efficacy of inter-governmental relations between London and Edinburgh even before the SNP assumed office in 2007.

The Herald obtained a leaked report by an official at the Scottish Executive in which it was claimed that 'Scotland's interests are being routinely forgotten, ignored and dismissed by Whitehall officials'. The report also warned that the 'Executive's views had been dismissed by Whitehall' and that a common complaint was that the latter 'tends to forget about consulting the Executive' (*The Herald*, 22 January 2007). This was by no means a novel scenario, as there had been similar examples before legislative devolution (Wright 2005; Gowland et al. 2009). Indeed potentially there has been greater scope for problems such as this following the establishment of devolution in 1999. The two administrations are separate political entities and this has ramifications for inter-governmental communications. For example, there have been instances where Scotland has been off the radar of a government department in Whitehall because the latter was under the false impression that the issue at hand fell within devolved matters. So, it was apparent even before the SNP's electoral victory that inter-governmental communication between London and the Scotland could have been better.

Finding New Ways of Working

The 2007 elections in the devolved territories set the scene for political upheaval in the UK, which in turn had consequences for inter-governmental relations. Wales was to be governed by a Labour–Plaid Cymru coalition. Devolved government was restored in Northern Ireland, with Martin McGuinness of Sinn Fein sharing power with Ian Paisley's Democratic Unionist Party (Paisley stood down in the spring of 2008 and was replaced by Peter Robinson). In Scotland, the SNP formed a minority administration under Alex Salmond, which at time of writing appears set to serve a full four-year term. In the immediate aftermath of the elections, Paisley suggested that all three devolved administrations should work 'in harness' when dealing with London and Salmond called for 'channels of communication to be put on a more formal basis' (*The Herald*, 18 May 2007; 28 May 2007).

But Salmond's hopes for closer ties proved to be unrequited and instead relations between Edinburgh and London soured during the summer of 2007. In part that was because the Scottish government had its own agenda. One such example was the belief that Scotland should take the lead for the UK when the EU's Fisheries Council met in Brussels (on the basis that Scotland was the dominant UK player in the sector). Salmond was also opposed to the replacement of the UK's nuclear deterrent at Faslane. The same could be said of the UK government's support for nuclear-generated power (energy is a power reserved to Westminster, as is defence, but planning resides with Holyrood).

Another example concerned the 'Lockerbie Bomber', Abdelbaset Ali Mohmed al-Megrahi, who was imprisoned in Scotland. When Tony Blair hinted in his final days in office that the bomber might serve the rest of his sentence in Libya, it caused consternation in Scotland because he had been jailed under Scots law and such a deal resided outwith Westminster's competence. When Jack Straw, the newly appointed Justice Secretary, visited Edinburgh in the aftermath of the dispute over al-Megrahi, he reportedly 'backed plans to re-establish regular meetings of ministers from the two governments' (*The Times*, 14 July 2007). Although Gordon Brown conceded that he was 'looking forward to working with Salmond', when the two met at the British–Irish Council at Belfast in July 2007, formal contact between the two was rather elusive thereafter (*The Herald*, 17 July 2007). In November 2007 Salmond repeated his demand for the reinstatement of the JMCs. He also called for the abolition of the Scotland Office and for the devolved administrations to be entitled to 'deal directly with the Downing Street Cabinet Office' (*The Herald*, 26 November 2007). His demand fell on stony ground, in part because of the subordinate status of his administration compared to its counterpart in London. Whilst leaders of the devolved administrations could call for more formal relations, including convening the plenary JMC, the outcome essentially rested in the hands of the UK government.

Brown could have been deterred from re-establishing the JMC, however, out of concern that the Scottish government might be tempted to use it as a public platform from which they could wrong-foot their counterparts in London. Central to this was the issue of confidentiality. One such example occurred during October 2007. Following an outbreak of foot-and-mouth disease in England, the origins of which were linked to a government laboratory, bans were placed on the movement of cattle and sheep across the UK. Although this was partially lifted, the consequences were devastating for hill farmers, as they could not get their sheep to market. Subsequently a dispute broke out between Edinburgh and London over an (alleged) £8 million-aid package for Scottish farmers, which the SNP claimed was withdrawn after Gordon Brown decided not to hold an election that autumn. A political adviser at the Scotland Office warned, in response, that 'it is hard to see how the UK Government can trust the Scottish Executive with confidential information in future'.

This was the first time such a breach of confidentiality had occurred between the two administrations. Nonetheless, Brown announced on 30 January 2008 that Paul Murphy, the Secretary of State for Wales, would be responsible for JMCs on devolution and Murphy subsequently met the leaders of the devolved administrations on a bilateral basis in readiness for the first plenary session (Hansard, 18 June 2008, Col. 945W; see also Hansard, 30 January, 2008 Col. 306). In April 2008 Salmond did meet Brown. At the time there were strikes at oil refineries across the UK, raising fears of fuel shortages. Whilst the session appeared to demonstrate that the leaders could work side by side, almost a year went by before they met again in a formal setting.

The plenary meeting of the JMC was held in London on 25 June 2008. The session was chaired by Straw, rather than by Brown. Amongst those who attended were the territorial secretaries of state and the First Ministers of the devolved administrations. Items on the agenda included the EU's renewable energy target in 2020 and the UK government's draft Marine Bill. There were also discussions about relations between the UK government and the devolved administrations (Cabinet Office, CAB/065/08 19 June 2008).

During the meeting it was agreed by all parties present that the dispute resolution mechanism needed to be looked at afresh. Superficially that appears somewhat surprising given that the JMC's secretariat could act as arbitrators and, potentially, if necessary a dispute could be dealt with at the plenary. However, as Murphy explained to the House of Commons, up until then, 'there had been no need to invoke formal dispute resolution processes, and accordingly the arrangements for dispute resolution have not developed beyond those set out in the founding documents' – that is to say the MoU and related papers (Hansard, 18 June 2008 Col. 946W).

Despite the breakdown in relations over the alleged aid for hill farmers the previous autumn, there were no breaches of confidentiality as regards the plenary session and there was no grandstanding in public. Quite the reverse occurred. Publicity bordered on the non-existent and little if any mention was made of the JMC on the Scottish government's website. This very much reflected the desire of the SNP government to demonstrate to its electorate in Scotland it could act in a responsible manner in dealings with London. In so doing, it deflected those who might wish to suggest that their time in office would be one of instability in terms of Holyrood's relations with Westminster. However, 2008 may have been little more than a blip, as the UK economy unravelled the following year and London looked set to cut the Scottish budget between 2010 and 2012, as part of the government's attempts at 'efficiency savings'.

Relations between the Scottish government and the UK therefore experienced some stress during 2009. The first hint of this occurred at First Minister's Questions on 5 February, when Annabel Goldie asked Alex Salmond when he had last met with Gordon Brown formally. The underlying issue for Goldie was that the economic crisis required joint action by both governments. Salmond consequently wrote to Brown requesting a meeting. This quickly came to fruition (all the devolved administrations were involved). Unsurprisingly economic measures topped the agenda, but Salmond also intended to raise the issue of the forthcoming cut to the

Scottish grant as a result of proposed 'efficiency savings'. According to *The Herald*, the session took place not in Downing Street but at Brown's office in the House of Commons. Although the meeting was described as 'cordial', it appears to have raised more questions than answers (*The Herald*, 26 February 2009). Given the existing economic climate, devolution finance has become more contentious. Presumably it was issues such as this which the plenary JMC and its secretariat were intended to address. However, Salmond's meeting with Brown appears to have fallen outside the JMC framework.

The same applied when Finance Secretary John Swinney met Yvette Cooper, Chief Secretary to the Treasury in March 2009. Also present were his colleagues from Wales and Northern Ireland. Although the session was described as 'constructive', the leaders of all three administrations were united in calling for Alistair Darling, the UK Chancellor, to reconsider proceeding with the spending cuts (*The Herald*, 13 March 2009) The lack of transparency as a result of confidentiality ensures that parliamentarians and citizens alike are none the wiser about what, if anything, was agreed. Given the parlous state of the economy, that is cause for concern. Even so, both senior figures in the SNP government and Labour have maintained channels of communication via the Scotland Office when it has been in their mutual interest so to do (thereby affirming that the latter does potentially retain a useful function despite Salmond's call for its abolition in 2007). Essentially, however, this is a bilateral arrangement between Bruce Crawford, the SNP Minister for Parliamentary Business at Holyrood, and Ann McKechin, Under-Secretary of State at the Scotland Office. Whether this is sufficiently robust to meet the strains imposed by the current economic downturn remains to be seen, but it does suggest that the SNP can be pragmatic with regard to inter-governmental relations and the same applies to its attitude towards 'Britain' more generally.

THE DEVELOPMENT OF SNP THINKING

Over the years, Scottish nationalists have differed on what Scotland's relationship should be with Britain. In 1928, when the National Party of Scotland (NPS) was formed, 'self-government' amounted to 'independent national status within the British group of nations'. According to Richard Finlay, the phrase 'British group of nations' had been used deliberately instead of 'British commonwealth of nations' (Finlay 1994: 80). However, senior figures remained divided on the issue. In 1932, it was also proposed that there should be 'joint co-operation with England on foreign and defence matters' (ibid.: 97–9). That persisted when the SNP was formed in 1934 although, as Finlay observed, the SNP was quite distinct from the NPS because there was no desire for Scotland to become a dominion (akin to Australia, for example). Instead, as one of the 'mother nations', Scotland 'shared with England' certain 'rights and responsibilities' with regard to the British Empire. Moreover, 'the new party stressed the continuation of a partnership with England which removed the possibility of independence in the international sphere' (ibid.: 153–4). Consequently, as Findlay remarked, 'the new party was more in line with the Home Rule movements of former times in that self government was firmly placed within the context of the continuation of some form of overall British Government' (ibid.: 154).

However, the matter appeared to be resolved in 1942 when it was decided that 'self-government meant independence from Westminster in the total sense of the word' (ibid.: 239). That position holds true to the present day, though the European Union also needs to be taken account.

Talking Independence (which was published in the run-up to the 2003 election) stated that, 'independence is full control by the people of Scotland over all their own affairs, apart from control in any areas where they have freely agreed to share power with others' (SNP 2003: par. 1.1). However, the attainment of independence, whilst divisive during the latter part of the 1970s (Hutchison 2001: 124), has become less contentious following the party's commitment to a referendum in 2010 (although the other parties at Holyrood have shown little enthusiasm for this with the possible exception of the Scottish Green Party). Yet independence is not tantamount to 'separatism', it would seem, because in a number of respects Scotland would not be wholly detached from the British State.

After its 2007 election victory, the SNP launched *Choosing Scotland's Future: A National Conversation* in a bid to stimulate debate about Scotland's future constitutional status. Some of the issues set out in this document were by no means new but it did flesh out in some detail the proposed institutional arrangements post-independence. The Queen (or her successor) would remain 'the Head of State of Scotland' (Scottish Executive 2007: par. 3.25 p. 24). If the Queen remained Head of State that raises the issue of how independent Scotland would be from the rest of the UK. According to the SNP's *A Constitution for a Free Scotland* (2002), the Head of State would have 'a ceremonial role rather than a position of power within the scheme of government' (p. 6). When the Queen or her successor was not physically in Scotland, the Chancellor of Scotland (whose duties also included acting as the Scottish Parliament's Presiding Officer) 'would exercise the responsibilities of Head of State' (par. 4 p. 7). It was also proposed that there should be a referendum on retaining the monarch as Head of State during the first term of an independent Scottish Parliament (p. 6). However, although some in the party are staunchly republican, that does not apply to the SNP more generally. According to *Talking Independence* it would appear that the SNP is not opposed to the monarchy per se. However, the pamphlet suggested that the monarch could 'have a more informal role than has traditionally been the case in the UK' (par. 11.5). Furthermore, after the introduction of a written constitution and Bill of Right, Scots would be citizens not subjects and sovereignty would therefore reside once again with the people. So, the relationship between Scots and their monarch would change. The party also favoured 'membership of the Commonwealth on independence' (SNP 1999: 31; SNP 2003 par. 11.4, par. 8.9).

In the aftermath of secession Scotland would also retain other connections to the UK. *Choosing Scotland's Future* stated that 'a range of cultural, social and policy initiatives would continue' and there could be 'a series of cross border partnerships and services' (par, 3.26 p. 24). Given that the two countries share the same island, that comes as no surprise. It was also conceivable that 'cross border or UK public bodies' would be involved in Scottish matters if the Scottish government so decided (and presumably so too Westminster). So, in some respects post-secession Scotland could still have connections with the British political system. It would be interesting to see what the SNP had in mind. Maybe it could agree to a British border agency, for example, whereby in the aftermath of independence there might be a form of passport union between Scotland and the rest of the UK, under the aegis of a British–Irish Council (BIC).

The SNP believed that the BIC, a by-product of the Belfast Agreement of 1998, 'could provide a model for future co-operation across Britain and Ireland following independence for Scotland' (SNP 2003: 30). In effect it would be somewhat akin to the Nordic Council which was originally conceived in 1952 as an inter-governmental body. The Nordic Council enabled five Scandinavian countries (Denmark, Iceland, Norway, Finland and Sweden) to collaborate where it was in their mutual self-interest to do so. That applied, for example, to the creation of 'a passport union, reciprocal extension of social security rules and a common regional labour market' (Neil Elder in Gowland et al. 2006, 164–6). The origins of the SNP's position on the BIC can be traced to an inquiry into how Scotland could become independent in Europe. A subsequent report stated that 'following independence a body analogous to the Nordic Council to be established for regional co-operation among the states of the British Isles'. In effect there would be a 'social union' (Murray 2000: 127).

Would 'Britain' therefore persist in some form or other and, if so, would Scotland remain part of 'Britain'? The SNP claimed that the Council 'would provide formal mechanisms for the governments of Britain and Ireland to work together to complement continuing relations across the islands in social and cultural fields, as well as the Union of the Crowns' (Scottish Executive 2007: 30). So it would seem that Scotland would remain a part of 'Britain'. Almost a decade earlier, speaking in the Republic of Ireland, Alex Salmond indicated his preference for the term 'the Council of the Isles' but then referred to it as 'an Association of British states which would embrace Scotland, Ireland, England, Wales and Northern Ireland' (Salmond 1998: 73–4). Whilst such a body would not encroach on Scottish autonomy, whether the phrase 'British states' is appropriate, given the Republic of Ireland's status, is open to question. But it could be argued that as Scotland and the rest of the UK share the same monarch as Head of State, such a descriptor is potentially tenable in relation to them. In effect being British (for those who wish to describe themselves as such) would be essentially a cultural and social phenomenon somewhat akin to being Scandinavian and not too much should be made of it.

However, until Scotland attains independence, the issue of inter-governmental relations remains contentious. As Jeffery rightly observed, 'asymmetrical devolution [. . .] encourages bilateral rather than multilateral (that is, UK-wide) discussion of policy areas and objectives' (Jeffery 2008: 203). Whether his concern that the current arrangements are 'ill-equipped to express and contain the new dynamics of territorial politics' (Jeffery: 207) have potentially adverse consequences remains to be seen. But at the time of writing it faces its greatest test not only due to the ideological divergence of the governing administrations in London and Edinburgh but also due to the deteriorating economic situation. To date the SNP government has respected the ground rules in its conduct of relations with London. Where possible it has sought to avoid confrontation with the UK government in public, but it remains to be seen how long that can be sustained given the absence of more formal mechanisms. In addition, whether or not Scotland now has a louder voice in London is a moot point. On the one hand having the same or like-minded parties in power in London and Edinburgh means that intra- and inter-party channels can be mobilised to influence outcomes behind the scenes. On the other, the SNP would be unlikely to tolerate the apparent flaws in inter-governmental communication and co-operation that were exposed in the Scottish Executive's leaked report early in 2007.

Whilst the desire for 'independence' lies at the party's core what it actually amounts to in practice is questionable in an era in which sovereignty in its purest sense is somewhat ephemeral (see for example MacCormick 1999 and Keating 2001). In part the erosion of sovereignty is the result of European integration. In addition it is a reflection of global economic interdependence, a by-product of which is the current financial crisis. Equally, it is inconceivable that in the aftermath of secession from the UK, Scotland and its people would chose to isolate themselves completely from their closest neighbours with whom they have much in common. From the SNP's perspective, therefore, independence is not tantamount to 'separatism', it is rather more incremental. The Queen would continue as Head of State unless Scots decide otherwise. Scotland would remain part of a monarchical and social union within Britain, the constituent territories of which would retain cultural and economic ties. Scotland would expect to become a member state in the EU in its own right. It would also seek membership of the Commonwealth and the UN: international organisations such as these not only offer Scotland the opportunity to work alongside other countries in the global community but also to collaborate with the territorial remnants of the UK where it is in their mutual interest so to do. Whilst such an incremental approach to 'independence' might be regarded as betrayal by some sections of the party, the SNP's pragmatism reflects a realism not dissimilar to some of its forebears in the 1920s and 1930s. Whether Scotland secedes from the UK or not rests to no small degree in the hands of the Scottish electorate, an electorate at the time of writing that appears to shows little appetite for 'separatism'.

Notes

1. Memorandum of Understanding and Supplementary Agreements between the United Kingdom Government, Scottish Ministers and the Cabinet of the National Assembly for Wales, SE 99/36 October 1999.
2. This point is made by Lord Falconer of Thorton when he was Solicitor General. HL Deb 588, cols. 1131–2, 21 April 1998, in Winetrobe 1999.

References

Bogdanor, V. (1999), *Devolution in the United Kingdom*, Oxford, Oxford University Press.

Bulmer, S., Burch, M., Carter, C., Hogwood, P. and Scott, A. (2002), *British Devolution and European Policy-Making: Transforming Britain into Multi-Level Governance*, Basingstoke, Palgrave.

Bulpitt, J. (1983), *Territory and Power in the United Kingdom: An Interpretation*, Manchester, Manchester University Press.

Finlay, R. J. (1994), *Independent and Free: Scottish Politics and the Origins of the Scottish National Party 1918–1945*, Edinburgh, John Donald.

Gowland, D., Dunphy, R. and Lythe C. (eds) (2006), *The European Mosaic*, Harlow, Pearson.

Gowland, D., Turner, A. and Wright A. (2009), *Britain and Europe since 1945: On the Sidelines*, London, Routledge.

Hutchison I. G. C. (2001), *Scottish Politics in the Twentieth Century*, Basingstoke, Palgrave.

Jeffery, C. (2008), 'Where Stands the Union Now?', in Devine, T. M. (ed.), *Scotland and the Union 1707–2007*, Edinburgh, Edinburgh University Press.

Keating, M. (2001), *Plurinational Democracy: Stateless Nations in a Post-Sovereignty Era*, Oxford, Oxford University Press.

Keating, M. (2005), *The Government of Scotland*, Edinburgh, Edinburgh University Press.

Kellas, J. G. (1989), *The Scottish Political System*, 4th edn, Cambridge, Cambridge University Press.

MacCormick, N. (1999), *Questioning Sovereignty: Law, State, and Nation in the European Commonwealth*, Oxford, Oxford University Press.

Midwinter, A., Keating, M. and Mitchell J. (1991), *Politics and Public Policy in Scotland*, Basingstoke, Macmillan.

Mitchell, J. (2003), *Governing Scotland: The Invention of Administrative Devolution*, Basingstoke, Palgrave.

Murray G., (2000), 'New Relations Between Scotland and Ireland', in Wright, A. (ed.), *Scotland: The Challenge of Devolution*, Aldershot, Ashgate.

Paterson, L. (1994), *The Autonomy of Modern Scotland*, Edinburgh, Edinburgh University Press.

Salmond, A. (1998),' Scotland and Ireland', *Scottish Affairs*, No. 25, Autumn 1998.

Scottish Executive (2007), *Choosing Scotland's Future: A National Conversation*, Edinburgh, Scottish Executive.

Sewel, Lord (2007), 'The Union and Devolution: A Fair Relationship', in Bryant, C. (ed.), *Towards a New Constitutional Settlement*, London, Smith Institute.

Sillars, J. (1986), *Scotland: The Case for Optimism*, Edinburgh, Polygon.

SNP (1994), *A Manifesto for the European Elections, June 1994*, Edinburgh, SNP.

SNP (1999), *Scotland's Party Manifesto for the Scotland's Parliament 1999 Elections*, Edinburgh, SNP.

SNP (2002), *A Constitution for a Free Scotland*, Edinburgh, SNP.

SNP (2003), *Talking Independence*, Edinburgh, SNP.

Trench, A. (2003), 'Intergovernmental Relations', in Hazell, R. (ed.) *The State of the Nations 2003*, Exeter, Imprint Academic.

Trench, A. (2005), 'Intergovernmental Relations within the UK', in Trench, A. (ed.) *The Dynamics of Devolution*, Exeter, Imprint Academic.

Winetrobe, B. (1999), *The Scottish Parliament*, SPICe, Research Paper 99/12.

Wright, A., (2005), *Who Governs Scotland?*, London, Routledge.

CHAPTER 15

Degrees of Independence:
SNP Thinking in an International Context

Eve Hepburn

INTRODUCTION

Independence is something of a minority preference amongst nationalist parties in Europe and beyond. Far from demanding sovereign statehood and a complete separation of powers from the host state, the vast majority of nationalist parties have opted for creative forms of shared sovereignty within larger state and supranational structures. This makes the Scottish National Party's constitutional goals quite distinctive within the nationalist party family (Lynch 1996; De Winter and Türsan 1998; Hepburn 2009a). For the SNP, independence is the only way to make Scotland a 'normal nation' (SNP 2009). Yet the SNP has refrained from advocating a nineteenth-century notion of statehood, based on the doctrine of indivisible, unitary internal sovereignty. Nor has the SNP been dogmatically committed to only one form of self-government for Scotland. Rather, the SNP since its inception has supported *degrees* of independence for Scotland within various larger political frameworks, including dominion status within the British Empire, self-government within a confederal British Isles and independence in an integrating Europe. The SNP has regularly revised its understanding of independence, and its goals for achieving this, in response to changing processes of spatial rescaling at the state, supranational and international levels. This fluid understanding of independence has been important in enabling the SNP to exploit opportunities resulting from state restructuring. Moreover, the SNP's support for varying degrees of independence has allowed it to endear itself to a Scottish electorate that is generally unfavourable to separation from the UK (McCrone 2009).

This chapter will consider how the SNP has interpreted the meaning of independence over the years. The first part begins with an examination of the SNP's early demands for self-government, before exploring in depth the idea of 'independence in Europe' (which became official party policy in 1988). In particular, it considers the paradox that although European integration has offered the SNP an external framework for supporting Scottish sovereignty, it has also undermined that very sovereignty by concentrating certain powers at the supranational level. The second section considers how the existence of a devolved Scottish Parliament has altered the context for pursuing independence, whereby the SNP's strategies have shifted to support for 'softer' forms of independence and 'devolution-max'. Following this, the SNP's understanding of independence is placed in an international context, through comparison with nationalist party demands in Wales, Catalonia, Quebec, and Sardinia. Finally, the concluding section reflects on how the meaning of independence has been irrevocably changed in a post-sovereign world, and considers the challenges small nations face from (in particular, economic) globalisation.

CHANGING NOTIONS OF SCOTTISH SELF-GOVERNMENT

The Scottish National Party, which was established in 1934, is one of the oldest existing nationalist parties in the world and its support for independence is very much of an historic nature. However, independence has not always been the main demand of the SNP. In its early years, the SNP's constitutional goals were of a vague and underdeveloped nature, lying 'somewhere between devolution and independence within the Empire' (Lynch 2002: 10). This to an extent reflected the uneasy confluence of demands for Scottish self-government during the party's formation. The merger of the pro-independence National Party of Scotland and the pro-Home Rule Scottish Party to form the SNP forced a compromise on the constitutional question. The end result satisfied neither party and produced a faultline that would plague the SNP for decades to come, between those members wishing to remain within the UK and those wishing to leave it. The newly formed SNP's goals were to establish a Scottish parliament within the UK, whereby 'Scotland shall share with England the rights and responsibilities they, as mother nations, have jointly created and incurred within the British Empire' (Finlay 1994: 153). A partnership of 'mother nations' would include joint machinery to deal with foreign policy, defence and the creation of a customs union (which the SNP would later propose sharing within Europe). Clearly, the SNP's first constitutional aims were marked by interdependence with, rather than independence from, England within the larger ambit of the British Empire.

In the 1930s and early 1940s, the divisions between 'independentist' and 'home rule' factions became more sharpened, and the home rulers left the SNP to set up their own rival political organisation in 1942. The Scottish Convention (and later the Scottish Covenant Association), headed by John MacCormick, sought to build a cross-party consensus as well as mass popular support for Scottish devolution. The departure of MacCormick's group allowed the SNP to develop a clearer position on the constitutional question. In 1943, the party re-wrote its constitution to focus on 'the restoration of Scottish national sovereignty, by the establishment of a democratic Scottish government, whose authority will be limited only by such agreements as will be freely entered into with other nations' (cited in Lynch 2002: 58).

In the following decades, the SNP would develop a much stronger commitment to separating Scotland from the UK and establishing it as an independent sovereign state with full powers over its affairs. But even then, there were still 'unifying' aspects of the party's independence line. In particular, Scotland was to remain a member of the Commonwealth and the Queen would continue to be the (unelected) Head of State for Scotland. Moreover, the SNP was never able to completely purge itself of pro-devolution sentiment. Some party members continued to support greater powers for Scotland within the UK, and with the demise of the Scottish Covenant Association (SCA) and the death of MacCormick in 1961, the arrival of new SCA members into the party further diversified the SNP's base and consolidated the home rule and independence wings of the party (Brand 1978). These days, this is referred to as the division between 'fundamentalists' and 'gradualists'. The former see independence as a zero-sum game, whilst the latter see sovereign statehood arriving in stages.

In the following decades, the SNP's position on independence was fundamentally altered by two processes of state restructuring. The first of these was the possibility of gaining devolution for Scotland in the 1970s. In response to the rise of the SNP and Plaid Cymru, the Labour governments of 1974–9 sought to implement devolutionary measures for Scotland and Wales. Although the SNP believed that Labour's plans did not go far enough to satisfy demands for self-government, it did offer tentative support for the Scotland and Wales Bill 1977 in the House of Commons. But the party's campaign on the streets was of a more fundamentalist nature. The SNP demanded 'Independence, nothing less' in an attempt to reassure grassroots supporters that it had not abandoned its ultimate goal. Support for devolution also had important policy implications for the party. At its annual conference in 1976, 58% of SNP members voted to accept an assembly with limited powers. Lynch (2002: 148) describes the outcome as 'a classic gradualist-fundamentalist compromise over devolution'. Yet whilst the SNP became active in a 'Yes' campaign for a Scottish assembly, it did not join a cross-party umbrella group with Labour and Scotland's other parties. Such divisions within the 'Yes' camp did not bode well for a favourable vote for a Scottish assembly and the referendum failed. SNP Leader Gordon Wilson blamed the poor result on 'the indecisive collective direction of the party, which has wandered in only two years from full-blooded independence to an obsession with devolution' (cited in Lynch 2002: 156). In the aftermath of 1979, the SNP moved once more to a more fundamentalist position.

During the same period, debates on UK membership of the European Economic Community forced a re-evaluation of the SNP's goal of independence. The SNP was during the post-war era highly suspicious of European integration. The EEC was viewed as centralist and elitist, and it was unclear how Scottish interests would be represented if the EC operated on an inter-governmental basis – with the UK government taking important decisions over Scottish affairs. During the referendum on continued British membership of the EEC in 1975, the SNP argued that UK membership of the European Community conflicted with the 1707 Treaty of Union and campaigned on the theme 'No voice, no entry' (Lynch 1996: 31). However, it misjudged the mood of the public and, with a turnout of 61.7%, Scotland voted 'Yes' by 58.4%. The referendum result forced the SNP to re-think its attitude towards the EEC and from 1979 the SNP's first elected representative in the European Parliament, Winnie Ewing, brought a new awareness of the European dimension into the party. The SNP also began arguing for a stronger role for Scotland in Europe, and with the enlistment of Jim Sillars, a former Labour politician, the SNP began to develop positive linkages between EEC membership and Scottish self-government (Hepburn 2006).

INDEPENDENCE IN AN INTEGRATING EUROPE

The SNP adopted a policy of 'independence in Europe' in 1988 in response to accusations of trying to 'divorce' Scotland from the rest of the UK. The justifications for this policy appeared to be largely pragmatic: the European context would provide not only an external political support system for a small country such as Scotland, but also an economic one, by removing the threat of economic dislocation from England through the European common market, and providing potential security safeguards without the need to join organisations such as NATO. The SNP became an avid supporter of economic and monetary integration, and high-ranking members of the Party, such as Roseanna Cunningham, indicated that the SNP would be happy to grant the EU powers over defence and foreign policy.

Membership of the EU therefore appeared to lessen many of the transition costs of independence through access to the common market, structural funds for underperforming areas, and a ready-made institutional system in which small states had a disproportionate voice. As former party leader Gordon Wilson stated, 'within the common trading umbrella, the move to independence can take place smoothly and easily' (cited in Lynch 2002: 6). Support for such integrationist measures, however, raised questions about how independent Scotland would actually be as a full EU member state, and to what extent independence would actually give Scotland the territorial capacity to manage processes of social and economic change, given that economic and social policy in European member states was largely impinged upon by EU regulations.

There has been significant contestation within the SNP about how the goal of independence in Europe should be achieved, and what kind of Europe the SNP would like to see being developed. For instance, when the policy was adopted in the late 1980s, there was ambiguity as to whether the party supported centralisation or decentralisation, or federalism versus confederalism in the EU. Those within the 'supranationalist' camp advocated closer European unification, in which a central authority would have control over foreign policy, defence and a single currency. Contrarily, those who positioned themselves within the intergovernmentalist camp argued for the primacy of states, whereby powers would only be transferred to the EU if the members states so decided. Allan Macartney MEP (1990) made an attempt to clarify where the SNP stood in these issues. He argued that the goal would entail the creation of a European confederation, that is, an association of member states which pool sovereignty in certain areas but do not surrender total control to an authoritative body. This would allow Scotland to exert equal influence over decision-making as other small member states. This view is reflected in *Scotland – A European Nation* (SNP 1992: 5), where it is stated that 'many decisions affecting the lives of every European will continue to be taken in Brussels. And . . . those decisions will be reached by representatives of independent member states in the Council of Ministers.'

However, despite aiming for a confederal Europe with power concentrated at the member-state level in the Council of Ministers, the SNP also became active in debates about the regionalisation of Europe. For instance, it favoured the creation of a Committee of the Regions (CoR) in 1993, an issue which split the party when SNP leaders made a secret 'deal' with the Conservative government to win more seats on the Committee for Scotland (*The Scotsman*, 9 April 1993). The SNP was also supportive of the establishment of Scotland House, the creation of a Scottish Minister for European and External Affairs, and the development of stronger links between the Scottish Parliament and other substate governments in Europe. The SNP has talked at length about the need to implement the principles of 'subsidiarity' within the EU's member states.

Since taking office in 2007, the SNP has furthermore argued that Scottish ministers in the devolved parliament should be given the right to participate in the EU Council of Ministers' meetings, and to take the lead in UK delegations on matters of relevance to Scotland. This strategy represents the triumph of the gradualist wing over the fundamentalists. By seeking to gradually expand the powers of the Scottish Parliament, in particular in its European relations, the SNP has realised how much a devolved parliament could do in Europe – something that other national-ist parties in Europe have long played towards. But SNP demands for a stronger Scottish presence in Europe has also put into question the fun-damentalist position of how much sovereignty the SNP really wants for Scotland. In particular, gaining Scottish representation on the Council of Ministers (albeit through the UK delegation) would arguably meet one of the main aims of independence in Europe.

So what could an independent Scotland in Europe actually do? Keating (2002) argues that the three main functions Scotland would seek to repat-riate from Westminster (defence and foreign affairs, fiscal and monetary policy and social security) would be highly constrained by European integration, globalisation and ties to the rest of the UK. On defence and foreign affairs, an independent Scotland would not be able to defend itself from foreign attack, and would rely on a future European defence and security system (given the party's hostility to joining NATO). However, as a small member state in the EU, it may not have much control over the direction of security policy. On fiscal and monetary affairs, there is a risk that Scotland becomes too dependent on oil revenues (which is danger-ous given volatile prices), or international markets (so Scotland would be fearful of doing anything to detract investors). The SNP also proposes to give up an independent currency in favour of the European currency (euro), though it would be vulnerable to fluctuations in the pound if the rest of the UK does not join. And on social security, an independent Scotland would no longer be able to pool economic shocks resulting from recession with the UK, though it could use social integration to adapt to change, as the Nordic countries have done (Keating 2002: 292).

From a different perspective, the SNP's principled support for integra-tionist measures, such as the Economic and Monetary Union (EMU) and the process of Eastern enlargement, have masked a subtle protectionist edge to SNP discourse. Since the early 2000s, the SNP has taken a strong stand on the Common Agricultural Policy (CAP) and Common Fisheries Policy (CFP) and has even threatened at times to opt out of these policies altogether in order to protect Scotland's fishing and agricultural sectors. This indicates that the SNP is unsure whether certain integrationist measures actually benefit Scotland's interests, or whether they may even threaten Scotland. For instance, the SNP has argued that although it supported the European currency, it also held a 'rigorously critical view of excessive Euro-enthusiasm, and creeping integrationism. We have a robust view of the need to set clear limits to what can properly be done at the all-Europe level and what must be retained by the states and their regions in accordance with subsidiarity' (SNP 2001: 1–2).

Therefore, a number of contradictions exist within the SNP's policy programme, whose support of further European integration in matters of monetary and economic policy, defence and security, sits awkwardly with the party's demands for an intergovernmental Europe with power residing among the states. As Keating (2002: 294) sums up, 'independence in Europe involves swapping classic sovereignty for influence within a complex system of decision-making.' The EU is not only an association of states; it can also be seen a normative order that profoundly affects the sovereignty of its members, undermining their claims to a monopoly of authority over its territory and eroding its functional powers (MacCormick 1999; Keating 2002). In the context of closer European integration, many important legislative decisions regarding defence, security and monetary policy are being increasingly centralised at the European level, leaving both independent and devolved parliaments with the same competences over social policy. This means that the difference between devolution and independence is not quite as clear cut as the SNP (and Labour) suggests.

DEVOLUTION AND DEGREES OF INDEPENDENCE

In many ways, devolution has benefited the Scottish National Party by giving it a new platform for its demands. Cross-national evidence demonstrates that nationalist parties perform better in regional than statewide elections, and the SNP is no exception, as we saw in May 2007. When taking office in Holyrood, one of the SNP's first actions was to publish a white paper setting out Scotland's constitutional options in August 2007, entitled *Choosing Scotland's Future* (Scottish Executive 2007) and to launch a consultative 'national conversation' on these options. As the party of government, the SNP is in a position to influence public opinion on the merits of independence and has a range of mechanisms at its disposal to do this. Furthermore, with the creation of new institutions including a Scottish government and a Scottish parliament, devolution has de facto lowered the institutional barriers to independence.

However, devolution has also created new barriers to independence. In the additional-member system (AMS) electoral system of the Scottish Parliament, governments will most likely be of a minority or a coalition nature. The SNP was forced into the former scenario in May 2007, when the Liberal Democrats refused to enter a coalition. Minority government presents significant challenges for the party, requiring it to compromise on policy issues and seek consensus with others. It also means that the unionist opposition – which represents a majority in the parliament – can veto any legislation to hold an independence referendum. Yet perhaps a greater problem is that devolution appears to have lessened popular demand for independence. Even though the SNP won the Scottish Parliament election in 2007, it was not on the back of popular demand for independence. Indeed, support for independence at that moment was 25% (less than half the support for devolution) (McCrone 2009: 93). So for the time being, it appears that devolution has managed to constrain popular support for independence.

Furthermore, the transformation of the SNP from opposition movement to party of government does not come without its problems. Governing at the regional level puts any independence-seeking party in a difficult position. The SNP's main demand is for an independent Scotland, but at the same time it must demonstrate that it can effectively implement its policies in a devolved Scotland in order to win the next election. To do so, the SNP has sought to downplay its main goal by delivering independence 'by stealth'. This means seeking to gradually build upon the 1998 devolved settlement to the point where independence seems the next natural step. This strategy of accelerationism might allow the party to make more 'constitutional progress through arguing for "more" independence for Scotland rather than absolute independence' (Lynch 2002: 253). Yet there is also the danger that expanding the powers of the Scottish Parliament (so that many of the general aims of self-government are achieved) undermines the actual need for independence. In this context, independence and devolution would become increasingly difficult to distinguish.

Given low public support for independence, Lynch (2005: 511) argues that the SNP must either somehow convert voters to the merits of independence, or offer a new constitutional option, like the Parti Québécois did in the 1995 referendum on Quebec's 'sovereignty-partnership' with Canada. The SNP has opted for the latter strategy, by demanding more powers for the Scottish Parliament (especially on Europe), fiscal autonomy and 'devolution max'. On the first issue, the SNP has advocated the expansion of the Scottish Parliament's powers on European matters, as well granting the executive a representative role in European institutions on a par with the German Länder or Belgian regions. Furthermore, the party wishes to expand the Scottish Parliament's control and influence over areas like energy, welfare, transport, defence and immigration – powers that are currently exercised by Westminster, but which the SNP believes a devolved Scotland should have. On the issue of fiscal autonomy, the SNP has proposed obtaining the right to set tax rates, define tax bases and raise the money that the parliament spends through borrowing. This would improve the devolved parliament's accountability to the electorate, as well as the responsibility of MSPs by forcing more discipline into spending decisions.

In 2008, the SNP repackaged these proposals as 'devolution max'. At the time, Finance Secretary John Swinney declared that he would consider a watered-down form of independence, whereby full financial powers would be devolved to Scotland, giving the Scottish Parliament control over everything except monetary policy. Cynics might argue that this strategy was only to gain Liberal Democratic or Conservative support for an independence referendum, to pass the legislation through the Scottish Parliament. Others might reason that the SNP was merely responding to public opinion, whereby the majority of support was for increased powers for the parliament and not independence. But another argument could also be made that devolution max represented a 'softer' form of independence that recognised the extensive interdependencies between Scotland and the rest of the UK and Europe, which was part of a long tradition of SNP accommodation of various forms of shared sovereignty in its constitutional goals.

Recently, the SNP has highlighted its commitment to continuing partnership with England and other parts of the UK were Scotland to secede. SNP minister Bruce Crawford speaks of a 'Kingdom of United Countries' of the British Isles, whereby it is necessary for 'governments across the UK and Europe to work together to face today's problems' (Crawford 2009). This reiterates SNP leader Alex Salmond's proposal to create a 'Council of the Isles' with joint decision-making machinery that brings Scotland, Ireland, Wales and Northern Ireland together to discuss issues of relevance (see Alex Wright's contribution to this book). It is clear that, owing to the deep unpopularity of the EU following the failed draft constitution, the SNP has focused once again on the 'UK partnership' dimension of its self-determination claims rather than the European dimension. This is noticeable in its paper *Choosing Scotland's Future* (Scottish Executive 2007). The SNP highlight the extensive linkages and interdependencies between

Scotland and the rest of the UK, including cross-border public services, policy initiatives and the unifying presence of the British monarchy. This softer position on independence may indicate that party members are following in the footsteps of the late Neil MacCormick MEP (son of John MacCormick) – an 'unrepentant gradualist' – in accepting more flexible interpretations of independence. As MacCormick (1999) argued:

> independence, freedom, sovereignty. All names, all labels. The SNP is part of a long, wide movement for self-government, autonomy. Now that in my definition would mean autonomy in whatever overall context of governance is sensible, constructive, forward-looking and also expressive of solidarity.

SNP Demands in an International Context

Whilst the SNP has focused its constitutional demands on independence, nationalist parties elsewhere have tended to seek unique forms of autonomy within state and supranational structures that fall short of full sovereign statehood. With the exception of the independence platforms of the ETA-associated Herri Batasuna and left-wing Eusko Alkartasuna, most nationalist parties have repeatedly rejected outright independence in response to the changing opportunities for self-determination resulting from globalisation and supranational integration. The Union Démocratique Bretonne (UDB) in Breton, the Unione di u Popule Corsu (UPC) in Corsica, the Union Valdotaine in Val d'Aosta, and the Bloque Nacionalista Galego (BNG) in Galicia have all developed autonomy goals that amount to something less than secession, where state sovereignty is no longer the issue.

To take some relevant examples, the Convergence and Union Party (CiU) in Catalonia does not believe that Catalonia must be independent to be self-determining. Instead, it frames Catalan nationalism within the Spanish and European contexts, emphasising the linkages and interdependencies that Catalans can take advantage of by operating in multiple spheres of influence. The CiU believes that Catalan nationalism has prospered with its integration into Europe, and to that end it is an avid supporter of a Europe of the Regions. Likewise, the constitutional aims of the nationalist Sardinian Action Party (Psd'Az) are more subtle than simply demanding independence (Hepburn 2009b). The party wishes to construct a federal Italy as part of a federalised Europe, in which Sardinia can exercise maximum autonomy. It supports the creation of a 'European Federation of the Peoples', in which the Italian federal state would have limited competences over currency, justice and defence, and the regions and nations would be responsible for everything else (Psd'Az 2003). But sooner or later the Psd'Az claims that these powers over defence, justice and monetary policy will be transferred to the European level in a federalising structure, so the Italian state is rendered obsolete and the regions obtain primary status in Europe. As a result, Sardinia would be freed of its ties to the Italian state without formally separating from it.

Similarly, Plaid Cymru has also rejected full independence for Wales in an integrating Europe. Instead, the party has sought to secure Welsh self-determination, first within a Britannic Confederation and then within a Europe of the Peoples. In each of the manifestations of Welsh nationalism, the 'principled rejection of sovereign statehood continued to inform Plaid Cymru's long-term constitutional thinking' (Elias 2009). Finally, what many scholars would argue is the closest comparator to the SNP, the Parti Québécois, has also taken heed of the realities of economic and political interdependence in a globalising world, and the need to maintain formal links with the rest of Canada. The party moved from supporting a form of 'sovereignty-association' in 1980, to 'partnership with Canada' in 1995, to support for a 'confederal Union' with a common Quebec-Canadian parliament in 2003 (Sorens 2004). The party presented these linkages to Canada as a form of insurance policy against the risks of full independence. Moreover, it believed that institutionalised interdependence in the form of the North American Free Trade Agreement (NAFTA) would provide the necessary external support for an independent Quebec (Keating 2001). Clearly, the CiU, Psd'Az, Plaid Cymru, Parti Québécois and others have been able to successfully integrate the notions of shared sovereignty in an integrating Europe and a globalising world into their core constitutional objectives – a trend that the SNP has not fully incorporated into its self-determination goals, but not fully rejected either.

CONCLUSION: INDEPENDENCE IN A POST-SOVEREIGN WORLD

The last few decades have witnessed enormous changes to the structure, competences, legislative framework, economy and political systems of states (Keating 2001; MacCormick 1999; Bartolini 2005). The twin processes of supranational integration and decentralisation have resulted in a far-reaching process of spatial rescaling. This transformation of the state has radically altered the meaning of independence, whereby the state is no longer the only source of ultimate authority (Keating 2001; Tierney 2005). Instead, scholars have begun to examine the implications of 'variegated' or shared sovereignty, whereby states are not so much independent as 'interdependent' (MacCormick 1999; Keating 2002; Walker 2002). This is part of the shift away from conventional understandings of sovereignty focused on the nation state and the (consequent) re-discovery that sovereignty was never as fully focused on the nation state as the conventions of post-war social science would have us think.

As a result, some scholars have asked why substate actors continue to demand independence when the very concept of state sovereignty is losing its meaning (Tierney 2005: 161). For instance, if we define sovereignty as consisting of 'a *plausible claim to ultimate authority* made on behalf of a particular polity' (Walker 2002: 345), how much sovereignty can a state in the EU now claim, when many of its competences have been shifted upwards? Tierney (2005) argues that in response to these developments, nationalist parties have developed a more nuanced approach, seeking complex constitutional arrangements within and beyond the state. Such aspirations are evident in the self-determination goals of nationalist parties in Catalonia, Quebec, Sardinia, Wales and elsewhere, who have not only responded to global interdependencies, but have further sought to radically transform the nature of the state itself. Seeking self-determination within larger political and economic structures is especially important if the territory possesses a small population and few resources, and its chances of 'survival', or being able to maintain pre-independence standards of living, seem small. This issue has become more pressing in the light of the current economic downturn, where small countries such as Iceland and Ireland have been rocked by collapsed banks and deep recession. Critics argued that an independent Scotland would not have been able to afford bailing out its two major financial institutions – the Royal Bank of Scotland and HBOS (Halifax Bank of Scotland). This puts the SNP's economic case for independence into question, despite the probability that if an independent Scotland were part of the Eurozone it would have received financial help from European institutions. But this fact in itself serves to highlight the dependent nature of an independent Scotland on Europe.

Because of these issues, the SNP has been forced to revise its notions of absolute Scottish sovereignty. It has moved to supporting 'degrees of independence' for Scotland, which have been informed by considerations of state partnership, European integration and globalisation. This has been evident in its reformulation of the goal of independence in Europe, its emphasis on the gradual accumulation of powers within larger political structures, and its commitment to maintaining close economic, public-services and symbolic ties to the UK. This move to an 'accelerationist' strategy places the SNP more firmly within the nationalist party family camp, which has predominantly sought to achieve self-determination within larger networks of decentred sovereignty.

However, contradictions still remain within the SNP's interpretation of independence, in particular, with regard to the implications of an integrating Europe for an independent Scotland. Whilst the SNP has expressed a principled commitment to European integration, in recent years it has articulated several reservations about the scope and direction of future integration. In particular, it has criticised the European agriculture and fisheries policy, threatened to oppose the draft constitution in a national referendum and opposed the encroachment of certain European regulations on current devolved competences and a future independent Scotland's powers (Hepburn 2008). One wonders: how feasible is independence in Europe, when the party does not support aspects of Europe? This is another tension in the party, alongside the gradualist–fundamentalist divide, that has historically plagued the party, and is set to continue to do so in the aftermath of the failed European Constitution and a notable rise in hostility to the European project amongst the British electorate.

References

Bartolini, S. (2005), *Restructuring Europe: Centre Formation, System Building and Political Structuring between the Nation State and the European Union*, Oxford, Oxford University Press.

Brand, J. (1978), *The National Movement in Scotland*, London, Routledge and Kegan Paul.

Crawford, B. (2009), 'Keynote Speech to Ten Years of the Scottish Parliament: Achievements and Futures', Edinburgh, 12 May.

De Winter, L. and Türsan, H. (1998), *Regionalist Parties in Western Europe*, London and New York, Routledge.

Elias, A. (2009), 'From Marginality to Opposition to Government: Mapping the Ideological Evolution of Plaid Cymru and the BNG', *Regional and Federal Studies*, 19:5.

Finlay, R. J. (1994), *Independent and Free: Scottish Politics and the Origins of the Scottish National Party 1918–1945*, Edinburgh, John Donald.

Hepburn, E. (2006), 'Scottish Autonomy and European Integration: The Response of Scotland's Political Parties', in McGarry, J, and Keating, M. (eds), *European Integration and the Nationalities Question*, London, Routledge.

Hepburn, E. (2008), 'The Rise and Fall of a "Europe of the Regions"', *Regional and Federal Studies*, 18:5.

Hepburn, E. (2009a) (ed.), *New Challenges for Stateless Nationalist and Regionalist Parties*, Special Issue of *Regional and Federal Studies*, 19:5.

Hepburn, E. (2009b), 'The Ideological Polarisation and De-Polarisation of Sardinian Nationalism', *Regional and Federal Studies*, 19:5.

Keating, M. (2001), *Plurinational Democracy: Stateless Nations in a Post-Sovereignty Era*, Oxford, Oxford University Press.

Keating, M. (2002), 'Independence in an Interdependent World', in Murkens, J., Jones, P., and Keating, M., *Scottish Independence: A Practical Guide*, Edinburgh, Edinburgh University Press.

Lynch, P. (1996), *Minority Nationalism and European Integration*, Cardiff, University of Wales Press.

Lynch, P. (2002), *SNP. The History of the Scottish National Party*, Cardiff, Welsh Academic Press.

Lynch, P. (2005), 'Scottish Independence, the Quebec Model of Secession and the Political Future of the Scottish National Party', *Nationalism and Ethnic Politics*, 11:4

Macartney, A. (1990) 'Independence in Europe', in Brown, A. and Parry, R. (eds), *The Scottish Government Yearbook*, Edinburgh, Unit for the Study of Government in Scotland, pp. 35–48.

MacCormick, N. (1999), *Questioning Sovereignty: Law, State, and Nation in the European Commonwealth*, Oxford, Oxford University Press.

McCrone, D. (2009), 'Conundrums and Contradictions: What Scotland Wants' in Jeffery, C. and Mitchell, J, (eds), *The Scottish Parliament 1999–2009: The First Decade*, Edinburgh, Luath Press.

Psd'Az (2003), *La nuova stagione della NON dipendenza*, Cagliari: Psd'Az.

SNP (1992), *Scotland – A European Nation: The Case for Independent Scottish Membership of the European Community*, Edinburgh, SNP.

SNP (1996), *A Real Scottish Parliament*, Edinburgh, SNP.

SNP (2001), *Scotland in Europe: The Fundamentals of SNP Policy*, Edinburgh, SNP.

SNP (2009), *Independence: The Benefits*, http://www.snp.org/node/240.

Scottish Executive (2007), *Choosing Scotland's Future: A National Conversation* Edinburgh, Scottish Executive.

Sorens, J. (2004), 'Globalization, Secessionism, and Autonomy', *Electoral Studies*, 23.

Tierney, S. (2005), 'Reframing Sovereignty: Substate National Societies and Contemporary Challenges to the Nation-State', *International and Comparative Law Quarterly*, pp. 61–83.

Walker, N. (2002), 'The Idea of Constitutional Pluralism', *Modern Law Review*, 65(3).

CHAPTER 16

Nationalist Movements in Comparative Perspective

Michael Keating

NATIONS AND NATIONALISM

The death of nationalism has long been predicted, during the nineteenth century, after the Second World War, and in the euphoria of globalisation at the end of the Cold War. Yet it always seems to come back. This is no happenstance. It is impossible ever to align perfectly the nation with the state, the economy and a single culture, given that these are perpetually changing their contours and meaning. Nationalism is a continual argument over the locus and meaning of political authority that has no end as long as history itself has no end.

Despite the ubiquity of the phenomenon, there are surprisingly few comparative works on nationalism. There are theories a-plenty, but these tend to be generalisations from a few cases, often starting from the author's own, and reflecting his/her own conceptions and preoccupations. Many of these come from physical or ethnic frontiers, where issues of identity and nationality are salient. People living in secure nation states, on the other hand, often take their nationality for granted, even insisting that their own national perspective is somehow not national at all but universal. Some scholars have denied the very possibility of a theory of nationalism. Others insist that, the essence of nationalism being the uniqueness of the nation in question, no systematic comparison is possible.

If we look for comparable cases to the SNP's then the field is perhaps reduced, with obvious examples being in Catalonia, the Basque Country, Galicia, Quebec, Flanders, Wales, Brittany, Corsica and the frontier regions of Europe. Yet what are we to call these cases? Can we distinguish between the nationalism of established states and that of stateless peoples, or is this a prejudicial way to frame the inquiry? For some, the nationalism of the stateless is somehow backward, tribal and divisive; for others, it is morally superior since it represents the urge for liberation rather than domination. Even the terminology to separate out the stateless national-isms is loaded. Many people have adopted Walker Connor's term 'eth-nonationalism' (Connor 1994; Conversi 2002). Yet as far as this suggests that the stateless are 'ethnic' and the state nationalisms are not it is surely prejudicial. Tom Nairn (1977) and others have written of 'neo-national-ism', but this risks losing the perennial nature of the national question. The term 'minority nation' has been employed, but I was rebuked for using this in Catalonia since the Catalans are the majority within their own land. With others, I have written of 'stateless nations' or 'nations without states' (Guibernau 1999) but got into trouble in Quebec, where they have their own 'state' within the Canadian federation. David McCrone (2001), in the second edition of his book on the sociology of Scotland, removes the adjective 'stateless', now that Scotland has its own autonomous insti-tutions. On the other hand, all three of these nations lack some element of stateness, since otherwise they would presumably not harbour nationalist movements at all.

Nor is nationalism any easier to define, since it is used to cover cultural, sporting, economic and political matters, which may or may not be closely related. Since we need to begin somewhere, let us make two specifications. A nationalist movement is one that seeks political autonomy on behalf of what it claims to be a nation. It is always a claim and nearly always contested. Nationalism differs from regionalism in that nationalists claim a *right* to self-determination based on their historic existence and present will, while regionalists merely argue for autonomy within an existing con-stitutional order. The claim for self-determination does not necessarily imply independence, although most of the literature treats the two claims as being the same. In its minimal form, self-determination means only that nations should be the subject and not the object of constitutional change, with the details to be negotiated with other self-determining entities. Nations and nationalist movements are not fixed for all time, but come and go according to circumstances. It is not uncommon for regionalist movements to develop into nationalist ones as they extend their support base and refine and deepen their claims.

Stateless nations (as I shall call them) have survived the state-building process at the periphery (of the state and usually of Europe) and at the interface between state-building projects or cultural/linguistic zones (such as the Latin, Germanic and Slavic zones). Their distinctiveness consists variously in language, culture, religion, institutions and historical memo-ries. Some European peripheries fragmented into separate states in the course of history, as in the Nordic, Baltic and Balkan areas. Others have maintained a precarious unity within complex multinational states, such as Spain, the United Kingdom and Belgium. In fact, even these three cases have secessionist experiences. Spain failed to unite the whole Iberian peninsula as Portugal, briefly under the Spanish crown, went its own way. The United Kingdom lost the larger part of Ireland. Belgium is itself the result of a secession from the Netherlands. The resulting state system has left a complex patchwork of identities. Western Europe contains stateless nations (notably in Spain and the UK), national minorities (for example between Germany and Denmark, Italy and Austria, Hungary and its neighbours and in Ireland) and regionalist movements that sometimes play the nationalist card (for example in Flanders or Brittany). In North America, Canada as part of the British Empire resisted incorporation into the United States but has an uneasy relationship with Quebec. The United States did incorporate a large part of Mexico in the mid-nineteenth century and now has a large minority population of Mexican and South American origin.

Developments in European and North American politics in the late twentieth century have favoured a revival of peripheral and minority movements and the emergence of new ones. Decolonisation in the 1960s gave a new respectability to nationalism in progressive circles and in some cases raised the question of where the empire ends and the metropolitan state begins. State-sponsored regional policies aimed at modernisation and the incorporation of peripheries into the national division of labour on the state's terms provoked a counter-reaction, in which themes of economic insecurity, cultural defence and political autonomy were combined. In some cases, this produced vibrant regionalist and nationalist movements, while in others the various strands of protest never coalesced.

By the 1980s, state-sponsored regional policies gave way to bottom-up development strategies in which regions were expected to find their own way to prosperity in competition with others. This 'new regionalism' (Keating 1998) weakened state instruments for territorial management and integration and encouraged autonomist movements inspired by the new economic thinking. European integration further weakened the state framework and encouraged new visions of a Europe of the Regions or Europe of the Peoples, in which small nations would have a role. The end of the Cold War weakened security concerns in Western Europe and opened new spaces for movements challenging the monopolies of the state. At the same time, the renewed emphasis on universal human rights spilled over into debates about national minorities and their collective rights to language, culture and self-government. In these circumstances, the nationalism of the stateless altered its image. Previously labelled as backward and anti-modern, stateless nations and regions came to be identified with the modern and even post-modern. They were now in tune with contemporary developments in the economy, society and state, and with new understandings of pluralism and democracy. Yet the responses to the developments differed enormously, so that it remains as difficult as ever to generalise about nationalism and nationalists, even among the ranks of the stateless.

DEFINING THE PROJECT

Nationalists tend to adopt the language and categories of their times and their claims reflect what is normatively legitimate and institutionally possible. So from the late nineteenth century they increasingly stressed the need for their own nation state and by the First World War this became almost the only formula deemed capable of satisfying the self-determination claim. Sabino Arana, founder of Basque nationalism, rapidly evolved from a defence of traditional formal rights under the Spanish crown to radical separatism. Scottish nationalism in the past stressed the Empire as a framework and later dominion status as a constitutional option. Only from the 1930s did independent statehood emerge as the dominant option. So now the spread of international interdependence is leading nationalist movements to adapt again.

Indeed one of the factors encouraging the growth of stateless nationalist movements is the very weakening of the state and its powers of cultural assimilation, social regulation and territorial management. Global interdependence has not entailed the disappearance of states but has curtailed their autonomy. European integration explicitly aims to overcome the old model of the separate and sovereign nation-state. This faces nationalist movements with the question of what sort of political order they are looking for. In the initial phase of European integration, nationalist parties (of the stateless nations) tended to hostility, aware of the limitations which the European Community/Union placed on national independence, and seeing Brussels as even more remote than their state capital. There were exceptions, certainly. The Basque Nationalist Party (PNV) was an early exponent of European Union and Catalan nationalists incorporated European themes into their discourse, but elsewhere opposition to the principle of integration was reinforced by leftist criticisms of the capitalist design of the EC/EU and worries about the impact of the single market on vulnerable peripheral economies. These attitudes changed gradually over time, with considerable movement in the 1980s (Lynch 1996). Now there is a tendency for nationalists to favour the European project, seeing the multi-tiered and complex order as a means of extending rather than restricting their autonomy and resolving the old problems about the viability of small units.

For some, Europe provides an external support system for statehood. Basque nationalists in the 1980s used to fly a flag with thirteen stars, the extra one being for themselves. Since its European turn in the mid-1980s, the SNP has used variations of the formula of independence-in-Europe. Some Catalans and Flemish nationalists dream of a future in which they would have the same status as the smaller EU members. Indeed each EU enlargement, bringing in member states smaller than many of the stateless nations, revives this argument. More interesting, however, is the way that the experience of Europe has transformed the meaning of the independence demand itself. Catalan nationalism has never been strongly separatist and has adapted easily to a world of limited independence and shared sovereignty. Moderate Flemish nationalists in the former Volksunie were similarly able to adapt, as was a large sector of Basque nationalism. These movements have adopted a discourse and strategy of 'post-sovereignty', in which the national claim is to be resolved within an overarching system of European and international order in which the old absolute state sovereignties have disappeared altogether (Keating 2001).

Yet the turn to Europe is not universal (Keating 2004). To play the European game, it is necessary to share the dominant European value system, on issues of human rights and democracy, and on liberal welfare capitalism. Extreme right and xenophobic movements like the Vlaams Belang (Flanders), the Lega dei Ticinesi (in Switzerland) and the Italian Lega Nord are unable to do this, and have lapsed into Europhobia. Leftist populist movements like the Bloque Nacionalista Galego (Galicia) have found it difficult to reconcile Europe with the defence of threatened sectors or an anti-capitalist discourse, although the BNG has come to terms with the EU over recent years. Radical nationalists like the Basque movement Batasuna (the political wing of ETA) or Sinn Féin, have also disdained the European project. On the other hand, pro-European attitudes have characterised Christian Democratic nationalists like the Basque Nationalist Party (PNV), the Catalan Convergència i Unió (actually a federation of liberal and Christian Democratic elements) and the Sudtiroler Volkspartei (Italy) as well as social democratic parties like Esquerra Republicana de Catalunya, Eusko Alkartasuna (Basque Country), the SDLP (Northern Ireland), the SNP and Plaid Cymru. Social democratic parties are overwhelmingly pro-European and this applies also to the nationalist versions. Leftist and Green parties, for their part, tend to oppose the existing EU but argue for a Europe of the Peoples free from domination by big states and big business.

Nationalism always makes an appeal to the past, the present and the future and nationalist parties' perspectives on the European future are influenced by whether they have a 'usable past'. Hence we find nationalists invoking the historical European vocation of their nation and calling for a return to a more outward-looking golden age. Flemish nationalists recall the glories of early modern Flanders and its trading prosperity, before borders closed the old European routes of commerce. Catalan nationalists similarly recall a fabulous trading past, making explicit comparisons with the European single market. Sometimes these claims have constitutional implications, invoking historic rights to self-government or older conceptions of sovereignty and shared rule.

Scots have often referred to their distinctive traditions of sovereignty and limited government, which even gained some legal backing in the famous case of *MacCormick v. Lord Advocate*. Catalans have a similar tradition of limited and mixed sovereignty, embedded in their experience as part of the Crown of Aragon, a federation nested within a broader federation, the Crown of Spain, and linked variously to the Holy Roman Empire and the Mediterranean trading area. Basque nationalists have in many cases abandoned the spurious history of Sabino Arana, who insisted that the Basque provinces (although he initially referred only to Vizcaya) constituted an independent nation state in the Middle Ages. Instead, they invoke the historic rights or *fueros*, under which Castilian and later Spanish monarchs had to respect the privileges of the Basque provinces, effectively providing for shared rule. Silesian activists and intellectuals, long divided over whether Silesia is German or Polish (or at one stage Prussian), now insist that it has historically been European, a classical frontier region that cannot be fitted into the neighbouring nation states. It is perhaps not surprising that in small nations facing powerful and aggressive neighbours, doctrines of limited and shared sovereignty and overarching supranational law have been developed. These are the doctrinal weapons of the weak against the brute force of the strong.

History is more difficult in central and eastern Europe, where shared sovereignty is associated with imperial domination, but there has been some revisionist thinking about the Habsburg and Ottoman empires. It is not that these are presented as models of liberal tolerance, let alone democracy, but they did permit a degree of national pluralism. The argument is that they could have democratised without this pluralism giving way to separate nation states, and that history has proved that the nation-state formula is impossible in such an ethnically complex region. Again, Europe is presented as a way of recovering this supranational political space.

The post-sovereigntist strategy, while it has sound intellectual foundations, is often very vague in practice. Europe is evoked as a new political space in which very different meanings can be invested. Some movements place great faith in the Europe of the Regions, yet the scope for regions in practice is very limited. Others see scope for creating new states, as in the proposal of the European Free Alliance (grouping many of the nationalist and minority parties) for 'internal enlargement' of the EU by separation. The Convention on the Future of Europe gave scant consideration or concessions to the regionalist movement. As a result, there has been a certain turning away from Europe and scepticism about the draft constitution. While the Basque Nationalist Party (PNV) and Convergència i Unió reluctantly supported it, Eusko Alkartasuna (a smaller social democratic nationalist party in coalition with the PNV) and Esquerra Republicana de Catalunya rejected it despite their pro-European ideology. Nationalist parties are also aware of the unpopularity of some specific EU policies and so are cross-pressured, as indeed is the SNP. The Parti Québécois has similarly been torn between its support for the North American Free Trade Agreement as something that would weaken the Canadian state, and the opposition of some of its core supporters, including trade unions and farmers, to the economic and social impact of NAFTA.

There have been only two fully worked-out efforts to formulate a constitution reflecting the new realities of national sovereignty in an interdependent world. The first was in Quebec, where similar formulas were presented in the referendums of 1980 and 1995, in both cases as compromises within the nationalist movement. Quebec would become sovereign but in partnership or association with Canada. The second was the Ibarretxe Plan for the Basque Country presented in 2004 and providing for the Basque Country to become a state 'freely associated' with Spain (Keating and Bray 2006). Neither plan was accepted by the potential partners as a viable or legitimate strategy; the Quebec plan also foundered on a rejection by its own voters by a large margin in 1980 and a very slender one in 1995. The political world in the existing states is not, it seems, ready to accept post-sovereignty in principle, however much sovereignty has been eroded in practice.

BUILDING THE NATION

Nationalists often favour a teleological history in which the emergence of the immanent nation is a matter of removing the obstacles and oppression that stifle it. For academic historians, however, nations are built in specific circumstances and using a range of historical and contemporary materials.

In practice, most nationalists have been aware of this since the nineteenth century and nationalism has been about building and rebuilding the nation in successive epochs. It is a remarkable feature of Scotland that this discourse about nation building and rebuilding is largely absent. Perhaps because of the unchallenged national identity and the defined boundaries, nationalists have merely assumed that the nation exists. Elsewhere, however, nationalist movements have sought to rebuild the nation for the modern era. This is not merely about constitutional change or independence. It is also about constructing a national civil society and a shared project. For Catalan nationalists, the task is *fer país*, to make the country. Quebec nationalists (whether sovereigntist or more federalist in their constitutional ambitions) sought since the Quiet Revolution of the 1960s to modernise their society, to build their economy, to secure control over their resources and to formulate a broader social project to maintain their identity and autonomy in a rapidly changing world. Flemish region- or nation-builders (it is an ambiguous case) have similarly stressed economic, social and cultural issues along with political autonomy.

New regionalist models of economic development de-emphasise traditional factors of production, such as natural resources or location, and emphasise the social construction of the market in particular places. This involves culture and its uses, collective identity, social networks and a capacity for adaptation and innovation. In an integrated European market and a global trading order, small nations may have advantages over large ones, in the form of a greater capacity for collective action, shorter lines of communication and denser networks in which issues can be decided (Katzenstein 1985). Since they cannot afford the costs of high unemployment, they must either put up with mass emigration (as in Ireland up to the 1980s) or have active labour market policies to get people into work and adapt rapidly to external economic pressures. The ideology and policy measures of nationalist movements are thus often deeply informed with a form of economic nationalism which differs from the protectionism of the past and emphasises change and modernisation. This is a debate that is almost completely absent from Scottish nationalism.

THE LEFT–RIGHT DIMENSION

Nationalist parties are defined by their position on the issue of autonomy or independence, but as parties competing in a modern electoral arena they also need to take a stance on social and economic questions. It is difficult to generalise here, since nationalist parties have historically ranged across the entire ideological spectrum. Traditionally, in many parts of Europe, the movements of the periphery were conservative and traditionalist in tone, pitched against the modernising and secularising nation state. This was the case in France, in the Alpine regions, in Flanders and in the Basque Country. Quebec nationalism was associated with the clerical right. Even in the nineteenth century, however, there were exceptions as the cases of Scotland and Wales show. Catalan nationalism, as it emerged in the early twentieth century, was associated with a modernising but socially conservative bourgeoisie. On the other hand, there are radical traditions even within Catalonia or Brittany. From the 1920s both European communism and social democracy tended to be centralist and favour the large states, which it was thought were better able to control the commanding heights of the economy and engage in large-scale redistribution. This opened a gulf between socialism and peripheral nationalism.

From the 1960s, this began to change under the influence of the 'small is beautiful' philosophy, disillusionment with centralisation, and the libertarian leftism of the 1968 generation. Peripheral nationalism and regionalism moved to the left, incorporating new social movements, notably in environmentalism and pacifism. The new left, in its turn, lost its disdain for nationalism. In time, social democratic parties came around, in France, in Spain, in the UK and elsewhere, rediscovering lost traditions of localism and cultural defence, although these new sentiments co-existed everywhere with the older commitment to centralisation. In Spain, peripheral nationalism was part of the struggle against Francoist dictatorship, bringing conservative nationalist parties into contact with leftist radicals and social democrats. In France, regionalism was incorporated into the opposition to Gaullist hegemony before the socialist victory of 1981. In Britain, nationalism was aligned with opposition to Thatcherism in a combination of class, national and ideological themes.

This is not to say that nationalisms all went to the left. There remains a moderate conservative nationalism akin to 'bourgeois regionalism' (Harvie 1994; Keating 1998) in prosperous regions. This is based on the support of a middle class and business community committed to local development and struggling against an inefficient state. Catalonia has long been home to such movements, which are now represented in Convergència i Unió (CiU), as in more recent years has Flanders. The social support base of such movements is not big business or transnational capital, but small- and medium-sized enterprises and the middle classes, including the professional middle classes. Among their grievances is the transfer of resources from their rich regions to support their poorer relations in other parts of the state and the argument that this hampers their ability to compete in global markets. Some of these conservative nationalisms are Christian Democratic in inspiration, combining modernisation, tradition and nationalism with a European vocation. This would include CiU, the Basque Nationalist Party and sections of Breton and Flemish nationalism.

Another type of movement is right wing, populist and often xenophobic. The Lega Nord has gone through many gyrations, from regionalist, to federalist, to secessionist, to Italian nationalist and has swung from a pro-European to a strongly Euro-phobic stance. The only constant theme is its right-wing populism directed at the 'other' who has in turn been southern Italians, immigrants, Muslims, the Italian state and then the European Union. Its support base is in small businesses and small towns in Lombardy and Veneto; it had only short-term success in Milan. The Vlaams Belang is also right-wing populist and racist, and has been able to replace the Belgian state or the Francophones with immigrants as the hated 'other'.

POLITICAL COMPETITION

The strategy and trajectory of nationalist parties and movements is strongly influenced by their competitive context. In the past they may have monopolised the national question, giving them a committed base but preventing them from reaching beyond it. In so far as they have moderated their position on independence while the other parties, notably the social democratic parties, have accepted degrees of home rule of autonomy, their policy is less distinct and there is more competition for the marginal voters. Similarly they are faced with competition from parties to the left and right who are also trying to reach out of their traditional bases. This accentuates competition on both the national and the social and economic dimensions of politics. In France the peripheral nationalist movements have been squeezed into insignificance as a result. In Belgium the split of all the parties into Flemish and Francophone components has left little room for nationalist parties, outside of the Vlaams Belang, whose main appeal is simple racism. In Galicia the veteran conservative politician Manuel Fraga combined conservatism with traditional 'regionalism', which he carefully distinguished from nationalism, as espoused by the Bloque Nacionalista Galego.

This has given rise to new political dynamics In the historic nationalities of Spain (Catalonia, the Basque Country and Galicia) the party system is balanced between nationalist and left or right parties, both of which need to handle both sorts of issue and to deal with each other. So when Galicia voted out the Fraga government, the Socialists and nationalists (BNG) formed a new coalition government. Another long-standing government, that of CiU in Catalonia, gave way to a coalition between the socialists and a more radical nationalist party, the Esquerra

Republicana de Catalunya. For years, the Basque Nationalist Party governed in coalition with the Socialists. The Lega Nord has been part of the centre–right coalition government of Silvio Berlusconi, albeit at the cost of massive incoherence in the coalition's policy towards the regions. The Hungarian minority party in Slovakia has participated in coalitions at the state level following the overthrow of the Meciar regime.

All this has served to 'normalise' nationalist politics as part of the regular democratic game. Proportional representation systems, making it difficult for any party to rule on its own, of course encourage this type of coalitional creativity. In only a few cases has a nationalist party become hegemonic in its territory and these are normally in minority enclaves. The Sudtiroler Volkspartei has dominated elections in its region until recently, giving it considerable room for tactical manoeuvre: while in principle in favour of self-determination, it plays the Italian political game, extracting large resources to feed a patronage machine, which in turn helps it to sustain its support base.

DEFINING THE NATION

One of the oldest questions in nationalist politics is how to define the membership of the nation. It is a logical necessity that the nation must be defined to include some people and exclude others, but the criteria can vary and include birth, descent, residence, cultural affinity, religion, language and the simple will to be a member. A recurrent but ever-disputed distinction is made between the ethnic and the civic criteria of belonging. Ethnic criteria are more exclusive and stipulate ancestry and narrow ethnic markers. The markers differ from one case to another, but may include religion or language. Sabino Arana notoriously specified descent as the criterion, requiring adherents to the original Basque Nationalist Party to have four grandparents with Basque names. Ethnic nationalists in Quebec make references to the *Québécois de souche*, or 'old-stock' Quebeckers. Irish nationalism has sometimes emphasised Catholicism. This is not to say that these ethnic criteria have an objective reality. Ethnicity is a social construction and can, as we have just noted, be based on various elements. The point is that these elements are then used to define a closed community. Civic nationalism, on the other hand, tends to regard all who are born and all who live in a given territory as members of the nation. This does not, as is sometimes thought, mean that it has no cultural basis or does not use historical myths; it is just that it is possible for people to enter into this culture and that the history be sufficiently open to recognise pluralism and mixing as part of the tradition.

If we can again generalise, there has been a trend across Europe and in Quebec for the ethnic definition of the nation to give way in nationalist discourse to a civic one. Sometimes the civic tradition is deeply rooted, as in Catalonia, which has incorporated generations of incomers since the nineteenth century. In the Basque Country the civic tradition, which was present weakly from the early days, has become dominant, but still competes with the occasional statement from traditionalists like former PNV president Xabier Arzallus about the distinct cranial dimensions of the true Basques. The official PNV policy is that all who live in the Basque Country and wish to be Basque are so; as are people of Basque descent living elsewhere. For the radicals associated with Herri Batasuna and ETA, the boundary is between real Basques and others, where real Basques are people, irrespective of their origins, who identify with the armed struggle. Indeed one purpose of the armed campaign, including street riots and intimidation, is precisely to create this boundary in the absence of a clear ethnic division within Basque society. Quebec nationalism is also civic in discourse although there are, as noted above, regular lapses by individuals. Irish nationalism has never officially been ethnic, which in this case means confining Irishness to the Catholic community. There is a regular invocation of the cross-religious alliance of the 1798 rebellion and even the republican flag represents both Orange and Green traditions. All these parties also stress their anti-racist credentials. The Vlaams Belang and the Lega Nord, by contrast, are racist to the core and the only liberalisation among the latter is the abandonment of the rhetoric against incomers from the south, most of whom are now socially integrated and many of whom indeed vote for the Lega.

On the other hand, there is still a strong tendency for voting for nationalist parties to be concentrated among voters who are born locally and/or are of local ancestry. The confessional nature of voting in Northern Ireland is beyond dispute. Support for Quebec nationalism is almost entirely confined to Francophones (although not all Francophones are nationalist). Basques and Catalans born locally and of native ancestry show a stronger nationalist inclination than others, although the contrast in these cases is not so stark.

There are several reasons for the shift to a civic focus. One is connected with dominant values in a world in which, unlike in the late nineteenth century, people do not talk lightly about the division of the world into 'races'. Claiming self-government for a group defined by territory is more legitimate than for an ethnic group and reflects the practice of states themselves. There is also a strategic dimension. In societies of large-scale immigration, like Catalonia, the Basque Country or Quebec, a narrow ethnic definition of the nation would condemn the nationalists to marginalisation. The civic criteria also demonstrate the outward-looking nature of the national project and its insertion into a pluralistic world order.

NATIONALISTS IN GOVERNMENT

As nationalist parties have advanced electorally, they have increasingly found themselves in government at their own level and even in state-level coalitions. The Parti Québécois has enjoyed two extended periods in office. Convergència i Unió governed Catalonia for 20 years and the Basque Nationalist Party dominated governments there from the transition until 2009. Nationalists have been in coalition in Galicia, in Flanders and Catalonia (where Esquerra Republicana is in government with the Socialists and the post-Communist/Green Iniciativa per Catalunya). In none of these cases has normal politics stopped. On the contrary, nationalist parties have carried through programmes in social and economic policy that do not depend on first gaining independence. Indeed on two occasions the Parti Québécois has fought and lost independence referendums and then gone on to be re-elected to govern for another term. Generally, nationalists have taken the view that, before proceeding to independence, they need to demonstrate that they are a credible government and can be trusted to manage existing devolved policy competences. In the meantime, they have proceeded with nation building in both internal dimensions and externally through forms of para-diplomacy and networking.

Nationalist parties have also shown themselves open to playing in state-wide politics. Moderate Catalan nationalism has long aspired to reshape Spain in its own image and both CiU and ERC have given external support to Spanish governments; in CiU's case, both to the Socialists and the conservative Popular Party. Basque nationalism, despite its more separatist tradition, has also traded support in Madrid for concessions at home. The Spanish electoral system, which makes majority governments difficult but favours territorially concentrated parties, encourages this. Quebec nationalism has played in Canadian politics, with the migration of prominent nationalists into Brian Mulroney's Conservative Party in the 1980s in exchange for a new deal for Quebec, and the more recent offer of the Bloc Québécois to support an effort by a Liberal–NDP coalition to unseat the current Conservative government. Moderate Flemish nationalists have long played coalition politics, and since the separation of all the parties into Flemish and Francophone wings all Belgian governments are coalitions across the two communities.

216

THE SNP IN COMPARISON

The SNP certainly fits into the family of nationalist parties of the stateless nations. Its ideology is impeccably civic, it is active in the European Free Alliance and it has adopted a generally pro-European stance. Electorally it is among the most successful of these parties and in any other system would be a natural coalition partner. That it has not been so is partly due to the British tradition of single-government parties only slowly being challenged by devolutionary politics. The SNP has participated in coalitions at local level and is open to coalition at Holyrood. There have been strong hints that it could play a brokerage role in the event of a hung parliament at Westminster. Like other movements, it is divided between a traditional independence-or-nothing wing and a more post-sovereigntist tendency, although this has been buried in the run-up to the proposed referendum. The party is also caught between a catch-all ideology, reflected in policies on charging, from prescriptions to universities to road tolls, and its official social democratic commitments. It support base crosses all social groups but peaks among the working class and the petty bourgeoisie, classes that, in other cases, might gravitate to two separate nationalist parties. The demise of the Scottish Socialist Party means that the SNP will not, in the near future, face competition to its left. Yet its policies in government, seeking to combine generous and universal welfare provision with tax-cutting, reflect choices not taken and suggest problems to come.

In other ways, the SNP is a rather traditional nationalist party. It has neglected nation building and failed to develop a narrative around identity, collective action, economic development and social solidarity, indeed neglected to exploit precisely the cultural advantages that small nations possess. It presents a vision in which the attainment of statehood itself will resolve its problems, calling in aid the oil wealth when the sums get difficult. Nor has it given serious thought to Europe, seeing this rather as a useful external support system for independence and proposing an instrumental, à la carte approach to integration that closely resembles British attitudes.

REFERENCES

Connor, W. (1994), *Ethnonationalism: The Quest for Understanding*, Princeton, Princeton University Press.

Conversi, D. (ed.) (2002), *Ethnonationalism in the Contemporary World: Walker Connor and the Study of Nationalism*, London and New York, Routledge.

Guibernau, M. (1999), *Nations without States*, Cambridge, Polity Press.

Harvie, C. (1994), *The Rise of Regional Europe*, London, Routledge.

Katzenstein, P. J. (1985), *Small States in World Markets: Industrial Policy in Europe*, Ithaca, Cornell University Press.

Keating, M. (1998), *The New Regionalism in Western Europe: Territorial Restructuring and Political Change*, Cheltenham, Edward Elgar.

Keating, M. (2001), *Plurinational Democracy: Stateless Nations in a Post-Sovereignty Era*, Oxford, Oxford University Press.

Keating, M. (2004), 'European Integration and the Nationalities Question', *Politics and Society*, 31.1, pp. 367–88.

Keating, M. and Bray, Z. (2006), 'Renegotiating Sovereignty: Basque Nationalism and the Rise and Fall of the Ibarretxe Plan', *Ethnopolitics*, 5.4, pp. 347–64.

Lynch, P. (1996), *Minority Nationalism and European Integration*, Cardiff, University of Wales Press.

McCrone, D. (2001), *Understanding Scotland: The Sociology of a Nation*, 2nd edn, London, Routledge.

Nairn, T. (1977), *The Break-Up of Britain: Crisis and Neo-Nationalism*, London: New Left Books.

Index

abortion *see* Corrie Abortion Bill
Achieving Our Potential (Scottish Government), 128–9, 131
'Activate' computer system, 86
agriculture, 196; *see also* foot-and-mouth disease
Aircraft and Shipbuilding Nationalisation Bill, 97
Alexander, Douglas, 152
Alexander, Wendy, 8, 90, 157
Anderson, R. D., 23
Arana, Sabino, 207, 209, 214
'arc of prosperity', 12, 106–10
Argyll by-election (1940), 25
Arzallus, Xabier, 215
Ascherson, Neal, 10
Ayr conference (1982), 169–71

BBC, 136, 137, 138, 139, 140, 141, 144
BBC Alba, 140
BBC Scotland, 139, 140, 141
Bain, Margaret (later Ewing), 45, 86, 123, 155, 169, 170
Basque nationalists, 207–8, 209, 210, 212, 214, 215, 216
Bayne, Ian O., 162, 163
Belgium: nationalism, 206, 213, 216
bills, 11
   Aircraft and Shipbuilding Nationalisation Bill, 97
   Corrie Abortion Bill, 167
   Creative Scotland Bill, 142
   Culture (Scotland) Bill, 142
   Referendum Bill, 90
   Scotland and Wales Bill, 192
   Scotland Bill, 99
   Scottish Convention Bill, 154
   Welfare Reform Bill (amendment), 103
Birt, John, 141
Blair, Tony
   and broadcasting, 141
   and Labour movement, 151
   and 'Lockerbie Bomber', 181
   and nuclear weapons, 156
   and social democracy, 4, 128
Bonnar, Anne, 142, 143
'bourgeois regionalism', 212
Brand, Jack, 163, 165
Bridgeton by-election (1961), 94
Britain *see* United Kingdom
British–Irish Council (BIC), 186–7
British Social Attitudes Survey (2005), 125–6
Britishness, 187
broadcasting, 135–6, 137–43, 144–5
Brown, Ewan, 142, 144
Brown, Gordon
   as a 'British figure', 3
   endorsement of *Creative Britain* report, 135
   and the economy, 116–17, 118
   and income tax, 80, 103
   and reinstatement of Joint Ministerial Committees, 182, 183–4
   and 'new social democracy', 4
   and nuclear weapons, 157
   on becoming Prime Minister, 79, 152

Brown, Gordon (*cont.*)
  Red Paper on Scotland, 9
  and Salmond, Alex, 182, 183–4
Buchan, Norman, 147
Buchanan, Stewart, 166
budgets, 87–9, 113, 183
business, 107–8, 109–10, 111, 112; *see also*
  industrial strategy
business taxes, 103, 131
Butler, Steve, 164, 165, 168
by-elections, 35–6, 86, 91
  Argyll, 25
  Bridgeton, 94
  Coatbridge & Airdrie, 171, 172
  Dunbartonshire, 22
  Glasgow Cathcart, 25
  Glasgow East, 15 n2, 91
  Glasgow Govan, 15 n2, 34, 36, 86, 173
  Glasgow Pollok, 30, 94, 149–50
  Glenrothes 15 n2
  Hamilton, 1, 2, 15 n2, 30, 31–2, 36, 41,
    55, 86, 94, 148
  Kilmarnock, 24
  Kirkcaldy, 26
  Moray, 86
  Motherwell, 15 n2, 26, 86
  Paisley, 26, 149
  Perth & Kinross, 15 n2, 173
  West Lothian, 94

Callaghan, Jim, 96
Calman Commission on Scottish
  Devolution, 13–14, 89–90, 103, 141
Campaign for a Scottish Assembly (CSA),
  154
Campaign for Nationalism in Scotland
  (CNS), 169
Campbell, Menzies, 3
Canada, 197, 200, 206; *see also* Quebec
Carson, Brenda, 171
'cash for honours' scandal, 102
Catalan nationalists, 199, 205, 207, 208,
  209, 210, 211, 212, 213–14, 215,
  216
Catholics: support for SNP, 6, 57
Cencrastus magazine, 164
Chancellor of Scotland, 185
Channel 4, 137, 139

*Choosing Scotland's Future: A National
  Conversation* (Scottish Executive), 89,
  185, 186, 196, 198–9
Churchill, Winston, 27
civic nationalism, 214
civil disobedience, 168–9
'Claim of Right for Scotland, A' (CSA),
  154, 155
Clarke, Tom, 149
class
  SNP voters, 6, 58
  Scottish politics, 32, 37
coalitions, 216, 217
  anti-Tory, 35
  Italy, 214
  Labour–Lib Dem, 11, 80–1, 87, 135, 142
  Labour–Plaid Cymru, 181
  Northern Ireland, 181
  SNP–Lib Dem, 86, 87
  Scottish Parliament, 76
  Slovakia, 214
  Spain, 213–14
  Wales, 181
  Westminster, 94
Coatbridge & Airdrie by-election (1982),
  171, 172
Commission on the Constitution (1973), 95
Committee for Scotland, 194
Committee of the Regions (CoR), 194
Common Agricultural Policy (CAP), 196
Common Fisheries Policy (CFP), 196
Concordats, 180
Connor, Walker, 205
Conservative governments, 13, 15, 33,
  152, 159, 194
Conservative Party
  and class, 6
  and elections, 8, 15, 30, 55, 56, 97, 154
  and SNP, 33
  Scotland, 9, 28, 29, 32, 35, 36, 45, 90,
    99, 126, 150, 153
  and Scottish Nationalism, 27
  and Scottish Parliament, 126
  see also see also 'tartan Tories'; Thatcher,
    Margaret; Thatcherism
Constitution Unit, 12
Constitutional Convention, 154–5
Convention on the Future of Europe, 210

Cook, Robin, 3, 152, 153
Cooper, Yvette, 184
corporation tax, 110, 132
Corrie Abortion Bill, 167
Council of Ministers *see* European Union: Council of Ministers
'Council of the Isles', 187, 198
council tax, 87, 91, 111, 112, 124, 130; *see also* poll tax
Cowan, Henry, 20
Crann Tara, 165
Crawford, Bruce, 184, 198
Crawford, Robert, 164
Creative Britain report (DCMS), 135
creative economy, 135–45
creative industries, 87, 136, 142, 143
Creative Industries Working Group, 143
Creative Scotland, 136, 142
Creative Scotland Bill, 142
Crossman, Richard, 148
Crowther, Lord, 33
Cultural Commission, 141
Culture (Scotland) Bill, 142
Cunningham, Chris, 162, 164, 171
Cunningham, George, 152
Cunningham, Roseanna, 157
    as committee convener, 81
    and leadership election (2004), 84
    wins Perth & Kinross by-election (1995), 173
    and 79 Group, 162, 164, 167, 171, 174
Cunningham 40% referendum rule amendment, 99
currency, 195, 196
Currie, Andrew, 163, 167
Cuthbert, Jim and Margaret, 11–12

Dalyell, Tam, 150, 152
Darling, Alistair, 184
'Declaration of Perth', 33
defence, 14, 74, 89, 114, 120, 184, 191, 193, 194, 195, 196, 198
Department for Culture, Media and Sport (DCMS), 142
devolution
    and politics of broadcasting, 141
    and independence, 196–9
    and inter-governmental relations, 187

Labour and, 96, 120
Northern Ireland, 178
referendum on, 152, 162
SNP and, 10–12, 33, 36, 39–40, 41, 55–66, 89–90, 126, 192, 196
Speaker's Conference on, 20
Wales, 178
'devolution max', 198
Dewar, Donald, 124, 154
Dewar Gibb, Andrew, 23
D'Hondt formula, 66 n3
Digital Britain, 139, 142
Doig, Andrew, 171
Doig, Peter, 152
Donaldson, Arthur, 27
Donoughue, Bernard, 96
Drucker, Henry, 5
Dudley Edwards, Owen, 9, 164, 170, 171
Dunbartonshire by-election (1932), 22

ETA (Basque nationalist movement), 215
Early Years Framework, The (Scottish Government), 129
Economic and Monetary Union (EMU), 195
economic nationalism, 211
economy
    creative, 135–45
    Scottish, 111
    United Kingdom, 183–4
Edinburgh: Royal High School building, 168
education, 80, 107, 109, 114, 124, 125, 131
    higher *see* Future Thinking Taskforce
Elder, Dorothy-Grace, 82
elections, 22, 31
    Additional Member System, 197
    European Parliament, 7, 8, 83
    female candidates, 42–52
    general, 2, 6, 11, 15, 24, 29, 31, 34–8, 39, 45, 46, 55–6, 61, 83, 85, 150, 163, 172–3, 181
    internal, 80
    local government, 7, 8
    Scottish Parliament, 1, 3–4, 6, 7, 8, 42, 43, 44, 55, 56, 57, 80, 157, 197
    Westminster, 7, 8, 37, 40, 60–2, 64
    see also by-elections; voting

employment, 107–8, 109
energy, 3, 111, 112, 181, 183, 198
Equally Well policy statement (Scottish
Government), 128
equity, 109
ethnicity, 214–15
Europe
SNP and 12, 96, 177–8, 179, 193–6,
202, 217
UK and, 177–8, 179
Europe of the Regions, 199, 206, 210
European Free Alliance, 210, 217
European structural funds, 115
European Union
Council of Ministers, 195
Fisheries Council, 181
and regionalism, 210
Euroscepticism, 12
Evans, Gwynfor, 94, 95
Ewing, Annabelle, 45
Ewing, Margaret *see* Bain, Margaret
Ewing, Winnie, 45
and Europe, 193
and Hamilton by-election, 1, 31, 40–1,
94
and Labour Party, 149, 151
as MEP, 193
political background, 156
and SNP, 43
reconvenes Scottish Parliament, 81
and 79 Group, 167, 169, 170
at Westminster, 95, 156, 167

Fabiani, Linda, 142, 144
Falconer of Thornton, Lord, 188 n2
federalism
Europe, 199
United Kingdom, 179
Federation of Small Businesses in
Scotland, 112
feminism: and SNP reform, 52
financial services: and recession, 132
Finlay, Richard, 184, 185
fiscal affairs, 195, 198; *see also* taxation
'Fiscal Autonomy in Scotland' (Scottish
Government), 89
fisheries, 122, 196
Five (broadcaster), 137

Flemish nationalists, 208, 209, 211, 212,
216
Foot, Michael, 32–3
foot-and-mouth disease, 182
foreign policy
Scotland, 195
United Kingdom, 14
Fraga, Manuel, 213
France: nationalism, 207
Free Student Press, 164
fundamentalist Nationalism, 39
Future Thinking Taskforce, 111

Gaelic language community: broadcasting
services for, 140
Gaitskell, Hugh, 156
Galician nationalists, 208, 213, 216
Gibson, Kenny, 84
Gibson, Rob, 164, 170, 174
Gibson, Tom, 27
Glasgow: broadcasting, 137
Glasgow Cathcart by-election (1942), 25
Glasgow East by-election (2008), 15 n2, 91
Glasgow Govan by-elections
(1973 and 1988), 15 n2, 86
(1973), 34, 36
(1988), 173
Glasgow Housing Association (GHA),
125
Glasgow Pollok by-election (1967), 30, 94,
149–50
Glasgow University Scottish Nationalist
Association, 21, 164
Glenrothes by-election (2008), 15 n2
globalisation, 13, 107–8, 127
Goldie, Annabel, 183
Government Economic Strategy, The (GES)
(Scottish Government), 127
Grahame, Christine, 82
Gray, Iain, 90
Great Depression, 23
Greens
and Europe, 208
as MSPs, 44, 76
Scottish, 69, 77, 87, 88, 90, 185
and Scottish Parliamentary elections,
7, 59
Gunn, Neil, 23

Habsburg Empire, 209
Halliday, James, 27
Hamilton, James, 149
Hamilton, William, 152
Hamilton by-election (1967), 1, 15 n2, 30, 31–2, 36, 94, 148
Hanham, H. J., 120
Harvie, Chris, 11
Hay, Ken, 142
health services, 80, 108, 121, 125, 128–9, 130
Heath, Ted, 33
Henderson, Douglas, 39, 98–9, 163
Henderson, Hamish, 148
Herald, The, 180, 184
Herri Batasuna (Basque nationalist movement), 199, 215
Highland Clearances, 29
Holloway, Richard, 142
Holyrood *see* Scottish Parliament
Holyrood magazine, 143
home rule, 20, 24, 149
Homecoming 2009 initiative (Scottish Government), 112
hospitals, 128
housing, 113, 121, 122–3, 125, 128
Houston, William, 168
Hughes, Bob, 96, 152
Hughes, Emrys, 95
human rights, 206
Hutcheon, Paul, 89

ITV, 137, 140
income tax, 80, 88, 122, 130
independence, 12–15
electoral support for, 49, 64–5, 66, 75
European Union, 73, 123, 173, 179, 208, 211, 213, 216
Labour and, 157–8, 159, 162, 163
and nationalism, 205, 207
political, 19, 27, 28, 30
Quebec, 216
SNP and, 22, 32, 36, 41, 81, 83, 86, 89–91, 94, 98, 101, 104, 105, 116, 120, 124, 133, 172, 187–8, 190–202, 217
Scotland and, 5–6, 116, 185
and self-government, 21
79 Group and, 164, 167

inequality, 103; *see also* sexual equality
Ingram, Adam, 133
Ireland
economy, 99, 108
home rule, 21
nationalism, 214, 215
as social welfare model, 127
see also British–Irish Council (BIC)
Italian nationalism, 213, 214, 215; *see also* Sardinian nationalism

Jeffery, C., 187
Jenkins, Blair, 107
Johnston, Thomas, 22, 25
Joint Ministerial Committee (JMC), 180, 183, 184

Keating, M., 196
Kellas, James, 35
Kennedy, Gavin, 164, 174
Kerr, Andy, 85
Kilbrandon, Lord, 33
Kilmarnock by-election (1933), 24
Kirkcaldy by-election (1944), 26
King, Robin, 148
'Kingdom of United Countries', 198
Kinnock, Neil, 153

Labour governments, 22, 32–3, 152–4; *see also* Blair, Tony; Brown, Gordon; Callaghan, Jim; Wilson, Harold
Labour Party
and class, 6
and corporatism, 24
and devolution, 120
and elections, 8, 28
ethos, 149, 156
female MSPs, 43, 44, 48
'London Labour', 150, 152
and Scotland, 8, 28, 36, 58, 65, 87, 88, 90, 103–4, 110, 121–2
and Scottish home rule, 22, 26
in Scottish Parliament, 80–1
and social democracy, 123, 128–9, 159, 175
see also New Labour; Scottish Labour Party
Laffer Curve, 5

leftist movements, 208
Lega Nord (Italian nationalist movement), 213, 214, 215
Levy, Roger, 168
Liberal Democrats
  elections, 8
  female MSPs, 44
  Scotland, 56, 86, 87, 88, 90
  Scottish Parliament, 80–1
Liddell, Helen, 153–4
Linklater, Magnus, 85
Lochhead, Richard, 86
'Lockerbie Bomber', 181–2
Lothian list, 82
Lynch, Jim, 165
Lynch, Peter, 172, 192, 197

MPs, 34, 39–40, 79, 102
MSPs
  and Creative Scotland Bill, 142
  female, 42–3, 44, 48, 49, 51, 69
  Green, 44, 76
  and referendum (2010), 90
  SNP, 39–40, 60, 76, 79–81, 82, 84, 87, 88–90
  and social issues, 133
  values, 126
McAlpine, Tom, 97
Macartney, Allan, 194
MacAskill, Kenny, 9, 131, 157
McConnell, Jack, 85, 141
MacCormick, John, 21, 23, 25, 26, 149, 192
MacCormick, Neil, 10, 199
MacCormick v. Lord Advocate, 209
McCrone, David, 205
MacDonald, Margo, 45
  backs Budget, 88
  and election failure, 97
  and Govan by-election victory, 36
  and Lothian list, 82
  marriage, 99
  referendum campaign speech, 162–3
  and 79 Group, 171
  and SNP, 34–5, 38, 43
MacEwen, Sir Alexander, 23
McGuinness, Martin, 181
McIntyre, Robert, 27, 31, 163

McKechin, Ann, 184
Mackintosh, J. P., 148
Maclaren, Duncan, 164
McLean, Chris, 9–10, 155, 168
Maclean, Fitzroy, 149
McLeish, Henry, 83, 87
McLetchie, David, 83
Macmillan, Harold, 156, 177–8
McNally, Tom, 96
McNeil, Angus, 40, 102
McNeil, Hector, 26
Macwhirter, Iain, 11
Mann, Michael, 14
Manuel, Archie, 149
Marshall, Will, 148
Martin, Campbell, 83
Marwick, Tricia, 84
Mason, John, 102, 133
Mather, Jim, 5, 110, 132
Maxwell, Stephen, 11–12
  and civil disobedience, 169
  and SNP, 39, 171
  Scottish Industrial Resistance, The, 165
  and 79 Group, 163, 164, 167, 173–4
media see broadcasting
Memorandum of Understanding (MoU) (Ministry of Justice), 179–80
middle class: support for nationalism, 69–70, 77, 163, 212–13
miners' strike (1984–5), 173
Minister for European and External Affairs, Scottish, 194–5
minority populations, 206, 214
Mitchell, James, 164, 172
moderatism, 22
monarch: as Head of State, 185–6, 187, 188, 192
Montrose, Duke of, 23
Moore, Ian, 168
Moray by-election (2006), 86
Moreno Question on national identity, 62
Motherwell by-election (1945), 15 n2, 26, 86
Motherwell conference (1976), 36
Muirhead, Roland, 22
Murphy, Paul, 182, 183

Nairn, Tom, 10, 205
'National Conversation' (Scottish Government), 14, 109
National Covenant, 26
National Party of Scotland (NPS), 21, 22, 24, 184
nationalisation, 26, 97
nationalism
  Basque, 207–8, 209, 210, 212, 214, 215, 216
  Belgian, 213, 215
  British, 2
  Catalan, 199, 205, 207, 208, 209, 210, 211, 212, 213–14, 215, 216
  civic, 214, 215–16
  definition, 205
  economic, 211
  ethnic criteria, 214, 215, 216
  and feminism, 52
  Flemish, 208, 209, 211, 212, 216
  fundamentalist, 38
  Galician, 208, 213, 216
  and history, 210–11
  Irish, 214, 215
  Italian, 213, 214
  and nations, 204–7
  peripheral, 206, 207, 212
  Quebec, 14, 197, 200, 205, 210, 211, 212, 214, 215
  Sardinian, 199
  Scottish, 2, 8–10, 23, 25–6, 211; *see also* Campaign for Nationalism in Scotland (CNS); SNP
  Silesian, 209
  states and, 204–8
  Welsh, 2, 178
nationalist movements: comparison of, 199–200, 202–18
nationalists
  in government, 216
  radical, 208
nations
  membership of, 214–16
  and nationalism, 204–7
Neil, Alex, 81, 99, 133
neo-liberalism
  definition, 5, 142

SNP and, 4, 103, 105–18, 131, 133, 144, 156, 159
NESTA think tank, 143
Network Rail, 114
New Labour, 79, 109, 135, 151; *see also* Labour Party; Scottish Labour Party
new towns, 6, 29
Nordic Council, 186
North American Free Trade Agreement (NAFTA), 200
North Sea oil, 33, 35, 122
Northern Ireland, 178, 181, 215
Norway, 122, 130; *see also* Scandinavia
nuclear energy, 181
nuclear weapons, 15, 29, 120, 156, 181

Ofcom, 136, 137
Orkney, 59
Ottoman Empire, 209

Paisley, Ian, 181
Paisley by-election (1948), 26, 149
party system, 32
Paterson, Lindsay, 49
Peat, Jeremy, 136
Perth: 'Declaration of Perth', 33
Perth & Kinross by-election (1995), 15 n2, 173
Plaid Cymru, 2, 94, 181, 192, 200, 208
Platform for Success report (Scottish Broadcasting Commission), 138
Plessey dispute, 165
politicians *see* MPs; MSPs
politics, modern: defined, 1
poll tax, 38, 101, 123, 155, 173
Pollok *see* Glasgow Pollok
poverty, 128–30, 131, 133
pressure groups, 20, 26
privatisation, 108
Protestants, 6, 55
Provisional Sinn Fein, 168–9; *see also* Sinn Fein
public procurement portal, 113
public sector, 98, 106, 108, 109, 111, 113, 116
Public Services Reform Bill, 144
Purdie, Sam, 95
Purves, Graeme, 168

Quebec, 14, 197, 200, 205, 210, 211, 212, 214, 215
Queen *see* monarch
Question (journal), 9

Really Effective Development Company, 11, 85
Referendum Bill, 90
referendums
    devolution, 152, 162
    EEC membership, 193
    head of state, 185–6
    independence, 185
    Quebec, 197, 210, 216
    Scottish and Welsh Assemblies, 152
regionalism, 205, 206, 212
Reid, George, 100
religion: SNP voters, 58; *see also* Catholics; Protestants
right-wing movements, 208
rights
    Basques, 207
    British Empire, 185, 191
    Catalonia, 209
    human, 206, 208
    Scottish, 178
    social, 4, 125, 129, 130
    women, 167
Robertson, Angus, 40, 85
Robertson, Douglas, 168, 171, 174
Robertson, George, 10, 55, 79, 156
Robertson, John, 99
Robinson, Peter, 181
Robison, Shona, 133
Ross, Willie, 147, 148, 150
Royal Commission on the Constitution, 33
Russell, Mike, 3, 9, 81, 82, 83, 84, 131–2, 143

SNP
    Aberdeen conference (1981), 166
    activists, 156
    administration, 11
    autobiographies, 2–3
    Ayr conference (1982), 169–71
    blackmail potential, 33, 41
    and Britain, 184–5
    and broadcasting, 135–6, 137–8, 141, 144–5
    and budgets, 88–9
    and business, 28, 90, 103, 107, 108, 109–10, 111, 112, 117, 132, 159
    and candidate selection, 45–6
    Catholic support for, 6, 57
    and Conservative Party, 33
    Constitution for a Free Scotland, A, 185
    and Constitutional Convention, 154–5
    cultural policy, 135–45
    and devolution, 10–12, 33, 36, 39–40, 41, 55–66, 89–90, 126, 192, 196
    divisions within, 98
    doctrine, 5
    early years, 22–3
    economic strategy, 105–18, 123, 127
    and elections, 34, 36, 37, 79, 80, 85, 172
    and electoral rivalry, 121–2
    ethos, 5, 156
    and Europe, 12, 96, 177–8, 179, 193–6, 202, 217
    foreign policy, 14
    and Fundamentalist Nationalism, 39
    and gender, 6, 9, 42–52, 68–9
    in government, 86–8, 124, 126–8
    and Greens, 40
    health strategies, 128
    histories, 2
    ideology, 36
    image, 29, 38, 39, 42, 50, 51–2, 70, 74–7
    impulses, 120
    and independence, 22, 32, 36, 41, 81, 83, 86, 89–91, 94, 98, 101, 104, 105, 116, 120, 124, 133, 172, 187–8, 190–202, 217
    and industrial politics, 166–7
    and inequality, 103
    and Labour Party, 32–3
    leadership elections, 83–4
    logo, 29, 49
    MPs, 34, 39–40
    as mainstream party, 32–3
    manifestos, 4, 35, 80, 91, 96, 109, 126–7, 129, 137, 175
    and the media, 35, 37, 50
    membership, 57–62
    and national identity, 62–3

National Executive Committee (NEC), 97
as a nationalist party, 217
and neo-liberalism, 4, 103, 105–18, 131, 133, 144, 156, 159
and nuclearisation of Scotland, 120
and oil, 121
organisation of, 28, 34
origins of, 1–8, 20–2, 191
political identity of, 19
and poverty, 123
power and place making, 3–8
and privatisation, 108
publications, 9
and recession, 115–16, 132
and referendums, 19, 38–9, 185
research on, 9
and reserved matters, 114
Return to Nationhood, 122
rise of, 35, 90–1, 192
Scotland – A European Nation, 194
and the Scottish Constitutional Convention, 19
and Scottish Parliament, 80–1
79 Group *see* separate entry
slogan, 5
and social democracy, 4, 35, 122, 124, 159, 175
and social justice, 120–33
and socialism, 173–4
socio-economic impact of, 28
staff, 35, 82, 84
Statement of Aims and Policy (1946), 121
strategy, 74–7
support for, 6–7, 9, 20, 28, 40, 55, 60–6
symbol, 156
Talking Independence, 185, 186
and taxation, 87, 97, 108, 122, 198
and tourism, 112
Towards a Better Scotland, 109
and UK government, 177–88
voters' ages, 57, 58
voters' social class, 6, 58
and Westminster, 40, 60, 62, 64, 80, 100
and women *see* SNP: and gender
STV, 137, 140
Salmond, Alex, 2, 3
and British–Irish Council, 187

and broadcasting, 141
and Budget (2009–10), 88
and 'Council of the Isles', 187, 198
and financial services, 132
as First Minister, 40, 55, 83
and global crisis (2008–9), 12
and independence, 91
unveils Independence White Paper, 89
and Nairn, Tom, 10
expulsion from the SNP, 162, 171
re-admittance to SNP, 172
and first SNP government, 86–8
and SNP image, 40
as SNP leader, 3–4, 10, 80–1, 86–7, 88, 89, 91, 181, 182, 183–4
and SNP policy, 170–1
and Scottish Broadcasting Commission, 135–6, 138
and 79 Group, 164, 166, 167, 168, 169, 172, 173
and Sillars, Jim, 101
and taxation, 131
at Westminster, 40, 83
Saltire Prize, 111
Sardinian nationalism, 199
Scandinavia, 131; *see also* Nordic Council; Norway
Schlesinger, Philip, 11–12
Schröder, Gerhard, 4
Scotland
border, 186
constitution, 185
economy, 111
GDP, 106, 109, 131–2
home rule, 22, 26
infrastructure, 107, 111, 113, 127, 131
independence, 5–6, 116, 185
nationalism, 2, 8–10, 23, 25–6, 211
nuclearisation of, 120
Secretary of State for, 178
sovereignty, 12–13, 122, 155, 186, 187, 190, 191, 192, 195, 201–2, 209
see also devolution
Scotland Act, 60, 100
Scotland and Wales Bill, 192
Scotland Bill, 99
Scotland (Scottish Convention) Bill, 154
Scotland House, 194

'Scotland in Europe' policy, 116
Scotland Office, 184
'Scotland plc', 5
Scotland's Voice, 80
Scots National League, 21
Scotsman, The, 148
Scottish Arts Council (SAC), 136
Scottish Assembly, 152, 154
Scottish Broadcasting Commission (SBC), 135–6
  Platform for Success report,138
Scottish Centre for Economic and Social Research, 9
Scottish Constitutional Convention, 3, 19, 47, 59, 101, 154–5, 167, 192
Scottish Convention Bill, 154
Scottish Covenant Association, 192
Scottish Development Agency, 33
Scottish Enterprise, 111, 142
Scottish Futures Trust, 108, 111, 113
Scottish Government
  Achieving our Potential, 128–9, 131
  Digital Britain, 139, 142
  Early Years Framework, The, 129
  Equally Well, 128
  'Fiscal Autonomy in Scotland', 89
  Government Economic Strategy, The, 127
  Homecoming 2009 initiative, 112
  'National Conversation', 14, 109
  Secretary of State for Scotland, 178
  and social democracy, 128–30
  Taking Forward the Government Economic Strategy, 127–8, 131
Scottish Grand Committee, 25
Scottish Home Rule Association, 21–2
'Scottish Independence in Europe' campaign, 179
Scottish Industrial Resistance, The (79 Group), 165, 169
Scottish International Review, 9
Scottish Labour Party, 99, 144, 148, 151; *see also* Labour Party; New Labour
Scottish National Convention, 25–6, 27
Scottish National Movement, 21
Scottish Nationalism, 2, 8–10, 23, 25–6, 148, 211; *see also* Campaign for Nationalism in Scotland (CNS); SNP
Scottish Network (broadcasting), 107

Scottish Office, 178
Scottish Parliament
  bills, 11
  coalitions, 80–1
  elections, 6–8
  electoral system, 58–60
  and Europe, 197–8
  first, 37
  move to Holyrood, 84
  Labour Party and, 22
  policy initiative, 132–3
  SNP and, 80–1
  and social policy, 97
Scottish Parliament Election Survey (1999), 125, 152
Scottish Party, 1, 23
Scottish Screen, 136
'Scottish Six' news broadcasting, 141
Scottish Skills Strategy, 111
Scottish Social Attitudes survey, 58, 61
Scottish Socialist Party, 171, 217
Scottish Trade Union Congress (STUC), 22, 97, 112–13, 148
Select Committee on Scottish Affairs (UK Parliament), 95
self-determination, 199, 201, 205
Seligman, Martin, 11
79 Group, 39, 162–75
  aims, 174
  Case for Left-Wing Nationalism, The, 165
  and civil disobedience, 168–9
  demise of, 171–5
  and Europe, 167
  guiding principles of, 163–4
  and independence, 167
  and industrial politics, 165
  membership, 164, 174
  origins of, 162
  and paternalism, 167
  political identity of, 165
  relationship with Provisional Sinn Fein, 168–9
  and republicanism, 174
  'SNP 79 Group Papers', 165
  and SNP ideology, 173–4
  Scottish Industrial Resistance, The, 165, 169
  79 Group News, 166, 170

sexual equality, 130; *see also* women

Shaw, Eric, 5

Shetland, 59

Silesian nationalists, 209

Sillars, Jim
defection of, 99
and direct action, 147
and Govan by-election, 36, 173
Scotland: The Case for Optimism, 151
and 'Scottish independence in Europe'
campaign, 179
and 79 Group, 166–7, 171

Single Transferable Vote (STV), 8

Sinn Fein, 181; *see also* Provisional Sinn
Fein

skills, 111, 112–13

Skills Development Scotland, 111

Slovakia: Hungarian minority party, 214

Small, William, 149

Smith, John, 79

Smith, Richard, 144

social democracy
definition, 4
Europe, 208, 212
Labour Party and, 123, 128–9, 159,
175
SNP and, 4, 122, 124, 159, 175
Scottish Government and, 123

social policy: opinion surveys, 125–6

Souter, Brian, 11, 90

sovereignty
Britain, 10
European Union, 177–8, 194, 196
nation states, 209, 210
nationalist parties, 199
Quebec, 197
Scotland, 12–13, 122, 155, 186, 187,
190, 191, 192, 195, 201–2, 209

Soviet Union, 15

Spain, 206, 207; *see also* Basque
nationalists; Catalan nationalists;
Galicia

Spence, Lewis, 21

Steel, David, 153

Stevenson, Stewart, 170, 173

Stewart, Donald, 2, 34, 36, 96, 103, 168

Straw, Jack, 182, 183

strikes, 173, 182

Sturgeon, Nicola, 84, 85, 90, 91, 133,
157

Sudtiroler Volkspartei (Italian nationalist
movement), 214

Swinney, John
as Finance Secretary, 88, 89, 132, 184,
198
as SNP leader, 3, 40, 49–50, 81–4,
90–1

*Taking Forward the Government Economic
Strategy* (Scottish Government),
127–8, 131

'tartan Tories', 148–50

taxation, 74, 80, 88, 107, 108, 109, 110,
111, 120, 122, 125, 126, 127, 129,
157, 198, 217; *see also* business taxes;
corporation tax; council tax; fiscal
affairs; income tax; poll tax; Selective
Employment Tax

television, 137–41

Thatcher, Margaret, 101, 123, 151, 152

Thatcherism, 10, 121, 124, 158, 173, 175,
212

The Work Foundation, 144

Thompson, Mark, 107

Thomson, George Malcolm, 23

Tough, Jim, 142

tourism, 112

Trade Union Congress *see* Scottish Trade
Union Congress

training, 107, 109, 111, 113, 117

transport, 111, 114

Treaty of Union (1707), 177–8, 193

Trump, Donald, 11

Union of Crowns (1603), 178, 187

United Kingdom
economy, 183–4
government *see* Westminster
nationalism, 207
and secession, 206
as unitary state, 178

United States, 206

universities *see* Future Thinking Taskforce

Vlaams Belang (Belgian nationalist
movement), 213, 215

voters
  and devolution, 188
  and general election (1974), 55–8
  and nationalism, 215
  priorities of, 19–20
  Scottish Nationalist, 6–8
  and Scottish Parliament, 60–1
voting
  Additional Member System, 59
  gender gap, 50
  SNP leadership, 83
  single-member plurality voting system,
    50–1

Wales, 178; *see also* Plaid Cymru; Welsh
    Assembly
Washington consensus, 116
water charges, 114–15
Watson, Mike, 144
wave-power technology, 111
Welfare Reform Bill (amendment), 103
Welfare State, 26
Welsh, Andrew, 169
Welsh Assembly, 152
West Lothian by-election (1962), 94
Westminster
  Department for Culture, Media and
    Sport (DCMS), 142
  elections, 8, 37, 40
  Joint Ministerial Committee (JMC),
    180, 183, 184
  Memorandum of Understanding
    (MoU), 179–80
  SNP and, 40, 60, 62, 64, 80, 100

Scottish Office, 178
Select Committee on Scottish Affairs, 95
Wheatley, John, 22
Wilson, Andrew, 82
Wilson, Bill, 3, 83
Wilson, Brian, 147
Wilson, Gordon
  and civil disobedience, 171
  and cold-climate allowance campaign,
    123
  and Government of Scotland (Scottish
    Convention) Bill, 154, 167
  and oil campaign, 121
  as SNP candidate, 36
  and SNP ideology, 38, 172, 175
  as SNP leader, 39, 193, 194
  and 79 Group, 163, 166, 169–70, 172,
    179
  and Wolfe, Billy, 98
Wilson, Harold, 2, 33, 55, 96
Wilson, John, 133
Wolfe, Billy, 34, 38, 93, 97, 98, 163
women
  Norwegian public life, 130
  political representation of, 42–52
  as SNP voters, 57
Woodburn, Archie, 149
working class: support for nationalism, 6,
    29, 70, 163, 165, 174, 217
Wyllie, Ron, 171

xenophobia, 208, 213

Young, Douglas, 25